T0380393

Stepfathering
STEPFATHERS' ADVICE
ON CREATING A NEW FAMILY

MARK BRUCE ROSIN

SIMON AND SCHUSTER

NEW YORK

Published by Simon and Schuster
A Division of Simon & Schuster, Inc.
Simon & Schuster Building
Rockefeller Center
1230 Avenue of the Americas
New York, New York 10020
SIMON AND SCHUSTER and colophon are registered trademarks of
Simon & Schuster, Inc.
Designed by Irving Perkins Associates
Manufactured in the United States of America
1   3   5   7   9   10   8   6   4   2
Library of Congress Cataloging-in-Publication Data

Rosin, Mark Bruce.
Stepfathering: stepfathers' advice on creating a new family.

Includes index.
1. Stepfathers.   2. Parent and child.   3. Parenting.
I. Title.
HQ759.92.R67   1987   646.7′8   86-31644
ISBN 978-1-4391-8327-4

The author gratefully acknowledges permission to use the excerpt from "On Children." Reprinted from *The Prophet,* by Kahlil Gibran by permission of Alfred A. Knopf, Inc. Copyright 1923 by Kahlil Gibran and renewed 1951 by Administrators C.T.A. of the Kahlil Gibran Estate and Mary G. Gibran.

*To my wife, Cynthia,
to my two stepsons,
Kevin and Timothy,
and to my mother and father,
Mildred and Robert.*

ACKNOWLEDGMENTS

I would like to thank all the stepfathers who allowed me to interview them for this book. I would also like to thank Claire Berman, Barbara Mullen, Joel Brenner and the other members of the Stepfamily Association of America who were so helpful to me, Mark Gerzon and my editor, Bob Bender.

Contents

Introduction

I HAVE BEEN A stepfather for the last fifteen years (thirteen years of marriage and two years of living together prior to marriage), so I have a very definite bias about stepfathering. I see it as one of the most significant and challenging experiences in my life. I also enjoy it. But I haven't always enjoyed it. In fact, sometimes, especially in the first few years, I found it overwhelming, painful, and confusing. The research I've done for this book, interviewing over fifty stepfathers, indicates that my experience is far from uncommon.

If you are a stepfather, or if you are living with a woman who has children and have taken on the role of stepfather without marriage, or if you are dating a woman with children and could be called a "stepfather-to-be," this book is written for you. Its purpose is to help you as a stepfather or a prospective stepfather in making the most of your opportunity rather than merely making the best of it.

Clearly, not every man and woman who live as a stepfamily with the children of either or both of them intend to get married. Some living-together situations are specifically meant to

prepare for an intended marriage, while others are a commitment that adults make to each other and to living in a stepfamily without marriage.

Since among the stepfathers I interviewed, marriage was
the rule rather than the exception, in writing this book I refer
to marriage as part of the formation of the stepfamily. But I
am not suggesting that it is the only choice for people living
together as a stepfamily. In reading this book, a man who has
taken on the role of stepfather by living with his partner and
her children without considering it a preparation for marriage
will find that many things I say about stepfathering after marriage are applicable to his situation as well.

THE NEW FRONTIER

We are all pioneers—not just us stepfathers, but all members of stepfamilies. Current statistics indicate that 1,300 new
stepfamilies are formed every day, that 4.5 million children
under age eighteen live with a biological parent and a stepparent, that 10 percent of all the children in the U.S. live in stepfamilies. By 1990 it's estimated that the percentage of children
in stepfamilies will rise to 12 percent. This is a recent phenom-
enon. In the past, when the divorce rate was a fraction of what
it is today, stepfamilies were usually formed only when one
parent died and the surviving parent remarried. Clearly this is
no longer the case. And all of us who today are already part of
a stepfamily or are becoming part of one are also part of an
evolving understanding of what it means to be a stepfather, a
stepmother, or a stepchild, as well as what it means to be a biological parent married to a stepparent.

In the early 1970s, when I first became a stepfather, there
were few books on stepparenting and none that I could find on
stepfathering. This isn't surprising considering the lack of research that then existed on stepfamilies and the fact that even
biological fathering was just becoming of more than secondary
interest to men. Until the late 1960s, men generally believed
and espoused the traditional line that as fathers their primary

responsibilities were making a living and enforcing discipline. In the 1970s, with the impetus and support of the women's liberation movement, we were suddenly encouraged to develop the nurturing sides of our personalities in our relationships with our partners and children. As many of us—and our partners—have since discovered, it was impossible to make this change overnight. Becoming nurturing husbands and fathers, especially for men who were reaching adulthood before the women's liberation movement, requires a new set of definitions, a new set of norms, and an understanding of how to fit ourselves into this new behavior.

Stepfathers and prospective stepfathers have an additional task. We are not only challenged to develop and express the nurturing sides of ourselves, we are challenged to define what our roles are. For myself the role of stepfather was such a new concept in my mental vocabulary that it took me years to get some sense of what my options, prerogatives, and responsibilities were. Especially in the early years, I often felt alone: not without support from my wife, Cynthia, but alone in the particular and frequently apparently rewardless challenge of being a stepfather.

Of course, like many stepfathers, in the initial stages of my relationships with my future wife and stepchildren I had no idea what I was getting into. In fact, at the beginning I didn't even know I was heading for stepfatherhood.

The day I first encountered my youngest stepson, Timothy, he was five years old. Despite the plaster cast on his broken arm he was riding his bicycle down a New York City sidewalk. I was immediately struck by his good-willed rambunctiousness, but had no idea that within two years I would be dealing with that rambunctiousness myself on a daily basis. I had met Cynthia only several weeks before through her sister, Enid. I knew I liked her but had no serious thoughts of dating her yet.

Several months later I saw Cynthia again at Enid's house. This time I met her older son, Kevin, who was nine. He seemed like a sweet, serious child. Although he was as active as

Timothy when the two of them were playing together, at other times, I noticed, he had a protective air about himself and a possessive attitude about his mother and little brother. While Timothy seemed to accept me and other people easily, Kevin was more wary.

By coincidence a year later Cynthia and "the boys" and I moved to Berkeley, California, at the same time. As soon as Cynthia and I became reacquainted with each other, I began visiting her regularly in the house she was renting, and we became close friends. During my visits I noticed the same distinction between the boys' behavior toward me that I had observed in New York. Once, however, several months into Cynthia's and my friendship, I took her and the boys out for dinner in San Francisco, and although Kevin remained slightly aloof from me, he was cooperative and even seemed to have a good time. I felt I was finally making progress; that he was beginning to realize I was a "good guy" after all.

Since Cynthia and I got along so well and the boys didn't seem to be a problem for me, Cynthia and I decided to solve our housing problems (we both had to move out of the places we were in) by renting a house together as roommates. We were lucky enough to find exactly what we wanted: a house big enough for the boys to have their own large bedroom, for Cynthia to have a bedroom, for me to have a bedroom with a studio in which to do my writing, and for us all to share a living room, dining room, and kitchen.

Once we were living together, my relationship with Kevin deteriorated rapidly. Kevin always seemed to be leading parties of children on running raids across the roof of our house, which invariably brought them stomping over my head when I was trying to write. Suddenly I found myself in the uncomfortable role of ogre, spoiling both boys' fun simply by standing up for my own need for peace and quiet, not to mention my belief that their roof-running wasn't the safest activity in which they could be involved.

Beyond having to deal with the demands of living with "free" children during a very free time in Berkeley, I now had to deal more intimately with Kevin's outrage. Whenever Cynthia and I went out by ourselves for the evening, his general wariness for me burgeoned into anger and hurt: Where was his mother going? How could she be leaving the house without him? When would she be back? He would scream, he would cry, he would yell, and after several minutes of Cynthia's trying to console him, she and I would leave, she assuring him that we would be home in a few hours, and he not deigning to look or communicate with me at all. Timothy, who seemed to accept our departure with equanimity, was left, along with the baby-sitter, to comfort him.

Fortunately Kevin's anger was not always so overt. Even at the height of his resentment, when we were all together, though he still remained very quiet around me, he seemed almost to accept my presence. When I was away from him, in my mind's eye I could see that underneath the negative emotions there was still that sweetness I had first observed in him. Even though I resented his hostility toward me, knowing that sweetness was there helped me to care for his general well-being and to support Cynthia as a mother. I found myself spending hours talking to her about the boys, discussing our perception of what life was like for them and what might be most beneficial for them regarding school, friends, recreation, and coping with the aftermath of Cynthia's divorce from their father, which had occurred when Kevin was five and Timothy one.

During the time Cynthia and I began sharing the house our relationship was evolving into a romance. When we realized that our impromptu living arrangement had turned into a deeper commitment to each other, we knew something had to be said to the boys. It was late April, and they expected to return to New York in June to the apartment that Cynthia had only sublet. As far as they were concerned, I was going to stay in California.

Late one afternoon they found out that although the lease on the Berkeley house was going to end in June, Cynthia and I were going to continue—which meant that I was going to remain part of their picture, too. And my part in their picture was changing: I was no longer their mother's friend; she and I were lovers—whatever that meant to a six-year-old and a ten-year-old. One thing it meant, they soon found out, was that she and I would no longer be sleeping in separate beds. Cynthia sat them down on the back porch of the house to tell them about the change in our relationship. She started out by saying how much she cared for me and how much I cared for her and them, and then she said that she and I were "involved."

"What does that mean?" Kevin asked, his eyes already filling with tears.

"It means we're lovers," she replied.

"What does that mean?" he asked with an edge.

"It means we have a sexual relationship," she said.

"What does that mean?" he demanded, his voice growing louder and less steady.

"It means we're sleeping together," she blurted out.

I was upstairs working on my novel when suddenly I heard both boys crying and shrieking, "No! No! No!"

With a sick feeling in my stomach I walked over to the window at the end of the second-floor hallway and looked down at Cynthia trying to comfort the disconsolate children. I knew at once the subject of the discussion.

Self-consciously I descended the stairs and entered the kitchen, where I began preparing dinner for the company we were expecting. Minutes later, when I had already begun to make a soup, Timothy wandered in, his face red from crying. Without referring to the scene I had secretly observed, he asked if there was anything he could do to help with dinner. I looked at his vulnerable round face, thanked him, and set up his stool near the stove so that he could stir the big pot of soup. As he stirred, I told him how appreciative I was of his assistance. For a while he continued stirring in silence, then he looked up at me and said, "Mommy said I would like you more if I got to know you better, and she was right. I already like you more." I knew that now he felt comforted; I felt comforted, too.

Kevin was particularly quiet that evening when our company came, and so was I. Our company consisted of a classmate of Kevin's and his mother and stepfather. He was the first stepfather I had ever met; he was also a former weightlifter and lifeguard, which, given my own very indoor life as a writer, made me feel, perhaps wrongly, as if we had very little in common. At the time it seemed absurd that they were scheduled to come in the middle of our first "family" crisis, but in some ways it was also a godsend to have them there. Every now and then Kevin and I looked up from our food and at each other, unable to talk about what was on our minds but sensing what the other was thinking. We both knew now that our relationship to each other was more than just a temporary one. The question was: What would that relationship be like? Would it hold any real rewards for either of us?

After dinner the stepfather of Kevin's friend played a particularly wild game of hide-and-seek with Kevin, Timothy, and his stepson. The four of them ran around the big old house hiding and finding each other in places I didn't even know existed. Kevin and Timothy let off a lot of steam yelling, shouting, giggling, and looking for the other child's stepfather, who was a master at hiding. I sat in the dining room with the two mothers drinking tea and feeling relieved that the kids'—and especially Kevin's—aggression had an outlet and didn't have to be aimed at me, at least for the moment.

A few weeks later, when Kevin and I seemed to clash even more resolutely over matters of discipline within the house, Cynthia and I went to a therapist ourselves for counseling. Relatively soon it became clear to me that at least for the time being it would be more effective for everybody concerned if I expressed my desires to Cynthia about setting ground rules for the boys, if she and I reached an agreement, and then she communicated our mutual decisions to Kevin and Timothy rather than my doing it on my own.

By the time the lease on our house was up and Cynthia and I left Berkeley, taking the boys to the East Coast to see their father for the summer, we had become an acknowledged stepfamily: myself and Cynthia out of deliberate choice; Timothy apparently with good-willed acceptance; and Kevin with great reluctance.

But a year later, when Cynthia and I, now living with the boys in Los Angeles, announced to them that we were going to be married, Kevin was openly happy about it and Timothy began to cry.

Kevin, now eleven years old, had not liked having his mother and me living together without the bond of marriage. He was at an age where he was very concerned about what "other people" would think. Whether or not he was wholly thrilled with the idea of his mother marrying me, our marriage would at least legally sanction our union and make us more like the "other people" about whose judgments he was so concerned. More than likely, although he never expressed it, he also regarded our announcement of marriage as a recommendation for me, since I was making a legal commitment, and thus showing my intention of being more than just a fleeting presence. Given his general reserve, Kevin's seemingly thorough acceptance of our marriage plans was as surprising as Timothy's emotional explosion.

Seven-year-old Timothy had two objections to our marriage: the first was that my wire-rimmed glasses were "too delicate"; the second was that I ate out of the refrigerator. I sensed that underneath Timothy's objections to my delicate glasses was a comparison he was making in his own mind between me and his father. What Timothy was really saying, I felt, was that I was not as rugged as his father. Since Timothy didn't verbalize this himself and I didn't know where it would lead if I did, I didn't feel good about bringing it up myself. Instead I moved on to his next objection: my eating out of the refrigerator.

My response was to answer with humor: How could Timothy, of all people, possibly raise an objection? His own bad table manners were legendary, at least in our house. Cynthia was always correcting him, while I had left him alone. So why was he criticizing me?

Cynthia and I sat in the living room looking at the still-crying seven-year-old. Soon the real cause of Timothy's complaints about me was brought out into the open. If his mother married me, he asked, then how could she ever marry his father again?

Given that Cynthia's ex-husband had been remarried for some time and that after the divorce Cynthia and he had not been particularly friendly, this question was surprising to both of us. It was even more shocking given Timothy's apparent fondness for me. Cynthia responded by reminding Timothy that his father was already happily remarried and making it very clear that she and her ex-husband would not marry each other again under any circumstances, even if he were not married and she were not to marry me; that she had divorced him because they didn't get along, which meant that they did not enjoy being married to each other. Timothy nodded, then burst out crying and announced another deep concern: What if after Cynthia married me we decided to get a divorce?

Cynthia and I spoke simultaneously, telling Timothy just about the same thing: We couldn't give him and Kevin a guarantee that we would never get divorced, but we certainly didn't think that we would, otherwise we wouldn't be getting married. We told him that we loved each other, we reminded him that all of us had already lived together as a family for over a year and a half, and I told him that I cared for him and Kevin as well as for Cynthia, and that when she and I looked into the future we saw ourselves sharing it with each other and with them. Timothy seemed to accept this. Kevin, who had not been a verbal participant in this discussion, paid close attention to it nevertheless. Several months later, when Cynthia and I married, both boys walked down the aisle with their mother. They listened earnestly as the rabbi conducted the ceremony and she and I exchanged our vows, and then they helped serve the wedding cake to our guests.

Cynthia and I spent a weekend honeymoon in Santa Barbara, then came back to Los Angeles, where the kids remained with us for a few days—and I got to use the name stepfather legally for the first time—before they flew back to the East

Coast to be with their dad and stepmother for the summer.

My fantasy at the time was that they would return in the fall and everything would be "perfect," that we would be a stepfamily that would interact like my ideal of a nuclear family. The reality was that in the fall the conflicts continued, and when these particular conflicts were resolved, new ones arose. The reality was that it took until Kevin's late adolescence for us to grow close, and that since then, to both his and my surprise and pleasure, we've grown to love each other very much. My relationship with Timothy changed, too, over time, straining with his adolescence, only to grow even closer and more respectful on both our parts as he entered his twenties. And all this time we've never interacted like my ideal of a nuclear family; we've always interacted as just what we are: a stepfamily.

My interviews with other stepfathers have taught me that my misconceptions about stepfamily life and stepfathering are extremely typical. As a recent stepfather with two biological children from a previous marriage and one stepchild from his new marriage reflected: "I, like most people, thought that the stepmarriage would be very much like the first marriage. It isn't. It's really a totally different experience. There really is very little information out there that can prepare you for it. I find it really would have been helpful for me to have that information before I remarried. It would have saved me from some very difficult and painful experiences and allowed us to form the stepfamily much more effectively and quickly."

As this stepfather's comment suggests, even today, with the increased coverage stepfamilies have been getting in the media and the valuable support of such groups as the Stepfamily Association of America, becoming a stepfather is still a pioneering experience. For many stepfathers it feels like setting out from Missouri to California in the early 1040s with no map. That was what I wanted for so many years: a map that would chart out the factors of stepfamily life for me, tell me alternative choices I might make as a stepfather, so that I could see if there were better options than the ones I was thinking of. I also wanted this hypothetical guide to tell me what I might reasonably expect in the way of challenges and rewards.

This was one of the major impetuses for me to write *Stepfathering:* to see if the collective experiences and observations of a varied sampling of stepfathers would provide such a guide. The other major impetus for me to write this book was to share the personal perspective I had gained in my relationships with my stepsons, relationships that over the fifteen years since I have come into their lives and they have come into mine have produced far more rewards than problems. Given the intrinsic problems of working out stepfamily relationships, that's saying something, and I'm very grateful to be able to say it and mean it.

A PROGRESSION OF STEPS

In the years since Kevin and Timothy have become my stepsons, the word "stepfather" has come to mean different things to me—particularly the prefix "step."

At first it signified my resistance to the whole idea of being any kind of father to Cynthia's children by her previous marriage. It also signified their resistance to me and the puzzlement I felt at even trying to define the role. At that point the "step" in "stepfather" stated that I was one step removed. How could I be a father of any kind to children who already had a father without any kind of "step" attached to his title at all? Since Kevin and Timothy undoubtedly had a *real* father, even if Cynthia's moving had put him at a distance of 3,000 miles, did the "step" before my title mean that I was a pseudo father, a figurehead of a parent who had no real function? Or did it mean that I had some mysterious other function that I *should* perform but had not learned about?

Since then I've learned by trial and error that I did and do have a very real function in my stepsons' lives. Today, because of the strong bonds that have developed between us, when Kevin or Timothy introduces me as his stepfather, sometimes I feel awkward that the prefix "step" is there at all. And yet I realize that it's entirely appropriate. Regardless of the warmth and intimacy that have evolved between us, I am their stepfather; they have a biological father, too, and in this case an active and loving one. This is a major fact of stepfamily life: that there are parents and stepparents.

In learning to accept this fact, I've also come to see another reason why the word "stepfather" is so very appropriate for the position in which we men who marry women with children find ourselves: because the process of becoming a stepfather happens in steps. While editing articles on parenting during my five years as senior editor of *Parents* magazine, much to my amazement I came to see that the process of becoming a biological parent also happens in steps or stages. With this discovery came the realization that in some ways stepfathering is not so different from fathering.

Just as one doesn't become an experienced stepfather the moment the wedding ceremony is over, one doesn't become an experienced father the moment a child is born. Learning the skills of parenting takes time. Adjusting to a child's personality takes time. A child adjusting to your personality takes time. Adjusting to the changes in a child as he or she grows and develops takes time. Getting over the idea of wanting to throw in the towel and chuck the whole thing takes time—and more than likely that idea is bound to come up cyclically for any parent, step or otherwise. But try telling any stepfather how much he has in common with a biological father at the moment he is being faced by his recalcitrant stepchild shouting, "You're not my father!" and if he's calm enough not to do something more violent he'll rightly ask you what biological father has ever had to deal with this type of frustration.

DIVORCE: THE INDELIBLE MARK

As anthropologist Paul Bohannan observes, the stepfamily is different in nature from the nuclear family simply because the stepfamily forms after a divorce, and "the divorce does not break clean. There is always a residue to be dealt with."*

As Bohannan points out, when a divorced couple has a child, the divorce doesn't stop the ex-husband and ex-wife from having a kinship relationship to each other, nor does it stop the child from having an ongoing relationship with both parents, whether they are present or absent. Even if a parent has abandoned a child, the child may still focus on him or carry on an imaginary relationship with him. Also, as many stepparents of both sexes have informed me, children have emotional bonds—sometimes very strong ones—with parents who have passed away. The bond between a child and the biological parent who is not in the household exerts a very definite influence on any person marrying that child's other biological parent and taking on the role of stepparent. Thus any man who becomes a stepfather must create his relationships with his partner and stepchildren not on the basis of a clean slate but with the residue of divorce or death as an aspect that must be acknowledged.

This makes stepfathering a very different experience from biological fathering. And since the specific results of divorce or death are unique to each stepfamily, the *way* a man creates his role as stepfather is unique to his stepfamily—and to some extent at least so is the *role* he creates. There are common characteristics of stepfamily life and common experiences shared by stepfathers, of course, common challenges that to a greater or lesser degree we all face. But *there are many ways to be a stepfather*—which is part of the reason that becoming a stepfather can be so confusing.

THE EXPERTS SPEAK

My objective in talking to over fifty stepfathers was to learn what they thought and felt about their roles as stepfathers,

* Bohannan, Paul, "Some Thoughts about Divorce Reform," *Divorce and After*, edited by Paul Bohannan (Anchor Books, Doubleday and Co., Inc., Garden City, New York, 1971), p. 285.

about what they were doing right, what they were doing wrong, and, given what they know now, what they would do the same and what they would do differently. I wanted to know what was unique about each stepfather's situation and what common threads ran through all of them; I wanted to know what stepfathers' goals were, what their expectations had been, what the realities were turning out to be, and how they saw the future. I wanted to know about their biggest problems and their biggest successes. Finally I wanted to know what rewards they had received and what advice they had for other stepfathers and men who were in the process of becoming stepfathers.

The stepfathers I've interviewed live in various parts of the country. They are men of different ages, educational backgrounds, professions, and experiences. Their only common denominators are their gender and their having taken on the role of stepfather. I spoke to men whose only children are their stepchildren; to men with both biological children and stepchildren; and to other men who, in addition to stepchildren and sometimes biological children, too, also have had biological children with their new partners. In all three categories I found men whose problems with stepfathering have been minor, others whose problems have been major, and others whose stepfathering problems have been so major that they threatened to break up their marriages.

These are the experts I quote. Some of these stepfathers are experts in the more conventional sense as well: psychologists and other health-care professionals, some of whom specialize in counseling stepfamilies.

Stepfathering covers the different steps of stepfathering from courting to marriage to the process of adjustment as a new family unit, and the continuing process of adjustment and readjustment that stepfathers, their spouses, and their stepchildren (and biological children) make—or fail to make— throughout the course of the children growing up and leaving home to go out on their own as adults. It is a synthesis of my own observations, insights, and experiences and those of all the men who have so graciously and candidly talked to me about their lives as stepfathers over the past twelve months. It is a more comprehensive book than I possibly could have written had I confined it to my own experiences. It presents the problems, solutions, rewards, and advice that came out of the stepfathering experience of each man I interviewed.

Stepfathering is also a fuller book emotionally because of the contributions of these other stepfathers. Whether the men I interviewed were sharing their joy, their frustration, or their pain, their words about stepfathering were so heartfelt and the subject was so clearly at the center of their lives that I began to have a fuller sense of the spectrum of feelings that is part of stepfathering, and I also gained an even fuller recognition of what I knew from my own experience: that the emotional issues of stepfathering are at least as critical to us as the practical ones like finances, and that very often the two are so intertwined that it's hard to say where the practical issues end and the emotional ones begin.

STEPFATHERING OPPORTUNITIES: NO PAIN, NO GAIN

Becoming a stepfather is an opportunity to change your experience of life. The way you react to this opportunity has as much to do with whether the experience is positive or negative as the way your stepchildren, your partner, and her ex-husband react to your entrance into their lives. Whether the experience starts out as a positive or a negative one, your willingness and ability to respond to the realities of the stepfamily of which you become a part determine how much or how little that experience may improve with time. Especially in the early stages of a stepfather-stepchild relationship, and sometimes again when the stepchild reaches adolescence, it may feel as if you as stepfather have no power compared to the child, the mother, or the biological father. In reality this is far from true; what's crucial is to see where your power lies, and how choosing to use it in one way is likely to produce positive results, while choosing to use it another way will most probably be ineffective or destructive.

The National Center for Health Statistics projects a 47.4

percent divorce rate among remarriages, which I believe clearly states the challenge for both husband and wife in forming a stepfamily. If you are a stepfather or a stepfather-to-be, I hope this book will help you to meet this challenge successfully in terms of your own emotional fulfillment as well as in terms of fulfilling the needs of the other members of your stepfamily.

CHAPTER ONE

First Impressions

As MEN WHO ARE stepfathers already know and as prospective stepfathers are finding out, some of the most important
days in any stepfather's life occur during the period prior to
marriage, the sometimes lengthy and sometimes all-too-short
"getting-acquainted stage."

A man contemplating marrying a woman with children is
not just contemplating marriage, he is contemplating stepfathering. As one stepfather remarked, looking back, "I didn't
just marry the mother, I married the children, too."

In the course of the getting-acquainted stage of forming a
stepfamily—which includes dating, courtship, and if the couple chooses, living together—we must get to know our partners and also all the other members of our prospective new
families. And if we have children, we must include them in
this getting-acquainted process, too. This is the time of learning, adjusting, and choosing. How much we learn about the
members of our new stepfamilies *before* we marry and the
kinds of adjustments to and choices we make about how we interact with them will have a substantial impact on the future

success of our new relationships, especially during the first years of stepfamily life.

Unfortunately, many stepfathers-to-be—including myself when I was in the dating and courtship and even in the living-together stage—are not seeing the signs all that clearly, nor are we thinking very clearly about the future. During this hectic and often dizzying time we are merely doing our best to cope with a situation that is likely to be more emotionally and logistically complex than any we have ever dealt with before. Sometimes we may feel confused by the complexity of it all and other times arrogantly self-assured by how simple it will all be, only to wake up to a new event that leaves us baffled and bewildered.

One reason so many stepfathers, like myself, choose to live with their future marriage partners and stepchildren prior to marriage is to have the opportunity to find out what living as a stepfamily will be like: to have an increased opportunity to learn, to adjust, and to choose. Indeed, for some prospective stepfathers living together is a test to see if they choose to get married. Whether you live with your stepfamily before or after marriage (or without intending marriage), this is the time when stepfamily members really begin to let their hair down. The old adage that you never really know anybody until you live with them is even more true for two adults contemplating stepfamily life, since they will be living not only with each other but with the child or children of at least one of them.

The question is, then, What can a man do prior to becoming a stepfather to prepare himself for stepfathering? One stepfather I interviewed told me in no uncertain terms, "There is no sufficient preparation for stepfathering." Although he may be right, there are things a stepfather can do prior to marriage that will help him. The more he can learn during this critical time about what stepfamily life is likely to be like the better he is likely to be both as a stepfather and a husband in entering a family situation that involves so many adjustments at once.

Given this, the getting-acquainted stage of forming a stepfamily is a time for us to synthesize our impressions and to begin arriving at a middle ground for our expectations of our prospective stepfamily members, somewhere between our most hopeful fantasies and our worst fears. It's a time to begin arriving at a realistic idea of the challenges and struggles we will be facing in forming relationships with our prospective stepfamily members. Finally, it's a time to see how we ourselves are reacting to these challenges, to evaluate our actions and reactions, and to begin imagining ourselves in our future lives as stepfathers.

TEN CONSIDERATIONS

The following ten points about stepfamilies provide a useful perspective for seeing beyond the details of your daily emotional experiences to the dynamics that are at work between you, your partner, your partner's children, and, if you have them, your children. These ten points were derived from analyzing the patterns in the stories of the stepfathers I interviewed, as well as my own. I feel they are essential for every stepfather and prospective stepfather to know. They may even help you to look into the future and see more clearly the exact nature of the challenges facing you as a stepfather.

1. Each child's personality and needs are unique. Each child will react to you as a potential stepfather in his or her own way. These reactions will be determined partly by simple compatibility and partly by factors in the child's life and personal psychology, such as the effects of his or her parents' divorce.

2. Each biological child of yours, if you have any, will react to your new partner and her children in his or her own way, based partly on simple compatibility and partly on factors in the child's life and personal psychology, such as the effects of your divorce from the child's mother. A corollary of this is that your new partner and her children will react to your children on an individual basis, forming unique relationships with each of them based on the same factors of compatibility and personal psychology.

3. Your stepchild's behavior prior to marriage will tell you a lot, but there may be much more that you will discover later.

4. Just as each child will have a different reaction to you as a stepfather, you will react differently to each child based on his or her behavior as well as on your own personality, psychological makeup, and life experience. These same factors will also determine your overall attitude toward becoming a stepfather.

5. However well or poorly your relationships with your prospective stepchildren begin, several factors are likely to produce a change. The first factor is when the children find out their mother is "serious" about you (your relationships with your own children, if you have them, may also change when they find out you are "serious" about a woman other than their mother); the second is when you and your partner announce that you are getting married; the third is when you begin to live together as a stepfamily, with or without marriage.

6. Your positive feelings about your partner overflow into and help to create your feelings about her children. And if you have children, your partner's positive feelings about you help to create her feelings about your children.

7. Mutual support and open, good communication between a stepfather and his partner are the most important elements in determining a stepfather's satisfaction with his marriage, and they are a crucial basis for building strong relationships with his stepchildren. If prior to marriage your partner and you genuinely agree about your role in her children's lives, if she supports you in your relationships with them in the way you want to be supported, and if you communicate well with each other, then even if you disagree about certain specifics of child-rearing, you are likely to function as a team in meeting the challenges ahead with your stepchildren. But if you and your partner disagree about your role in her children's lives, or if you and she have continuing communication problems in settling disagreements in your views of child-rearing, then these are likely to remain intense areas of conflict. Unless each of you learns to negotiate and compromise, these conflicts may undermine your marriage.

8. The best way a stepfather can alleviate stepfamily problems is to learn to step back emotionally from the difficulties

confronting him and to act in a way that will tend to defuse conflicts rather than encourage or perpetuate them. Sometimes counseling is helpful in providing the detachment and insight you need to come up with more constructive ways of responding to a situation.

9. Whether the children's father is alive or dead, single or remarried, geographically close or distant, in continuous communication with the children or totally absent from their lives, he is a presence in the life of the stepfamily. If you are divorced and have biological children, your ex-wife is a presence in your stepfamily, too.

10. Everyone in a stepfamily needs time to adjust, and everyone needs a different amount of time. Children especially need time to adjust to stepparents, whether stepfathers or stepmothers. Some children need a great deal of time—some may need years, in fact. Where there are severe problems in a stepfamily, time's greatest benefit for a stepfather may be to help him adjust his expectations of what he will get from his stepchildren and what they will accept from him.

Some of these ten points may seem obvious. But as many of us have discovered, especially when in the throes of forming not one new relationship but several, it's easy to overlook even the obvious.

For the rest of this chapter, I'm going to use the ten points for stepfathers as a frame of reference within which to look at the pre-marriage experiences (and some post-marriage observations) of some of the stepfathers I interviewed. In these stories we'll encounter the major themes we will be exploring in the rest of the book.

GETTING TO KNOW THE CHILDREN

The uniqueness of each child's personality, needs, and reactions to you as a prospective stepfather seems self-evident, but it comes as a revelation to many men who never had any significant contact with children prior to dating a woman who has them. Although most stepfathers said that at the point of marriage they had a good idea of the individual qualities of their prospective stepchildren, a stepfather who doesn't spend much time with his stepchildren prior to marriage may not have this insight. Witness the stepfather who told me, "When we got married, I guess I thought all five children were one person, and I found they were five different people. And that made it five times more difficult."

"I was totally naive about my stepdaughter," commented another stepfather, whose courtship like that of the stepfather of five was traditionally formal and who did not live with his future stepfamily prior to marriage. "Her father had died of cancer three years earlier, and apparently she felt her mother was turning her back on her father and the memories of him—everything—by getting married, going in a whole different direction. My stepdaughter didn't want it, didn't want any part of it. She thought her little brother [she was age fourteen at the time, her brother was five] would never know anything she did about her father, because her mother got married again and pulled the curtain down on this experience that she was determined to preserve. I didn't realize it at the time of marriage, but she was behind the scenes trying to educate her little brother about her father. It didn't cause all that much of a problem with my stepson, but I'm saying my stepdaughter had problems I in no way anticipated."

"Dating's a tough word," another stepfather told me, describing his getting-acquainted experience and why he didn't get to know his stepson better during this stage. "Let's just say we knew each other for about two years. I'm not quite sure what was dating and what was friends, but it spanned two years, the last one and one half years being more intensive friendship changing into more of a romantic relationship. I only knew my stepson before the marriage a month or two months. The time I spent with him was negligible. I think maybe before we got married we went to the movies maybe or some other place three or four times at most. When Ginny asked him how he felt when we were getting married, he said, 'Great. Now we can have two TVs.' That was probably an accurate summation of his attitude."

For this stepfather, there were no problems with his stepson during the dating phase because, as he explained to me, "there were no significant experiences with him. We would just go to a few places and the interaction was mild. It was only done more to make him feel comfortable about what was going to happen rather than to really build something pre-marriage.

"It was such a turbulent road to get married that I'm not quite sure I had definite thoughts about him prior to getting married. I knew a lot about him, because during our friendship Ginny and I would talk about him; I would give her advice and stuff like that. About a lot of the problems she had with him; a lot of the questions, conflicts, conflicts he had with his father; advice; general support. So I knew a lot about his life, his habits, and things like that. But I can't really say that I knew him or had many thoughts about him."

When prospective stepfathers don't make it a priority to get to know their future stepchildren more than superficially prior to marriage, or when circumstances prevent them from doing so, it's no wonder there is often a sense of surprise following the wedding ceremony. Little wonder, too, that for some stepfathers there is even a sense of having been tricked. This is why the pre-marriage first-impressions period can be so valuable for building the foundation for potentially more stable and fulfilling relationships within the stepfamily and why many prospective stepfathers and their partners do live together prior to marriage.

It's helpful to remember that the children involved in a stepfamily are just as surprised by stepfamily life as we are, perhaps more so. If we keep in mind that we, not they, are the ones who made a choice about forming a stepfamily, it may give us the patience to take the time to get to know them— and to let them get to know us.

SECRET COURTSHIPS

For a small minority of the stepfathers I interviewed, either they, their future wives, or both were married to their former spouses when they began dating each other. In these cases the secrecy of the courtships prevented the men from really knowing what their future stepchildren were like and what reactions they might expect from them, until later.

For one stepfather who had been in this situation, as for others I spoke to who had also been involved in secret courtships, the children were an important topic of conversation during the dating period. "We talked about the kids a lot. That kind of talking, that kind of preparation, was a very significant part of the courtship," this stepfather told me, looking back after five years of marriage.

"Our whole secretive courtship was geared more toward insuring that the children would come to us," he went on. "The children's mother was very afraid that if the father found out about us seeing each other while they were still married, he might have made a problem in our taking the kids."

When the children's mother and father separated, the prospective stepfamily began living together almost immediately. "Once the children and I moved in together, they were sort of immediately stepchildren even though we weren't married. It was a full-type living together–dating period," this stepfather told me, describing an experience shared by other stepfathers involved in secret courtships who then live with their partners and stepchildren prior to marriage. "It wasn't easy for the children and it wasn't easy for me. But it was a beginning."

QUALITIES STEPFATHERS SEE IN THEIR PROSPECTIVE
STEPCHILDREN

As expected, the most common problematic reactions of stepchildren cited in my research were: resistance to the prospective stepfather as a potential new husband for their mother; feelings of conflict of loyalty between allegiance to their biological father and being open to their future stepfather; resistance to the prospective stepfather as an authority figure; and protectiveness of their mother.

Although one might expect that older children would manifest all of these qualities more strongly and would therefore present more difficulties than young children, this isn't always true. As one stepfather observed: "During the dating phase, the biggest problems with Hank, who was ten at the time, were in terms of his feelings about loyalty to his father and liking me. But with Rachel, who was two, there was more of a problem of tending to be somewhat protective of her mother. And because it was less with Hank, I think there was a little less friction for me with Hank than with Rachel. Rachel's protectiveness was partly because she was home so much and so tight with her mother. She expressed her protectiveness by wanting her mother to herself, clinging to her, constantly interrupting, making demands, shielding her from me."

Frequently, older children's feelings are very much the same as those of younger children, and often they do include a sense of protectiveness as well as feelings of conflicted loyalties. A stepfather of three years whose biological children and stepchildren were in late adolescence and older during his courtship prior to remarriage commented, "Initially, I think the greatest challenge was just reassuring the children that my wife was not taking me away from my kids or vice versa; just *trying* to get to know them. My wife's oldest, who was twenty-one when we were dating, just wouldn't talk to me at all, just did not like me." Even though this kind of cutting off of communication occurs more than occasionally in the early stages of stepfamily life, often, with time, communication resumes (point 10). In fact, in the next breath the stepfather of the silent twenty-one-year-old girl informed me, "Through a course of events she moved in with us, and we're pretty good friends now; we get along quite well. That was a big change."

Another stepfather, who today has what he characterizes as a "basically very loving relationship" with his stepdaughter, said their relationship also got off to a difficult start. The reasons he attributes this to—as well as the kind of behavior he describes on the part of his stepdaughter—are common to the experiences of many stepfathers who also have dramatic problems in the early stages of their relationships with their stepchildren. "During the first period, I think Jacqueline, who was eight years old, was quite upset about a lot of things in her life—particularly having lost her mother's previous boyfriend, whom she was very close to, on top of having lost her father through the divorce," this stepfather told me.

"I don't think Jacqueline had a very clear picture of what had actually happened, but she blamed her mother for these things as well as for having to leave the house they lived in, and to leave her friends at school. When your life gets disrupted like that, after it hasn't been easy to begin with, I think there's a lot of heavy anger. To Jacqueline's credit, she reacted strongly rather than internalizing.

"With me, Jacqueline was unpredictable, rather arbitrary and emotionally explosive. I hate to say this, but the first six months I met her she would call me insulting names. She made it very clear that I was never allowed anywhere near her thoughts. She hoped that we wouldn't get married and probably that was her strategy, to not give and not talk.

"The first time I was ever alone with her for any period of time—my future wife did it on purpose—I was given the assignment to take her to a little zoo. I remember standing around the gift shop, and I could tell what she wanted. She was kind of putting the signal out that this was a major test, that if I didn't get her what she wanted she was going to be angry, and so on. I remember that very pointedly, because I didn't know what the hell to do. She's doing a George Meany number on me, I thought. Do I give in to it, do I not give in to it? How do I deal with it? I don't actually remember what I did. I'm pretty certain I didn't buy her what she wanted me to buy, but I bought her something else.

"It was an absolutely crazy relationship at that point between future stepfather and future stepchild, because you don't know each other. She was testing me in all kinds of ways."

" 'Test' isn't a hostile word for me," another stepfather commented in describing his stepson Sandy's behavior toward him during the two years of courtship and living together that preceded marriage. While Sandy's behavior was certainly provocative, by contrast to Jacqueline's tantrums and name-calling it was mild and in fact seems to be more typical of what prospective stepfathers are likely to encounter during the early stages of their relationships with their partners' children.

"Testing just sort of means you lay out your measures to see what's going to happen," Sandy's stepfather said, describing his early relationship with his future stepson. "That's pretty much what it was—Sandy measuring me up to see what was there, just compared to other men in his life. That's what we each had to do; he was 'learning' me and I was 'learning' him.

"Sandy was eleven when I first met him, so for him it was the end of an old era and the beginning of a new era, an era of growing up. A lot of times at the very beginning I noticed that when we were all together, he wouldn't talk to me; he'd only talk to me through his mother and all the stories he'd tell were directed directly at her. And I had to interject myself, so to speak. There were times when that would happen and we'd have arguments; and I'd take it out on his mother and he'd take it out on me, because he and I weren't talking to each other. We developed lines of communication as we went along.

"Every now and again he'd also act in a protective way about his mother and I'd just let it be. The situation was that he had lived with her since he was just three, and when I came along he definitely was at the age where he was ready to get more protective. Every now and then he'd be acting as if he were saying, 'Wait a minute, you can't do that.' So I'd say gently, 'Yes, I could; yes, I will; yes, I am able to; I can.' That was that. I just went along, one step at a time, and in that mode we developed the trust in each other we have now three years later."

WHEN CHILDREN AND STEPCHILDREN MEET

Many of the stepfathers I interviewed felt that during the initial stages of forming combined stepfamilies (stepfamilies where both partners bring children into the family), having children of their own about the same age as their partners' children gave them an advantage. For one thing, they were already "broken in" regarding the ways of children in general, which stepfathers like myself were not. For another, having part-time or full-time responsibility for their own children made these prospective stepfathers more conscious of the necessity of spending time not just courting the woman in whom they were interested but with her and all the children together.

These men perceived another important plus for themselves in the early stages of becoming a stepfather. For the most part, they reported, the children seemed to get along with each other and thus took some of the burden off them for forming relationships with their prospective stepchildren. Indeed, some stepfathers said they met their future wives through the children, who were already friends from school, from the neighborhood, or from a community organization.

One stepfather of three and a half years seemed to sum up the advantage many biological fathers felt they had in already having a child when dating a woman with children: "It was easier for me during the dating period than most other stepfathers because I had a kid, too. At the time I met my wife, hers were eight and four, mine was six. So it was a good situation. My son would play with her two boys, so it wasn't a big deal for me. I just brought him over, he played well with them, and I said, 'Isn't that nice?' So if anything, having my son helped the whole situation."

Another stepfather, married almost seven years, has two daughters of his own who are now ages ten and twelve; his wife has a son age thirteen and a daughter age fifteen. He knew his wife about six months before dating her, and then dated her for a year. Both he and his future wife had full custody of the children during the entire courtship, and the children were very much a part of their developing relationship. "I met the kids when I started dating Mary. We spent weekends together. We'd have picnics and little things like that. We'd get together and take the bicycles and the kids and run around the park, this kind of thing; a little family outing, so to speak, to get to know one another.

"My children liked Mary's children and vice versa, and everybody seemed to get along real fine. After doing this for several months, we decided to work on getting married. The children enjoyed one another. The only objection came from Joey, the boy, of course. He said, 'What's it going to be like with three girls?' But then he found that my two daughters had a lot of things in common with him."

In rare instances, stepfathers in combined stepfamilies reported that from the beginning either their children or their partners' children rebelled at the prospect of remarriage and the potential formation of a combined stepfamily. In such situations, the children rejected their future stepsiblings or their parents' future partners or both. In some cases, such behavior did not occur until it was clear that marriage was actually pending. Often, this behavior occurred with older children, even post-adolescent, where children did not want to accept a change in their parents' status.

Such behavior was painful, of course. In some cases involving children who were still minors the children went to live with the other biological parent and discontinued association with the parent who was getting remarried. Frequently in these situations, given the commitment of the rejected parent and stepparent to each other and to working out relationships with their children and each other's children, this kind of outright rejection dissipated with time, and bonds were formed. In more extreme cases, if the children were old enough, they cut themselves off from their parents and stepparents; and sometimes the parents and stepparents cut themselves off from the children as well.

But according to the stepfathers I interviewed, the major problems of forming and living in a combined stepfamily have nothing to do with children rejecting parent, stepparent, or stepsiblings. For many stepfathers, the major problems arise from the conflict they themselves feel about being loyal to their own children while also attempting to be good stepfathers, and the conflict their partners feel about wanting to be loyal to their own children while attempting to be good stepmothers. Often these situations cause problems between stepfathers and their partners. One stepfather spoke for many when he told me, "The boys never had a problem with each other. It's always been my wife and I who have the problems. The problems mostly occur with my wife feeling I give Michael more attention than her two."

For some stepfathers, the challenge of treating their biological and stepchildren equally is a difficult one that begins during courtship and gets easier with time. For others, the issue isn't equal treatment but learning how to fulfill different roles for their children and stepchildren.

SURPRISES

That there may be surprises for you about your stepchildren, regardless of how much you learn about them prior to marriage, is true not just because they are stepchildren but because they are children. Major events in children's lives are certain to bring out feelings, thoughts, and needs that may have been dormant when the children were at an earlier stage in their development. Time itself—children's interactions with the world and whatever internal changes they are experiencing as part of their growth process—brings out thoughts, feelings, and needs that may throw us stepfathers as well as the children's mothers for a loop.

On the positive side of the changes children exhibit as they grow, I and many other longtime stepfathers to whom I spoke were happily caught off guard by the deep love and appreciation our stepchildren, who had been initially distant from us, began to show us as they grew older. This doesn't always happen, of course. A stepfather of twenty-one years told me, "One child who was a teenager at the time I dated and married her mother did resent my relationship with her mother. I didn't know to what depth until many years later. I don't know if it was me or the marriage or the mother and father's divorce or what it was. But it built. To this day, she is very bitter."

One problem many stepfathers eventually find themselves facing with stepchildren has to do with grades and/or behavior problems in school. Such problems often arrive with the approach of the well-known Jekyll and Hyde period, adolescence. While these "surprises" also occur in a nuclear family, a stepfather's reactions to them are colored by the fact that, unlike a biological father, he has neither a genetic link to the children nor the opportunity to bond with them or influence them from birth.

SEEING YOURSELF

Point 4, that your attitudes and background will play a major role in your relationships with your stepchildren, has many facets and begins with the observation that you are bound to like some children more than others. Undoubtedly you will feel more of an affinity toward one stepchild than his or her sibling. If, like myself, you've never had children of your own and you find it upsetting to realize that for a time at least you like one child more than another, remember the observation of a stepfather I interviewed who has two biological children as well as two stepchildren: "Accepting this liking one child more than another is part of parenting, not just stepparenting."

In my own case, not only did Timothy respond to me more warmly and more openly than Kevin did from our first meeting, Timothy and I also immediately seemed to have more compatible personalities. From my perspective this gave us an immediate bond. During the early years of my relationship with Kevin, his shyness and quietness around adults—and me in particular—made me see him as "different" from me. This conviction was both heightened and confirmed by his wholesale rejection of me and his frequent sullenness in my presence. In my mind I linked Timothy to me and Kevin to his biological father, whom I had never even met. This mental association created an attitude that served neither Kevin nor myself.

This brings us to the second part of point 4, about our life experiences and psychological makeup influencing our attitudes about becoming stepfathers. Since I had had conflicts with my father during my childhood and adolescence, I was inclined to reproduce similar conflicts in my relationships with my stepsons. That was my idea of how it was *supposed* to be for a father or a stepfather. In my mid-twenties my father and I resolved our conflicts and developed a close and loving relationship—something that occurred during the first few years of my life as a stepfather. Consequently I had more of a sense that conflicts with both Kevin and Timothy could be resolved and that we, too, could form close, loving relationships with each other.

On a broader level, since family life has always been important to me and having a good family life as an adult was a major goal of mine, during the getting-acquainted stage my general attitude toward creating a stepfamily was a positive one.

Most stepfathers, whether they had close or distant relationships with their own parents and stepparents while they were growing up and at the time of our interviews, also said they had had a generally positive attitude about the idea of creating a stepfamily. Most told me they regarded forming a stepfamily as part of the "package deal" that came with marrying their partners, and viewed it as a highly acceptable package. Many saw the existence of the children simply as a fact, "not as a plus or a minus"; they looked at becoming a stepfather as a necessary consequence of being with the partner they were choosing to live with or marry.

Among stepfathers who said they had been enthusiastic about forming a stepfamily, many reported a degree of ambivalence as well. A stepfather who formed a combined stepfamily with his own and his wife's children commented, "The existence of kids, in terms of getting married, I think we considered a plus in some ways. We enjoy children, and we basically like each other's children. Yet at times I think we talked in terms of each of us bringing our baggage, and part of that baggage was the kids, and the baggage has pluses and minuses, I think. It certainly complicates whatever difficulties there are in the two adults relating to each other."

For other stepfathers, the children were wholly a plus, because there was a real desire not only to marry but to have a family. As one stepfather who had no children of his own told me: "My love for my stepson seems to me to be part of my desire to have a connection, to have a family."

In terms of life experience, being a biological father prior to being a stepfather can be an advantage or a disadvantage in forming a prospective stepfather's attitudes. Experience as a biological father can be a positive influence on one's attitudes as a stepfather; but on the other hand, preconceptions that one's stepchildren will be like one's biological children—which, of course, they probably will not be—and preconceptions that being a stepfather will be like being a biological father can be the cause of an initial sense of disappointment or even failure.

THE PLOT THICKENS

When prospective stepchildren find out their mother is "serious" about you and that you are about to get married and will all begin living together, a change in your relationships with the prospective stepchildren is inevitable.

Regardless of how children learn about the deepening of a commitment on the part of their mother—whether through open discussion, an open bedroom door, or just their own canny sense of things—it almost always produces a change, at least in degree, in their reactions to their potential stepfather.

As one stepfather told me: "It's different with a child when they realize that it's serious. We went to a park once before we started living together. We went on a picnic with lots of people; I was just one of many. We had organized the whole thing in such a manner that I would just be one of many. There was a child's bicycle, and I spent lots of time taking kids on rides, holding them by the saddle. I was very much accepted as such. This was a role that Alexandra, who was five years old at the time, could accept quite graciously. I was a lot of fun and could be used. That stopped immediately when she realized that her mommy and I were romantically involved with each other."

Another stepfather, whose stepchildren were fifteen, eighteen, and nineteen when he and his wife became engaged, commented, "They accepted me fine as long as we were dating. Then it was 'What do you mean you're getting married? You can't get married!' It was almost—I don't want to say a complete turnaround or reversal and rejection—but it was a 'You're not supposed to do those kind of things' type of attitude." Stepfathers reported this same attitude on the part of children, both step and biological, even over forty years old!

Not all the feelings brought out in children by the announcement of marriage are negative, however. There was no question in my mind that in addition to Kevin's wanting Cynthia and me to be legally married instead of just living together because he was at an age when he wanted us to conform to society's rules, he also received the news of our marriage as a sign of my commitment to making a family. Looking back, I can see that the marriage itself signaled the beginning of his being open to me—trusting that I was indeed going to be there—even though the process of forming a close relationship took many years beyond that. Another stepfather who had lived with his future wife and stepson prior to marriage also reported a positive change in his stepson's attitude as a result of the marriage. "I noticed that as far as Sandy's concerned, I've had an ace in the hole since his mom and I married. It was just a plus that added to all the other pluses."

MOVING DAY

As you may have seen already in your own life, moving in together creates changes in stepfather-stepchildren relationships, and it creates a need for adjustment on the part of all stepfamily members.

One stepfather who is also a therapist and a specialist in stepfamily counseling told me little children are often very confused by suddenly being thrust into a household with their mother's new partner (and possibly his biological children, as well), especially if this arrangement precedes marriage. "I thought it would be just understood that it meant that we were going to be living together. But when my wife told my stepson, who was eight at the time, that I was going to be moving in, that we were going to be living together, he said, 'Does that mean I have to give up my daddy?' Little kids don't understand. That's why everything has to be talked about, has to be opened up and explained, and questions allowed to be asked all the time. It's very important."

For many stepfathers, living within a stepfamily means more than just explaining things to stepchildren and being supportive of their emotional adjustments. It also means getting used to living with children, and almost invariably it means conflicts over territory. "While we started living together," one stepfather told me, "the main sore area was a feeling of a lack of being accepted or a lack of room. I moved into their apartment, so we put a wall of closets up in the bedroom, and I used one of the closets as my desk area. We moved my furniture in. But it didn't feel like there was really a place for me. Like I was an outsider a lot. And I think they were feeling the opposite, that there was an intruder coming in; they didn't want to give the room that they had all carved out. That was a biggie."

One other very real issue stepfathers face as soon as they begin living with their stepfamilies was brought up by a stepfather who told me that a large problem he encountered "was simply trying to find enough privacy. It's hard to carry out a courtship with a third person there. It constantly means having to negotiate with a third party."

Another way that stepfathers and prospective stepfathers often find themselves negotiating when they move in with their partners and their partners' children is in working out conflicts over lifestyles. "I'd say the major problem was that basically I moved in with a woman and her three children; it was like moving into an establishment in that sense," one stepfather explained, "with the different patterns, different routines than I had been used to. Quite different. It was a totally different tone—much more active and social than anything I had been used to."

This stepfather-to-be found that he confronted another area of conflict as well when he moved in: the area of discipline and authority. "Early on, when I was disciplining my future stepdaughter in one way or another," he told me, "she would throw a tantrum and say, 'Who are you to exercise that kind of authority over me?' "

Whenever the battle over discipline and authority begins for a man assuming the role of stepfather, whether it is during courtship, living together, or after marriage, it is definitely *just* the beginning.

Your Relationship with Your Future Spouse

Given the likelihood of continuing battles over discipline and authority with stepchildren, it's fortunate that point 6, that your positive feelings about your partner overflow into and help to create your feelings about her children, was almost universally expressed by the stepfathers I interviewed.

One man, who after two years of dating and courtship had recently begun living with his fiancée and her son and acting as a full-time stepfather to the fourteen-year-old boy, summed up the feelings of almost every stepfather I've interviewed when he said, "My desire to work with Tommy as a parent springs from my love for Elizabeth."

Even when there are severe problems regarding the children, often the stepfather's love for the children's mother seems to give him the desire and the will to continue. Consider the comments of a stepfather who after four and a half years of marriage is still having considerable difficulties with his stepchildren, one of whom has had serious emotional problems for which he has had to be hospitalized: "Stepfathering is a difficult and often thankless job. The relationship with your wife . has got to be primary and very important to make the effort worthwhile."

This stepfather, who says that he is still "hopeful" about his stepchildren "opening up and reciprocating with love and consideration," stresses that as a stepfather you "cannot have a good relationship with your wife without satisfactorily resolving your relationships to the children." In order to resolve your relationships with your stepchildren, he emphasizes that "it is absolutely crucial that the children's mother have the same view as you do of what your function as stepfather should be."

Stepfathers unanimously said that a strong marital relationship is the key to a stepfather's satisfaction within the stepfamily. Most also feel that prior to marriage, the higher the degree of agreement between you and your partner about what your role as a stepfather should be and about child-rearing in general, and the better you are at communicating with each other, the more likely you will function as a team in meeting child-rearing challenges in the future. Conversely, the more disagreement there is about these issues early on and the harder it is for you to communicate about them, the more probable it is that your role in child-rearing will be a major area of conflict later.

Prior to marriage, many stepfathers have deep reservations about the relationships between their future mates and stepchildren, and this heightens their fears about finding a place to fit in. One stepfather, for example, said, "This is probably classic. Emily and Jacqueline were essentially a single mother-daughter relationship. Even though Emily had been living with this guy after her divorce, Emily was by far the central person in Jacqueline's life. How that would be renegotiated with me around was quite unclear."

The situation of being a single mother with a child seems to generate a particularly strong mother-child bond. Whether that bond is a positive or a negative one depends on the individuals and circumstances involved.

Jacqueline's stepfather, like many other stepfathers I interviewed, sensed difficulties as well as great intensity in the relationship between his future wife and stepdaughter almost from the time he first met them. As a consequence of the intensity between mother and daughter, he felt anxious about what his relationship would be once they became a stepfamily. In getting married, men in this situation often do what Jacqueline's stepfather told me he did: try to push their anxieties aside with the hope that by becoming part of the family they can overcome these problems by restructuring the relationship between mother and child in a healthier way.

As Jacqueline's stepfather told me and as many others confirmed, this goal is far more easily stated than accomplished. Some stepfathers referred to it as "the superman fantasy." According to the stepfathers I interviewed, men who marry with the expectation that with their presence and insight they can change the relationships between their partners and stepchildren quickly—or even at all—are doomed to disappointment and years of struggle. That's why in order to get a realistic rather than a fantasy view of the future it's particularly useful in the getting-acquainted stage to get to know your prospective partner's attitudes about mothering and about your future role as stepfather to her children. Integral to this, of course, is the process of examining your own thoughts and feelings about becoming stepfather to her children.

MAKING THE MOST OF YOUR POWER

You have to learn to exercise detachment as a way of working out problems in stepfathering or prospective stepfathering. Let's go back to my own story as a perfect example of what *not* to do to defuse a situation.

In retrospect I can see that I exacerbated Kevin's negative feelings toward me by taking everything he did personally and resenting his behavior even when it was not directed at me. While I would never have said it, I felt that even his unhappiness over his parents' divorce was directed at me. If I could go back and do it over again knowing what I know now, I would observe my own behavior more carefully and see when I was reacting inappropriately. Instead of being so emotionally incensed myself, I would strive for enough emotional detachment to bide my time with Kevin and keep a respectful distance. I would also seek opportunities for one-on-one activities with him that would bring us in close contact with each other and would thereby give us opportunities to talk without making Kevin feel obligated to talk.

I'll never know if any of these strategies might have worked, because I didn't employ them. I didn't even think of them, because I was so entrenched in my own emotional reactions. Not surprisingly, most stepfathers reported a similar experience. As I mentioned, a brief stint of counseling for Cynthia and me improved the discipline in our home when we followed the counselor's suggestion that for the time being Cynthia should be the disciplinarian and I should communicate my needs and thoughts about disciplining the children to her. After that, Cynthia and I each saw a therapist individually, which also benefited our stepfamily. Counseling or therapy isn't always necessary to help a stepfather stand back from the stepfamily situation, but it was a great help to me and to many other stepfathers I interviewed. Many stepfathers also told me they benefited from the support offered by other stepparents through local chapters of the Stepfamily Association of America.

YOUR ALTERED EGO

It is important to realize that your stepchildren's biological father has an influence on the life of your stepfamily. Here I'll confine my discussion simply to how the biological father may affect the initial stages of forming a stepfamily.

In the course of developing relationships with our stepchildren or our prospective stepchildren, all of us are contending with their relationships with their biological fathers, whether we are aware of it or not. Often, even in the getting-acquainted stage, we are also contending with the children's biological fathers themselves and with the challenge of creating workable relationships with them in order to foster communication within the stepfamily and best serve the children's needs.

Stepfathers whose partners are widows or whose ex-husbands abandoned them and their children are frequently inclined to feel they should replace their stepchildren's father. Stepfathers in this situation may even try to act as if the biological father had never existed, an attempt that is certain to fail. Stepfathers who find themselves living in close proximity to their stepchildren's biological fathers are less vulnerable to this temptation.

Even so, stepfathers and prospective stepfathers may still *wish* they could eradicate or at least deny the existence of the children's biological fathers, while, paradoxically, they may also wish the fathers would "do more" or "be better." And it's not hard to see why these negative feelings arise. Divorce almost inevitably produces disappointment, disillusionment, and anger; often there is a feeling of abandonment even by the partner who made the decision to leave. Since a prospective stepfather first learns about his prospective stepchildren's father from the woman who divorced the man, his impressions of him are bound to be negative. And if a stepfather has an ex-wife, he will similarly prepare his new partner with impressions of her. There is also the factor of jealousy, which may well affect both the stepfather and the biological father.

We can begin taking steps toward building a positive relationship with our partner's ex-husband simply by acknowledging rather than deploring his rights and influence over the children, and by developing as open an attitude as possible toward him as the children's biological father. Obviously the more clearly positive an influence the biological father is on his children the easier and more appropriate this is to do.

TIME: CONSIDER THE ALTERNATIVE

Point ten states that everyone in a stepfamily needs time to adjust. And the fact that everyone needs a different amount of time pervades every other aspect of stepfamily life. This may be the most significant fact of all for a stepfather to remember in order to maintain his sanity in periods of stepfamily crisis. I'm including here a few stepfathers' comments about time and timing during the early stages in the formation of their stepfamilies.

After thirteen months of marriage following a two-and-a-half-year courtship, one stepfather reported that he has had "no real problems" in making adjustments to stepfathering his stepdaughter, age fourteen, and his stepson, age six, for whom he and his wife have joint custody (the children live with their biological father every other week). "I went very, very easy," he said, reflecting the advice many stepfathers gave me about how to build relationships with stepchildren effectively. "I didn't push myself on them. Sort of early on in the relationship I told them I didn't want to be their father. I already was a father, and I don't think they wanted me to be their father. They already had a good relationship with their father. All I wanted to be was the male influence in the house, and that seemed to be agreeable."

Another stepfather told me that after six years of marriage, which followed a four-year courtship, his overall experience of stepfathering had been "excellent." But he also commented, "I'd say there was a *long* period of adjustment. Of my three stepdaughters, two of them I had a fairly easy time with, though it took them some time to accept me as really the 'father' of the household. The third I still have a bit of a hard time with, though I think my relationship with her—and her mother's relationship with her—has developed a little better in the last year since her oldest sister has moved out."

It's not only children, of course, who need time to accept and adjust to their new situation. Stepfathers, even after making the choice, also need time to come to terms with becoming stepfathers. While *no* stepfather I interviewed said he regretted the choice, *almost every* stepfather mentioned that his ambivalence didn't end with the getting-acquainted stage. Especially if their stepchildren live with them full time, many stepfathers, even after years of marriage, still find themselves struggling, at least occasionally, in order to accept continually a challenge that involves so many years of commitment to children who in many cases are uncooperative and often seem unwilling to form mutually affectionate relationships with them.

I know that even in my own experience, which has been a blessedly positive one, every time I had a problem with either child I would mentally ask myself why *I* had to deal with the problem instead of the children's biological father.

At the other extreme from me are stepfathers whose internal struggles are constantly fueled by stepchildren who are enormously difficult. The painfulness of such a situation as well as the time involved in coming to terms with it are implicit in the comments of a man who for three and a half years has been stepfather to his wife's two sons, ages twenty-three and twenty-two, and daughter, age twenty, whom he describes as "juvenile delinquents." Although they are now legally adults and currently do not live at home, they are still a daily negative presence in his life and thus represent what I think of as the stepfather's worst nightmare: having stepchildren who, even as adults, continue to haunt him and their mother with their problems. "If I had a magic wand," this stepfather said, "I'd wave it and keep my second wife but not her children. But life's not like that, and my wife wouldn't like that either." Since this man's experience is at the extreme negative end of the spectrum of stepfathering, I'm going to quote him from time to time throughout the book to remind us what the furthest parameters are for having, and coping with, or not coping with, problem stepsons and daughters.

In Conclusion: Getting Off to a Good Start

I go back to the stepfather who told me that "there is no sufficient preparation for stepfatherhood." While few stepfathers would argue with this, few would also recommend becoming a stepfather without any preparation. The consensus among stepfathers is that the more time a stepfather-to-be spends with the members of his future stepfamily prior to marriage, the more realistic his expectations are likely to be about the challenges he will be facing. If there are going to be trouble spots—and undoubtedly there will be—he will have at least some sense of what they will be.

Of course there will be surprises. Living together prior to marriage is one way to mitigate the surprises that follow marriage, but even then, given the nature of life, it's impossible to eliminate the unexpected. And given the nature of stepfamily life—and the variations in time required to make the necessary adjustments to it—it's impossible to chart the expected. So when looking at the getting-acquainted stage of stepfathering and the whole initial period of forming a stepfamily, I believe the issue comes down to laying as good a foundation as possible for the future relationships in the stepfamily. This means acting as responsibly and with as much consciousness as possible from as early in the relationships as possible.

CHAPTER TWO

The Stepfather's Role

B EFORE RESEARCHING THIS BOOK, my concept of the role of stepfather was based solely on my own experience. Even though I had some inkling that both the role and a man's experience of it varied from stepfather to stepfather and from stepfamily to stepfamily, I had no idea just how much variety there was until I began my interviews. Here is what I mean:

"Since Sara has always had a very close ongoing relationship with her father and her new stepmother, I've never been forced into the role of really having to decide to be her father," one stepfather told me. "I think of myself as kind of her uncle."

"My role as stepfather is to try to be something of a friend," another stepfather explained, "somebody my stepchildren can turn to, somebody they can trust, somebody that will care about them."

Another stepfather said, "I've really come up with a definition for myself for what it's like to be a stepfather. For anybody that's ever gone to a sleep-away camp, I think the feeling between stepfather and stepchildren is much like that for the camp counselor and the kids in the bunk. It's very close, very intense, very important, but yet it's not like a parent."

"I really don't think there's any difference between stepparenting and parenting," another stepfather told me.

"Stepfathering is not at all like parenting, which surprised me," another stepfather observed. "It's more like being a scout leader."

"As a stepfather, I feel rejected and inessential," another stepfather said.

"Compared to my expectations before marriage, stepfathering is the pits," one stepfather told me. "Certainly more valleys than peaks. I constantly hear how my stepson's father is bigger, better, has more, does more with him."

"Prior to marriage I thought stepfathering would be a little more difficult than it's turning out to be," another stepfather commented. "I expected more resistance as a stepfather, more problems."

"I didn't think about stepfathering very much before marriage," another stepfather told me. "When I did, I figured I'd be raising a 'little-me.' It's a lot tougher than that."

"I thought stepfathering would be a blending of families," another stepfather said. "It didn't turn out that way. You must treat each child individually."

"Compared to my expectations, being a stepfather has been highly disruptive because my stepkids have been juvenile delinquents," another stepfather told me. "My wife has been brokenhearted, but she has defended them too often when I told it like it was. Stepparenting to me has been absolutely horrible."

"I think my expectations were that stepfathering would be a fairly small aspect of my life and sort of routine. I don't mean this as a pejorative metaphor but not unlike taking care of a pet or something like that, you know. You feed them, you pat them on the head, you do a few nice things for them; and they grow up and they respond with adulation and that's about it. That was my expectation at least—but it's not like that at all."

Listening to different stepfathers describe their roles is like listening to the blind men in the fable describing an elephant. Each stepfather gives a definition based on his own experience; and while the experiences of some stepfathers are similar, some are polar opposites.

But unlike the blind men describing the elephant, *each stepfather's definition of the role of stepfather is valid in and of itself.* A stepfather's role is defined first of all by the general factors that shape the life of all stepfamilies, and secondly by the numerous individual circumstances that shape the life of each stepfamily. These circumstances and factors are different in fundamental ways from those shaping the life of a nuclear family and the roles of biological parents. This is why we can't look to biological fathers as our models, nor, if we have biological children, can we look to our relationships with them as models of what our relationships with our stepchildren will be like. Instead we must look for our role models among other stepfathers—and even then we must adjust our role to accommodate the factors that are unique to our own stepfamilies Most of all, we have to remember that being a stepfather is a process of education and discovery—and a lot of it is self-discovery.

MAJOR DIFFERENCES BETWEEN STEPFATHERS AND BIOLOGICAL FATHERS

A large part of the education and discovery process that is inherent in becoming a stepfather has to do with our learning and then adjusting to the general characteristics that distinguish a stepfather's role from a biological father's. While our stepchildren calling us by our first names rather than "Dad" may be acceptable, many of us find some of the other characteristics that seem intrinsic to the role far more problematic. Primary among these is what one stepfather described as the "conditional" nature of the stepfather's relationships to his stepchildren.

As this stepfather explained it: "I think the biggest problems of stepfathering have been constantly being reminded in one way or another that the relationship between a stepfather and his stepchildren is different from the biological parent's, in the sense that there is an element which is conditional. To put it in a strong way that I don't quite mean, it's that one is always in some sense on probation as a stepparent in a way in which one is not as a biological parent. Feeling that the children's feelings toward you to a great extent but not totally are conditional on the way in which you behave toward them, and to some extent vice versa. That's a hard thing to own up to. A mother's love of her child, except in extraordinary cases, is unconditional and perpetual and eternal. The relationship with a stepfather, on the other hand, if one is honest with oneself, is to a greater extent dependent on how the kids turn out and how they relate to you and what, in effect, they're able to give back."

One of the other major characteristics that stepfathers continually pointed to as distinguishing the stepfather's role from that of the biological parent is the incontrovertible fact that for at least some of our stepchildren's lives we had absolutely no connection to them, genetic or otherwise. This lack of history not only means that our building a bond with them must begin at a later stage than it did with their biological father— and without the identification with the children that comes from a genetic link—it also means that our influence on them and our responsibility for them begin at that later stage. Often this is hard to accept with equanimity.

As one stepfather told me: "I think the hard thing about being a stepparent is that if you're a biological parent and you have problems, then you can say, 'Oh shit, I screwed up somewhere in the beginning, which is leading to this hassle now.' As a stepfather you come in, and you've already missed a certain period. With my stepson I missed the first eight years. If you make too strong a point of it, then the spouse says, 'Well, you're telling me that I really screwed up as a mother.' That leads to hassles. You have to accept that you start your input much later. I think that's the hard part of stepparenting; it's *hard* to deal with and accept. I don't think we ever fully accept it, nor can we ever fully deal with it.

"Regardless of what you and your spouse agree on, they've

already had so much input that you haven't agreed on that they've already created the base off which this kid operates. And that might be totally different from what your in-put would've created. It's like moving in a house that somebody else built. You can redo some of it, but weight-bearing walls you can't change. They're there."

Another factor that sometimes makes stepfathering "a process apart" from biological fathering is working out relationships between blood relatives and stepfamilies when the blood relatives refuse to accept the validity of the stepfamily. One stepfather who found himself encountering this problem commented, "I have actually felt that one of the hardest things for me to accomplish is integrating my current family with my other family. The relatives have not been particularly accepting. I think it's both a combination of problems of accepting a second wife—they always liked my first wife a lot, and they're still in contact with her. And I have had a hard time getting them to treat my stepchildren as my children, and they basically still don't do it. It's been frustrating from my point of view."

Another stepfather added this further twist: "I've had a real problem with my parents accepting that my wife and I aren't going to have any more children, that it's a decision we've both made. They keep dropping hints to my wife like 'I know you already have three children, but my son would really like one of his own.' I've had a lot of fights with my parents about this. It's been tough for them to accept that I'm really happy in my role as a stepfather."

IT'S A PROCESS OF EVOLUTION

Stepfathers' roles must evolve; one doesn't simply inherit the role by becoming a stepfather. Since time is a necessary ingredient in this process of evolution, a stepfather, especially in the early stages of his stepfamily's existence, may be unsure about what his role is or will be. As a stepfather of just over one year ("one year and two days," he made sure to tell me) said: "Role confusion is one of my major difficulties." And as another stepfather observed: "Since stepfathering is a new ballgame and most of us, being raised in nuclear families when we were kids, don't have much historical background for it personally, when we suddenly are thrust into this new role that has a lot of new rules that we don't know, it's understandable that we don't know what to do. I think you have to read books, you have to go to organizations like the Stepfamily Association of America that have data to give you. I don't think it's necessarily a therapy process; I think it's a relearning process—a lot of education."

To one extent or another, confusion over what our roles should be is appropriate, especially because *a stepfather cannot define his role just on the basis of his own preferences and assessment of what he wants and what he thinks his family needs.* In addition to his own ideas and personality, a stepfather's role is also determined by the ideas and personalities of the other stepfamily members and by the circumstances out of which his stepfamily is formed. The ten essential points about stepfamily life that are outlined in Chapter One influence what our stepfamily life is like at any given moment, and they also shape our roles as stepfathers. Some of the factors encompassed in these ten points are largely or totally outside our influence.

Regardless of how clear-seeing, well-intentioned, and committed we may be, we cannot necessarily transform our role from being like an uncle to our stepchildren to being like a father to them just because *we* may want to. If our stepchildren are antagonistic toward us, we cannot even go from what we might accurately describe as an inessential role in their lives to the role of being their friend. Our stepchildren have to cooperate with and support this type of a change; it cannot happen unless they do.

Although we can't change the factors outside ourselves that limit our roles as stepfathers, we can improve our experience of our role through our own attitudes and actions. How we *feel* about the role and how we *act* in it are up to us. The key to being productive as a stepfather, whichever way the role is defined, begins with having a productive attitude.

Of course, maintaining a productive attitude is a challenge in itself. Commenting on the nature of this challenge, one stepfather, reflecting a perception shared by many others, said, "Stepfathering is much more complex than I ever thought it would be." Another stepfather added, "In order to deal with the complex process of stepfathering, one has to be ready to commit a great deal of time, thought, feeling, and energy to it. Each day is a surprise and unpredictable and also very ordinary. Stepfathering is a process that demands a willingness to be flexible, to enter into conflict, develop trust, change, stand firm, negotiate differences, let go, cry, state needs over and over again, accept disappointment, blow up, calm down, and laugh from someplace deep inside that you never knew was there."

Part of what makes stepfathering so complex and demanding is that we are dealing with situations that are defined by so many variables, and, especially in the early stages of a stepfamily, some of these variables may vary from day to day. In the following section, I'm going to focus on those aspects of the ten essential points about stepfamily life that shape our roles as stepfathers. These are the variables that determine what role we have within our stepfamily and also how we feel about our role. Once you see these variables clearly, you can begin to sort out which ones you can change and which you cannot. This is the first major step you can take toward having a productive attitude.

ON OUR STEPCHILDREN'S AGES, GENDERS, AND ATTITUDES

The first variable that affects a stepfather's role is the age, number, gender, and attitude of his stepchildren.

The testimony of many stepfathers suggests that the younger the stepchild at the time a stepfather enters his or her life, the easier it generally is for the stepfather to form a bond with the child. The younger the child, the more he needs adults to do things for him and the less formed the child is generally. One stepfather's comment about his stepson reflects this: "He was only five when I became his stepfather, so, unlike his teenage sister, he was pretty open to me." But age isn't the only factor that determines a child's receptivity toward a new stepfather. One stepfather, for example, observed to me about his stepdaughter, who at age two and a half was unusually close to her mother, "She was not even three when we met each other and she wanted nothing to do with me."

One generalization that by and large holds true about the age of stepchildren is that it's difficult for a new stepfather to form a bond with an adolescent or even a post-adolescent stepchild.

One stepfather, commenting on the attitude of his step-daughter, who was fifteen when he entered her life, remarked, "She was very full of herself and wanted little to do with her mother or me. She had all the answers herself." Another step-father indicated by his comment about his fourteen-year-old stepson that despite this generalization stepfathers don't *always* face enormous resistance or rebellion when they enter the lives of adolescents. "Right away he thought of me as a friend, and he respected me," this stepfather reported about his stepson, who as a result of his biological father's physical and emotional distance missed having an adult male as a regular presence in his life. Perhaps the reason that this stepfather's experience with his adolescent stepchild has been largely positive is contained in his comment: "Of course, I respect him, too, and I make sure not to come down on him too hard. I respect his space, and I talk to him as a friend. I don't try to 'play father.' "

Again we come back to the temperament and attitude of the stepchildren and of the stepfather as being at least as important as the children's age at the time their stepfathers come into their lives or any of the other variables influencing the bond between stepfather and stepchild.

Stepfathers almost unanimously agreed that the gender of stepchildren, like their age, had some effect on their roles and their feelings about being a stepfather, but they varied widely on how and to what extent gender was an influence.

Some felt that while their role toward their stepdaughters was influenced to some degree by the gender difference, the different genders did not make their role as stepfather more distant. One stepfather of three stepdaughters said, "Having stepdaughters has its advantages and disadvantages, and a lot of them are just male-female relationships. To some degree, being a male in relationship to girls can be a little easier. Girls are typically more rebellious against their mother than their father. So that's a plus for me as a stepfather. The disadvantage, in terms of making my own turf or whatever, is that I was not only in a whole new family, which was foreign to me, but it was also a family of all women. So I had no male companionship—watching a football game for example or just sort of male reactions to things, which can be different from female reactions."

Other stepfathers reported that the gender of their stepchildren greatly influenced their roles, and that having teenage stepdaughters could create problems for some stepfathers. "The Oedipal conflict in terms of daughters is accentuated with a stepfather, and I've felt sexually self-conscious with my stepdaughters," one stepfather told me. "They are very, very attractive teenagers, and one is aware of being in a household with very attractive women. I think that's natural. What's important is how one responds to it. I think on the one hand it's important for young people to be affirmed by their parents and stepparents in their attractiveness, in their physicalness, and yet one has to be very aware of maintaining appropriate boundaries. I'm almost ready to say that it's perhaps natural in father-daughter relationships, and especially in stepfather-daughter relationships, that the relationship on some level be characterized by a particular distance. And so it's been for me. That doesn't mean in other ways we're not close; that doesn't mean that there isn't a mutual sense of love."

Another stepfather saw the differences between stepfathering boys and girls in terms of the role models and different types of parenting children need at different stages: "There has to be a difference stepfathering boys compared to stepfathering girls. I feel that girls need to have a woman around. There are so many things that the girls can talk to my wife about that I'm sure they would be reluctant to talk with me about, especially as they get older. Like the oldest [age fifteen] likes boys, and she's not dating yet, but she'd like to. I'm sure she'll spend more time talking to her mother than she would me. She'd be more comfortable talking with her mother about that. My stepson Joey, in turn, can be more open with me than he would be with his mother. There are a variety of things that boys like to do that girls don't want to be bothered with. I think they make a difference in raising boys and raising girls, not only stepsons and daughters, but also biological sons and daughters. I know that at this point in my life if I had not remarried and I was still raising a ten- and twelve-year-old girl, I'd be most appreciative of some woman stepping in and helping me and talking with the kids from time to time. They need the interaction of a female."

Whatever the age or gender of the stepchildren, the problem of forming close bonds with them is of course most severe when the children are resistant to the stepfather. For many stepfathers, this is the biggest problem they encounter in the role. As one stepfather said, summing up the experience of many, "It was a very rude awakening to find out how unwanted I am by my stepsons."

ON CHILDREN'S RELATIONSHIP WITH THEIR FATHERS

The second major variable shaping our roles as stepfathers has to do with the relationships between our stepchildren and their biological fathers.

As we've already noted in Chapter One, the more our stepchildren's biological fathers participate in their lives, the less likely our stepchildren will need us to play a predominantly father-figure role for them, and the less support we'll get from them if we are inclined to try to play this role. This is especially true if our stepchildren live full time with their father and only visit with their mother and us. The converse is also true: The less of a regular presence our stepchildren's fathers are in their lives, the more likely it is we will be called upon to play at least some variation of a fatherlike role.

This said, however, a stepfather may still play a fatherlike role in his own household in terms of discipline, authority, and creating an environment in which stepchildren can share their confidences with him.

It bears repeating—indeed, many of the stepfathers I interviewed emphasized and re-emphasized this point to me—that whether our stepchildren's fathers are regular and active presences in their lives, intermittent presences, or totally absent, we must be clear to ourselves and to our stepchildren that we are not attempting to take the place of their biological fathers, to take over the unique relationships they have with them, or to eradicate their memories of them. In such cases we may be fatherlike as the children's stepfathers, but unless we adopt the children we are still their stepfathers, not their fathers.

It's important to realize, too, that although many stepfathers cited problems with their stepchildren's biological fathers ("I don't like him and I don't think he likes me and we don't see eye-to-eye on just about everything" is one stepfather's comment), generally speaking these problems reach a point of stasis or even diminish with time. Only two stepfathers said that their primary problems in the role of stepfather were due to the biological father. In one case, the father, following the divorce, put his children in the extreme position of having to reject their mother and stepfather in order to continue having a relationship with him. In the other, the father "miraculously got custody and is now using it as a weapon" against his ex-wife and the stepfather, who are in the process of appealing the custody decision.

How Our Own Attitudes and Personalities Affect Our Roles

Some stepfathers explicitly cited their own attitudes and emotional makeup as being the biggest problem confronting them in their role. One stepfather I talked to was particularly sensitive to his own temperament and attitudes, acting in tandem with those of his stepchild, as the primary causes of his problems in the role. "My biggest problems," he said, "are behavioral problems on the part of my stepson that result from emotional confusion over the losses he has experienced and his fears of being abandoned again. I also have a problem because of my own expectations of myself, without the time to build the relationship adequately. Also I have a problem with self-doubting and being overly critical about decisions I should make. And it's all compounded because I have no role models to observe."

Another stepfather included his wife with him and his stepdaughter as the responsible parties for family disharmony. "My three biggest problems are my stepdaughter's reaction to me—jealousy and rage; my reaction to her—jealousy and rage; and my interaction with my wife—jealousy and envy," he said.

Rigidity in a stepfather's attitudes and emotional makeup contributes greatly to the problems he is apt to face in a stepfamily. Success is possible only when one remains flexible. As one stepfather commented: "There are few problems in stepfathering if one knows how to maintain harmony and a friendly attitude. Else—disaster!"

Ironically, a stepfather who feels he is "right" and that his stepchildren and/or spouse are "wrong" and that they are the exclusive cause of disharmony in his home frequently cannot see the problems his self-righteousness is causing. Even if such a stepfather *says* he is willing to "talk about the situation," what he *communicates* to the other members of his stepfamily by his rigid attitude is a lack of empathy for them and an unwillingness to bend himself. It is difficult for other members of the stepfamily to hear his point of view when they feel he is not hearing theirs; it is difficult for them to take a step closer to him if his posture suggests that he is standing in judgment of them. As one stepfather observed about himself: "My biggest problem is that I'm *always* being too critical of my stepchild. This causes animosity between my stepchild, my wife, and myself."

TRANSCENDING OUR OWN PRECONCEPTIONS AND DESIRES

A stepfather's attitude and emotional makeup will cause him tremendous problems if his preconception of the role is substantially different from the reality. This may be especially difficult if he has a strong desire for the role to be something other than what it is. At one extreme is the stepfather who feels that being a stepfather makes too many demands on him and requires too much closeness. At the other extreme is the stepfather who feels that being a stepfather does not allow a close enough relationship with his children.

One stepfather summed up the latter situation like this: "My biggest problem as a stepfather is learning how to live with very painful disappointment, sadness, and anger when the realization cuts in that they really are 'someone else's children.' " Another stepfather, who after sixteen years feels very close to his grown stepchildren, reflected about the pain he felt while they were growing up: "One of the biggest problems of stepfathering is to be able—how to say it—to be able to endure 'without love'—no return of love from the stepkids until they've reached adulthood. It's a long, lean time."

While biological parents frequently feel—and in fact may be—unappreciated by their children until they are adults, stepfathers tend to feel their stepchildren's lack of appreciation even more strongly because there is no biological link and no prior history. This is why a stepfather's affection for his stepchildren tends to be more conditional than a biological father's. "Look at all I'm doing for another man's children, and look how they act toward me!" I sometimes said to myself. Mentally adding up all the energy, time, and emotion I was investing in Kevin and Timothy, I felt I was not being amply compensated. I was unaware that, in fact, the future would bring me the emotional rewards from them I wanted so much.

In regard to the difference between the way children act with their stepfather compared to the way they act toward their biological father, a stepfather of eighteen years, also a psychiatrist, observed, "One way or another, the child feels freer in expressing the negative side of love to a stepfather. You have to have a special wisdom about that. If you take that personally, you're doomed."

Another stepfather who counsels stepfamilies said, "A problem arises with many people because there is a psychological need for them to have a daughter or their first daughter or their first child, and they really want to be a father. They want to be just like a biological father, and that in many cases creates conflicts. The first thing is to be very clear in the difference between your stepchildren's needs and your needs and to make sure that you know the differences and that they don't get muddled and clouded together.

"For instance, you may need to be close right away, while your stepchildren may need to take time.

"You also have to understand that 'The Brady Bunch' is fiction and things just don't and can't work that way. But on the other hand, 'Cinderella' and 'Hansel and Gretel' are also fiction, and the wicked stepparent also doesn't have to exist. Being a stepparent of either sex can be a very positive situation; it can be full of exciting kinds of things as long as you don't try to fit the new into the old mold. When you start to do that, then you're going to get friction and trouble. You have to take each thing that comes along as being new, and both stepchild and stepfather have to grow with the thing and learn from it together. You've got to be very flexible as a stepfather, extremely flexible."

OUR PARTNERS' ATTITUDES AND PERSONALITIES

The next variable influencing a stepfather's role is the attitude of his partner toward his role, and her abilities to be flexible and to communicate with the stepfather. These are, in fact, the primary factors stepfathers cited as necessary in order to find some degree of satisfaction in their role.

Some stepfathers felt it was necessary to have total agreement between them and their partners in areas involving child-rearing and in defining their roles. One stepfather commented, "It's 100 percent crucial that the children's mother have the same view as you do of what your function as stepfather should be. There is no life worth living getting in between a biological parent and her offspring." A stepfather of three-and-a-half years who doesn't have the agreement he seeks from his partner made the same point with a negative example: "My biggest problem is trying to discipline and correct them without being mutilated by their mother."

Stepfathers agreed that they have to form their own relationships with their stepchildren and that their partners should support them rather than trying to make the children like them. But stepfathers—and their partners—differ as to how much they think mothers should talk to children about how they relate to stepfathers. Some stepfathers felt that, if their stepchildren were consistently rude to them, not only they but the children's mothers, too, should speak to the children about their manners. "Rudeness is unacceptable behavior, even when it's directed against a stepfather," one stepfather said, "and I appreciated my wife's speaking to her children when she was alone with them about how rude they were to me all the time. I told them myself, of course, but it made a difference to have their mother tell them they didn't have to love me right away but they should at least treat me decently. After all, I was decent to them." Another stepfather, whose stepdaughter treated him with open hostility and constant ingratitude for several years, said that his partner left him to fend for himself with her daughter's surliness. This stepfather said he accepted his partner's reluctance to get involved—her belief that her daughter had a right to express her feeling any way she chose. That was who her daughter was. As this mother saw it, she had no role in working out her new husband's relationship with his stepdaughter.

Other stepfathers felt that total agreement isn't crucial as long as a stepfather and his partner are able to have open and honest discussions. "It's not critical to have the *same* view," a stepfather explained. "But it is critical that we are *united* as a team, working out things together, listening to the other's input. If we cannot be united, the child will follow his mother."

Some stepfathers reported that a partner's unconscious attitude was a major obstacle not just to their effectiveness as disciplinarians or authority figures but also to their getting close to their stepchildren. "My wife supports me verbally in getting close to my stepchildren in the role of stepfather," one stepfather said. "But when it comes to actions, she understands that there is a difference, and she is into a very strong mothering role. The father's role/place is a lesser thing in her mind, so she operates that way. I at times find that frustrating, and I find myself shut out from trying to be close to my stepchildren because of the intensity and the strength my wife puts into motherhood. They tend to be closer to her."

Another stepfather suggested that the closeness that develops between a mother and her children after a divorce may pose a real problem in a stepfather's getting close to the children. "I think that the bond between the single mother and the child is of such a strength and such a dimension that nobody can break in there," he said.

Many stepfathers said they sometimes felt that they were part of a "triangle" consisting of them, their partners, and their partners' child (or children). One such stepfather told me, "I've been in therapy, and it's been a bit of an issue in terms of what sort of triangle exists between Debby, Rachel, and me. Debby and Rachel are so close that it sometimes seems like a fusing of the two of them, and I end up like I'm dealing with them as one. That's the biggest problem I've had."

A stepfather of twenty-five years felt that by allowing time for all the members of his stepfamily to resolve their feelings, the "triangle" dissolved. "At this point I couldn't be any closer to my stepdaughter if she were my biological daughter," he said. "But I think that when you're not the natural father of children there tends to be more competition among the three of you in terms of affection and group dynamics. You tend to compete with the children for the mother and you tend to compete with the mother for the children, so I think there's more of a jealousy factor operating."

ON HAVING BIOLOGICAL CHILDREN

When stepfathers have biological children, their roles are influenced by either the absence or the presence of these children. A we've seen, for stepfathers like myself who don't have children of our own, this factor in itself can add fuel to our desire to get married and have an "instant family." We are also more prone to try to take on fatherlike or surrogate father roles to our stepchildren. Too, we are likely to be far more ignorant about the ways of children. This means that on a practical level we have to learn about how to live with children and how to handle the challenges of parenting generally as well as stepfathering in particular.

For stepfathers who have biological children, almost universally the biggest problem for them in their role is "learning to balance relationships with all the stepfamily members, including biological children, without developing jealousies," as a stepfather of four-and-a-half years said about his own experience.

Another critical factor in determining the stepfather's role in a combined stepfamily is whether his biological children live with him only part time while his stepchildren live with him full time. When a stepfather finds himself in this situation, he may feel that if he is too close and too caring with his stepchildren then he will be betraying his biological children, even when they are not present. A stepfather in this position may hold himself back with his stepchildren and define his role as a more formal one than the circumstances of his stepfamily may demand. He may feel frustrated both by his emotional distance from his stepchildren and his physical distance from his biological children. Until these feelings are resolved, a stepfather won't be able to reap the rewards in his role as stepfather or as a father.

Some stepfathers with biological children feel that the complicated logistics of working out connections among the differ-

ent households puts a burden on them. Often if you read between the lines, these stepfathers are really saying that they
don't feel their own needs are being met. "One of my biggest
problems," one stepfather told me, "is feeling that you are
supposed to be a part of the household while having your
schedule, household, and life oriented to everyone else—wife,
children, ex-spouse, stepchild, grandparents, et cetera."

FIVE VARIABLES

Put in their most basic form, the five variables we've just explored as shaping a stepfather's role are:

1. the age, number, gender, and attitudes of the stepchildren;
2. the relationships between the stepchildren and their biological father and the amount of time he spends with them;
3. the attitude of the stepfather toward what his role should
   be and his ability to be flexible and to communicate with
   the other members of his stepfamily;
4. the attitude of the stepchildren's mother toward what the
   stepfather's role should be and her ability to be flexible and
   to communicate;
5. whether the stepfather has biological children, whether
   they live with him full time or part time, and what all
   members of the stepfamily feel about forming a combined
   stepfamily.

Although at any given time one of these variables may have
a greater impact than the others, it's the interaction of all of
them that determines a particular stepfather's role and how he
feels about it. Let's look at a case in point. The stepfather
quoted at the beginning of this chapter as being like an
"uncle" has a biological son he doesn't often see. He prefers to
think of himself as an uncle to his stepdaughter so he can still
think of himself as father to his biological son. This has been
supported by the fact that his stepdaughter, Sara, has always
been close to her biological father as well as her mother. Recently, however—ever since he, his partner and Sara moved

several hundred miles—Sara has been growing closer to him and has needed more from him. Thus, while up to now being like an "uncle" has been a satisfactory role, Sara's increased dependency has made him question whether he should be feeling closer to her and giving her more affection. At times, this has made him feel inadequate in the role of being like an uncle. He keeps feeling he *should* be feeling more.

Other stepfathers I interviewed see themselves as "camp counselors," and "scout leaders," "friends" or any of a number of other possibilities in relation to their stepchildren; some are content in their roles and some are not. For all of them, their roles fit the dynamics of their personal situation: their relationship to the mothers, the children, the biological fathers, and their own biological children. But the stepfathers' *happiness* in their roles depends largely on whether these roles meet their own expectations and needs, as well as the dynamics of the family situation. As the example of Sara's stepfather suggests, stepfathers' happiness in their roles depend not only on what they expect of their stepchildren and their partners, but what they expect of themseves.

In any event, it's crucial to recognize that because there is no single definition of what a stepfather should be, it's fallacious to assume that a stepfather who describes his role as "like a father" is succeeding while a stepfather who describes his role as "like an uncle" or "like a friend" is failing.

IN CONCLUSION

In thinking about and seeing the commitment so many stepfathers are making to work through the problems they experience in their roles, I was reminded of the beginning lines of a passage in Kahlil Gibran's *The Prophet*. After interviewing dozens of stepfathers and reflecting on my own experience, I found these lines not only moving but helpful.

Your children are not your children.
They are the sons and daughters of Life's longing for itself.
They come through you but not from you.
And though they are with you yet they belong not to you.

Gibran's prophet is talking to parents about the ideal of unconditional love. For biological parents, the challenge of meeting this ideal is the challenge of being able to love their children without feeling they own them, to love them *and* allow them their uniqueness. It is the challenge of loving children as truly separate beings rather than trying to control them and make the children totally like themselves.

For stepfathers, the challenge of meeting the ideal of unconditional love is even greater, because our love for our stepchildren cannot be generated, even initially, by the *illusion* that we own them. Our challenge is to be able to love them for their uniqueness when in the most fundamental ways it cannot possibly bear any resemblance to our own (and may very well have something in common with their biological fathers'). This is where the absence of the biological link tends to push us toward a more conditional type of love. As one stepfather told me: "I think for stepfathers the special problem is to acknowledge the narcissistic problem that this child is not a physical reflection of yourself. And that that in a way is always disappointing for human beings, because it's a biological reality that we want immortality through that particular aspect of procreation. We get pleasure in the mirror of our own beauty in the child. And when you don't get that, it requires a certain amount of charity and grace that you wouldn't normally have. And you have to acknowledge that there's a special demand being made of you."

As stepfathers, we *know* our stepchildren are not our children; we *know* they have not come through us. Thus our challenge is to love them simply because "they are with" us and because "they are the sons and daughters of Life's longing for itself." It is the challenge of not making our love for our stepchildren conditional even if our stepchildren make their love for us conditional. This is indeed a challenge and a very personal decision whether to strive to meet it.

The reason so many stepfathers do try to meet this challenge, despite the resistance with which they are being met by stepchildren and the often difficult process of communication and negotiation with their partners, is found in the concluding lines of Gibran's chapter "On Children," which address the parents' role in sending children out into the world.

You are the bows from which your children as living arrows are sent forth.

The archer sees the mark upon the path of the infinite, and He bends you with His might that His arrows may go swift and far.

Let your bending in the archer's hand be for gladness;

For even as He loves the arrow that flies, so He loves also the bow that is stable.

Regardless of whether at the moment we define our role as stepfather as being like an uncle, a friend, a camp counselor, a father, a scout leader, or even an unwanted intruder—whatever the specifics of our situation and whatever our experience—many of us feel that just being in a child's life, just bearing the title "stepfather," just being the partner of the child's mother, means that we are part of the bow that sends that child forth. As such, we have a responsibility to that child, and what Gibran's prophet is telling biological parents holds true for us, too. We may not be as significant a part of the bow as our stepchildren's biological parents are, and if we have children we may not be as significant a part of the bow that sends our stepchildren forth as we are of the bow that sends our own children forth. But nevertheless we are part.

CHAPTER THREE

Adjustments

"PERIOD OF ADJUSTMENT? I think it's worse than that. Maybe the 365-day war or something."

"The period of adjustment lasts about two years. It's like holding your breath under water, hoping you come up for air before you drown."

"I'm married three years and we're still in the period of adjustment. How long does it last—I wish I knew! I can describe it like this: It feels like being an organ transplanted into a body that can't accept it or reject it."

"I understand that the first four to six years are the hardest. And we're definitely going through the hardest stage."

"We are just beginning to breach the walls after nearly four years."

"It took about two years to develop any relationship. After four and a half years my stepson still refuses to acknowledge my role as the man of the house and provokes arguments and is disrespectful. My stepdaughter, though cool at first, has warmed up, and I have a fairly good father-daughter relationship with her."

"The period of adjustment for us went on for a few—three or four—years. In some ways it's still going on, and we're in our sixth year now. I would describe it as quite traumatic."

"There was a definite period of adjustment for the first few years, but even after seven years I continue to experience adjustment."

"I'm not sure there is a definable period of adjustment, but after ten years of stepfathering it seems to me a minimum to accept the adjustment is probably two to three years. I am not sure it ever ends, since it is a position that requires continuous work."

"After sixteen years of stepfathering I would say the period of adjustment lasts as long as the stepchildren are under the same roof. I would describe it as somewhere between devastating and unbelievable."

For a long time, I didn't think of what was happening in our stepfamily as a period of adjustment. I just thought in terms of survival. This seems to be a common attitude. As one stepfather said: "My goal is to survive as a family, to live happily (whatever that is), and to raise my stepdaughter to the best of my capacity."

In my case, I first got the idea that there might be an acclimatization period in stepfathering after about ten years, when all of a sudden I realized that stepfathering had changed for me in a fundamental way: The good times were better and the bad times were better, too. Although I still sometimes found myself disappointed, frustrated, even slightly traumatized by my stepson's behavior—Kevin was twenty years old then and Timothy was sixteen—I also had a definite sense that they were in my life and I was in theirs and that had become a reality with which neither they nor I would quibble. In earlier years, sometimes the fact that we were in each other's lives was not quite as acceptable to me or to them (though I never asked). At some time during that tenth or eleventh year a new era began, a new level of acceptance.

To be sure, this wasn't the first adjustment I felt in our stepfamily, but it was the most major for me personally. It was also the first I recognized fully. Before that had come adjusting to living with children—that took about two years—and my adjusting to Kevin's overt resistance to my presence in the family, while he adjusted to being less overtly resistant to my presence in the family—which took between two and three years. When I first became stepfather to Kevin and Timothy, these were the primary areas in which adjustment was necessary so I would have a sense that harmony, though not a continual presence in our household, was possible.

Strangely enough, despite the extreme moments of frustration I felt prior to these adjustments taking place, when they did I took no notice of them. I failed to stop for even a moment to appreciate my fortunate change of fate. Instead, when all was not going well—meaning when the boys were fighting with each other, with their mother, with their friends, or with me, or were having problems with school—I often found myself preoccupied by the unfairness inherent in being a stepfather. This was my way of expressing to myself what one of the other stepfathers I quoted referred to as the conditional aspects of a stepfather's relationships with his stepchildren.

This, as I said, was the biggest adjustment I personally had to make: to accept what it means to be a stepfather rather than be frustrated or upset by it. And this was what I suddenly noticed took place after about ten years. As I now know, that didn't mean more adjustments weren't necessary on my part or on Kevin's, Timothy's and Cynthia's parts as Kevin and Timothy continued to mature and go out into the world. What it did mean was that these adjustments would be made within a new context. Finally I felt completely that I was their stepfather and they were my stepsons; I had adjusted to that. Once I had made this adjustment, I no longer felt our relationships to each other were in jeopardy because of disagreements. On a subtle level I also came to realize that my relationships with Kevin and Timothy were not in jeopardy as a result of their growing closeness to their biological father.

❊   ❊   ❊

As you can see from the stepfather's quotes I presented at the beginning of this chapter, stepfathers have varying thoughts about how long the period of adjustment lasts—with some of them feeling it never ends at all. Like so many aspects of stepfathering, the exact scenario and duration of the adjustment period depend on the individuals. The consensus among stepfathers is that adjustments do have to be made, and that making them is often far harder—and takes far longer—than they thought.

There is also a consensus that the primary adjustments stepfathers have to make are: to new living arrangements; to different lifestyles and values of their partners and stepchildren; to the needs, demands and expectations involved in relationships with partners, stepchildren and biological children; and to feelings regarding ex-partners. The issues stepfathers confront in all these areas are issues that stem from the ten facts I listed about stepfathering in Chapter One.

The period of adjustment begins, stepfathers say, when a stepfather and his stepfamily find themselves housed under the same roof. Whether it lasts one year, two years, three years, ten years, or if it never ends at all, seeing what other stepfathers experience is the best way to prepare for it.

UNDER ONE ROOF

My own feelings about adjusting to the simple facts of life with children were summed up by the stepfather who said, "Getting used to living with children was tough. There wasn't as much privacy as I was used to. They were sort of all pervasive."

Although some stepfathers I interviewed began adjusting to living with the all-pervasiveness of their stepchildren prior to marriage, most began their adjustments and their full-time resident status after the wedding. And for many of these stepfathers, especially those who had never lived with children before, a great many adjustments were necessary.

One stepfather who had never had a child before used the

word "mystification" to sum up his reaction to his stepdaughter in the early stages of his relationship with her. He explained: "She was the first child I had ever dealt with so closely. I think that's the major thread of the whole thing— mystification. In the sense of, with a first child, what kinds of allowances do you make? And then it's further complicated because with a stepchild it's a negotiated relationship, if only because the child is negotiating a relationship, regardless of what you want to do. So I kept trying to think what the terms of the negotiation were and what my obligations were, and, at the same time, I had very little understanding of what it was to be seven or eight years old. It's a classic parenting problem, although maybe it's more difficult when you're brought into the middle of someone else's life."

Even a stepfather who has had children but has not lived with them for a long time may find he has some readjusting to do when he begins living with his stepchildren. A stepfather in this situation explained it this way: "The issues for me were privacy and just getting used to having all these other people in the space. Kids tend to take over whatever is there. That was hard. During all my years on my own I had sort of developed a system. You know, you put something here, and that's where it always is: stamps live here, the flashlight lives there, that sort of thing. All of a sudden the stamps were never there, the flashlight was never there. You'd always have to hunt for them. Those kinds of things could be very annoying, and they sort of built up, I suppose."

It's at those times when things do build up that we stepfathers are especially grateful if our stepchildren's biological fathers live nearby and are active in the children's lives. As the stepfather I just quoted said: "I think the saving grace was that the children did spend time with their father on a regular basis from the beginning. I think that's what kept me sane."

Another stepfather said of the adjustments he had to make when he began living with his partner and stepdaughter, "When my wife and I and my stepdaughter moved together to a new apartment, the most acute problems were simply little feelings of whose turf is where—territorial conflicts. Things like where does my stepdaughter's stuff go, and my study is off limits—and she didn't seem to appreciate that—a certain sense of trying to draw boundaries, this was the biggest hassle."

Although this stepfather referred to his feelings about "turf" as "little feelings," he also called them "the most acute problems," which I think is nearer the truth of how some of us experience adjustments in living with our stepchildren and our partners. The clue to why we may feel so strongly about drawing boundaries and about having privacy is contained in the comment of another stepfather, who said, "I think the hardest single part of being a stepfather for me was feeling it was my home as much as the other people's home—that sort of general feeling that it's your turf as well as theirs."

Stepfathers tend to be almost apologetic about the intensity of their feelings about their difficulty adjusting to sharing living space with their stepfamilies. After all, it seems petty to be upset about our stamps being moved from one place to another or our stepchild entering our study, especially if we aren't working in it at the moment anyway. If, however, we see that negotiating for physical space for ourselves is really part of negotiating our relationships within the stepfamily, then we can see that the intensity has a basis in deeper issues that we are working out. Once we see this, we can devote ourselves to working out these larger issues productively instead of blowing up over a book that one of our stepchildren has moved from the desk to the top of the bookcase—an explosion that will probably push the child away and leave him bewildered about what we really want from him.

One critical observation many stepfathers shared with me was that it helped everyone adjust to each other if the stepfamily moved into a new living space rather than the home of either the stepfather or his partner. As one stepfather put it: "I think all new families should get a new home, a neutral territory, when it's time for them to live together, before or after marriage. That way there are no old memories haunt-

ing the rooms or the furniture. The house has no associations
with the biological parent or any other person who used to live
in the house and doesn't anymore. That way everyone can
make a fresh start making it their home."

DIFFERENT HABITS, STYLES, POINTS OF VIEW

"In our stepfamily, we've had clashes of style with table
manners. We've had fights over messiness versus neatness.
We've had fights over almost anything that has to do with
things like that," one stepfather told me.

In fact, almost every stepfather I spoke to told me about
similar clashes, and it would be astonishing if they didn't. Biological parents, too, have disagreements about values, styles,
and habits based on the differences in their own upbringing.
While resolving the differences on these matters is difficult
enough for biological parents, in stepfamilies we encounter
two further complications: Our stepchildren are, at least to
some degree, preformed when we meet them, not the prover-
bial tabula rasa infants on which both parents put their negotiated imprint. And in addition to bearing their mother's
stamp they have a biological father whose input has added to
the sum total of who they already are and whose values, lifestyle, and habits will continue to affect their identities even if
he isn't a continuing presence in their lives.

Thus, although we stepfathers and our partners may tend to
fight about and negotiate over issues from trivial to major, just
as biological parents do, we have the additional challenge of
respecting the influence of our stepchildren's biological fathers
and also of respecting the fact that our stepchildren may have
certain "preformed" values.

In general, the stepfathers I talked to reported that the
major clashes about these things were not between them and
their stepchildren or between them and the children's fathers,
but between them and their partners vis-à-vis the children.

As one stepfather of two years told me: "The biggest problem for me in terms of adjustment has been the relationship of

my wife and her two daughters and me. A couple of examples: Before marrying I was fairly stern with my own children. My children had to learn to do for themselves. They can cook, do their own clothing, et cetera; they were self-sufficient. My wife's children not only couldn't cook, they were the type that wouldn't—and they were raised this way. They wouldn't take a TV dinner out of the oven. My main problem has been my wife's feelings about her children in this respect—her defending them, her begging them to do things or overexplaining why they should do things, or not wanting them to do things at all. That has been our biggest problem—and it's not with the children. I think they understand me and they probably may talk to my daughter about me, but they don't seem to resent the way I am. My wife has the problem with me explaining to a child what I think they ought to do. I find myself holding back at times, whereas if it were my child, I'd tell them to do it. I find myself resenting the fact that I'm holding back. I'm not told directly to hold back, but I do hold back, and the resentment is there.

"Also, my family is huggers and kissers, and my wife's family is not."

Again the point is that in a stepfamily there are bound to be differences about everything. The more passionate stepfathers feel about getting their own way, the more intense the clashes will be, and the more unhappy they may find themselves when they don't get their own way.

One stepfather expressed a unique perspective on these matters, precluding the need for fighting or negotiating about such differences. "For myself, there is an active, loving biological father who has a different philosophy of child-rearing than I do, and I believe—and this is personal for me—that my philosophy should not interfere with his philosophy; they're his children, and I don't want to promote my philosophy onto his children," he said. "I also disagree with my wife, the children's biological mother, on some issues. On the subject of curfew, for instance, which only applies to my stepdaughter right now, I tend to be stricter than my wife and the child's father. But they are the child's parents and they talked about it and they knew what they wanted to do and I really didn't feel I had a right to impose my philosophy on this child that was not my child."

ADJUSTING IN RELATIONSHIPS WITH STEPCHILDREN

The adjustments we've been talking about thus far in getting used to living with our stepchildren and the differences between how they've been brought up and how we wish they had been brought up are a part of the larger process of forming bonds with them. About this—the basic challenge of stepfathering—one stepfather said simply, "In my case, the period of adjustment lasted two to three years. We had to come to know each other."

Another stepfather, who is also a therapist and stepfamily counselor, observed, "I believe something you have to be educated about is that it takes at least two to three years for trust and love to develop, if it ever will. There's no such thing as instant love. As a stepfather, you have to learn that because you may be bringing money into the house doesn't mean the child has to love you or even respect you. The child may need two or three years or longer to develop that, and that's hard for some people to understand. In my therapy with stepfamilies, it seems to take a minimum of two to three years before trust will develop, and with that, maybe love."

How much time it takes to make adjustments in relationships with stepchildren and how much emotional difficulty it presents are of course dependent on the five variables we discussed in the last chapter. Commenting on this, a stepfather I quoted earlier about his extremely negative situation said, "The time it takes to get adjusted to each other is dependent upon the type and quality of people involved. In my case, it's been three and a half years, and the end is nowhere in sight because of the bad character of the stepkids, who are juvenile delinquents."

A less extreme but still upsetting and far from uncommon situation is reported by the stepfather who told me, "Initially I found it very trying to be a stepfather, because there was a belligerence to my stepson that defined the way he interacted with his father and which naturally carried over to another male. Statements like 'Who cares?' or 'So?' stated in a belligerent way, never really showing much of an interest, and being kind of fearful. And when he needed to talk to his mother, he would call her into the room to talk to her alone. These were typical of his behavior. So in a lot of ways I felt kind of angry, living with someone I really didn't care about as a person, and yet having my life impacted in a major way."

Like so many of us, this stepfather was prepared neither for the belligerence he met nor the time it takes even to begin to adjust to each other given that resistance, and the stepfather's own disappointment and anger. "I think the danger, especially if you're unfamiliar with kids, is having unrealistic expectations of what you should be doing," he told me, "rather than in some way realizing there is a very strong relationship pre-existing between a natural parent and the child that just can't be there with you.

"This is how I've come to think of it now: that he's to a large degree formed. He's had a very close and supportive relationship with his mother, a highly troubled one with his father. He's going to have to work his own conflicts out in his own way. I'm not responsible for them. As much as I might want to help him in some ways, it's not possible. I think there's a certain sense of powerlessness certainly, because with a child you may affect them, but only over a longer period of time."

Commenting on the adjustments he has noticed in his relationship with his stepson over the last two years, this stepfather said, "In my more peaceful times I think of all the things we do now—a lot of the really constant interaction and working through of our problems—and I realize it's been a big change from day one to today. Sometimes when things are hard and he wants me to do something and in some way I don't really want to but I know that he needs it and that maybe if I was him I would need it, too, unless I'm on the ropes emotionally for one reason or another, I'll do it.

"A lot of things go into how we relate to each other: myself, who I am, what I need as a person; who he is, what he needs as a person. I think in some ways I'm willing to put out now to build a foundation with him. I know that the time I spend—if I can do it without really being upset—is something that's worthwhile. Not that I expect him to give anything back to me."

We come back again to that critical word "expect." As this stepfather observed, unrealistic expectations are "the danger." Our expectations set us up for frustration and hurt and increase the time and the pain involved in our adjusting to the real needs that are part of forming relationships within our stepfamilies.

Sometimes, as this stepfather indicated, unrealistic expectations come from a stepfather's previous lack of contact with children. But even having biological children is no guarantee against feeling mystified by stepchildren in the process of what one stepfather referred to as "negotiating" relationships with them. In fact, as I pointed out in the first chapter, having biological children may lead to unrealistic expectations about what stepfathering will be like. As another stepfather said: "Becoming a stepfamily has been very diffcult at times. I thought it would be an easy transition. I was a very active and participating father in my previous marriage, so I thought I could jump in and be a second father to my two stepdaughters. The 'period of adjustment' was about two years with the oldest girl, and with the younger one it's still ongoing. The counseling we have just completed has helped a great deal. The older one and I are really developing a caring relationship. The younger one still sees me as the enemy."

This stepfather pointed to another important fact: that the time it takes to form a relationship with one stepchild is bound to be different from the time it takes to form a relationship with another. Another stepfather told me: "There were differences between Scott and Alexandra. Scott was very accepting; to him I was just another buddy; Alexandra had a great deal of trouble accepting me. It took her a long time. Alexandra went through a jealousy period. She did not want her mother and me interacting."

What made adjusting to his stepdaughter during this period

particularly problematic for this stepfather was that her rejection of him was interspersed with moments of warmth, which led him to having expectations of her which she then wouldn't fulfill. "During the first year, there were times when we were having a good time," he explained, "but it would turn on and off. There would be a time where I was accepted, but then if my stepdaughter stubbed her toe it was my fault, and immediately I was on the outside again, and it was 'Get this man out of my life.' It's really hurtful, especially during that turn-off/turn-on period. As long as it was all solid 'Get this man out of my life,' I was all right, because I could accept that; it made sense. But then you sort of get your hopes up because she's including you, and then bingo! Suddenly you've had it again. That was real hard. Fortunately, I got a lot of support from my stepson. He'd come up and put his arm around me and say, 'It's all right, Pete, I like you,' and I would talk about it a lot. It was not easy, and occasionally it was read hard. But it was all right."

One of the factors this stepfather saw as complicating his stepchildren's adjustments to him was their relationship with their father. As he explained: "It was at those times when we picked the kids up from their father's or dropped them off there that we really noticed how difficult it was for both the children, because they'd be saying hello to Dad and goodbye to me or goodbye to Dad and hello to me. How to handle that with both of us there was very difficult. So in the first period of living together as a stepfamily, we spent lots of time talking about 'It's all right to have a dad and a stepdad. You can have them both, and they're both interested in you and your welfare.' That sort of thing. It takes a big amount of work and lots of time."

Some stepfathers have special adjustments to make in regard to their stepchildren because of the children's physical or emotional condition. Describing the evolution of his relationship with a stepson who has physical handicaps, one longtime stepfather said, "I was afraid of Danny because of ignorance. Eventually I learned to treat him just like any other child.

There was no favoritism to be shown him other than the necessities that he physically could not take care of for himself. He was punished and he was rewarded just like any other child. After a few years I started to feel a tremendous admiration for him for what he was doing."

In talking about his feelings about his biological children and his stepchild, another stepfather reminds us that while there may be an overall progression toward closeness in our relationships with stepchildren, there may be cycles of greater distance even after an apparent closeness. "The bond with my stepchild began pretty well, then it got pretty bad in the third year. I actually felt like I could strangle that kid I had so much anger toward her. But in the last year it's improved considerably, and in the last six months I can say that it's even at the point where it's enjoyable most of the time."

Another stepfather, in describing his experience of forming relationships with his stepchildren, observed that during what he calls "the breaking-in period" stepchildren are engaged in one primary activity: "testing—pushing the stepparent out— doing things to make both parents angry—trying to push them apart. Now, after four and one half years," this stepfather observed regarding his situation, "there is recognition that there are pluses to be gained by my presence. There's also an awareness that I as a stepfather won't go away! More acceptance, less pushing."

Stepfathers in general agree that, like the getting-acquainted stage, the process of adjusting to stepfamily life is characterized by stepchildren "testing" and "pushing" them. This is part of the negotiating process that one of the stepfathers I quoted earlier talked about. It is part of "coming to know each other." One stepfather described it this way: "There's been testing by my stepson and by my stepdaughter—wanting to see how far they could go and if I was willing to back up my words with consequences if they didn't pay attention to me."

Many stepfathers found that one of the areas in which adjustments were most necessary was in the opening up of communication. Often stepfathers feel—and are—excluded from the exchange of even vital information between the children and their mothers. As one stepfather said: "In the beginning my stepson would never let me be privy to his conversations with his mother. Often I didn't know about things until they were settled and it was a moot point. I'd have to say, 'Hey, look, you didn't tell me this. I need to know. I'm here, I'm this, I'm that, I'm the main man in this house and if you expect me to know certain things, you're going to have to tell me and we're going to have to hammer them out together or else I'll be at a loss. I'm not going to live like that. Why bother? That's not real rewarding as far as a living situation is concerned.'

"I have four R's for my running. They go like this: reach, roll, relax, and run. It's the way your foot hits. You reach with it, you roll with it, you rest with it, and you run with it. To me those four R's apply to adjusting to stepfamily life, too. It starts out with reaching."

It's helpful to keep in mind that even factors that have nothing directly to do with our stepfamily may keep us, at least temporarily, from reaching out to our stepchildren and their mother as we all get adjusted to each other. One stepfather emphasized this to me when he said, "The biggest problems of the initial adjustment had nothing to do with my stepdaughter. There were my own problems with my job and working out my feelings about my former marriage, which had dissolved only a year before. These seemed to add pressure to everything else."

ADJUSTING IN A COMBINED STEPFAMILY

Stepfathers who bring biological children into their stepfamilies have even more adjustments to make in terms of relationships, as do their partners, children, and stepchildren. In Chapter Four, "Yours, Mine, and Ours," I'll examine in detail the experiences of various stepfathers in combined stepfamilies; here I'm going to use stepfathers' observations to suggest some of the challenges presented to a stepfather within a combined stepfamily.

"Keep in mind it wasn't a case where I didn't have children and I just had to adjust to a child," one stepfather in a combined stepfamily told me. "We had interactions going on between the children, too. My son saying to my stepdaughter, 'You can't talk to my sister that way,' and we would have to separate them and rationalize for them why they feel that way. We did a lot of interpreting for them.

"During what I call the 365-day war," he continued, "the children would gang up against us at all times—my two biological children and my stepdaughter. Sometimes one would start the ball rolling, and the others would jump in. 'Because I can't have twenty-five cents to buy an ice cream, that's unfair,' one would say. And then the littlest one comes along and says, 'Sure that's unfair. You always did that for us.' But mostly because my wife and I would talk a whole lot and hopefully decide things ahead of time, we would sort of be prepared. We'd say, for instance, 'Summer's coming and if you do the wash and you do the trash, then you'll get your twenty-five cents a day for ice cream. That's the rule.' None of it was ever perfect. There are always minor problems and arguments to be dealt with. I'd say that type of thing lasted a good solid nine months, but it was not a constantly hectic period. There were weekends they'd be upset, or there'd be a day, or they'd get upset over schoolwork. After nine months we could finally say, 'Gee, they're getting better, we really see they're getting better.' "

The addition of a new baby makes further adjustments necessary in a stepfamily. Suddenly there is a new type of bond between a stepfather and his partner and a new relationship that must be established between the children in the household and their new stepsibling. Most stepfathers reported that their stepchildren and children don't regard their half sibling as an intruder. In the words of one stepfather: "Fortunately, my two stepchildren *adore* their new half sister."

Some stepfathers said the new baby brought them and their wives closer. As one stepfather said: "I knew that Sheila wanted a new child prior to marriage, so I had already addressed that question before, and it was a good thing, because some other people I know did not and it created a lot of conflicts. I was willing to have another child, I enjoy children. And for Sheila and me, it really has been a bonding agent, and a helpful one. I really, truly enjoy the child we have between us, much more than I enjoyed the children that came earlier in my life. I love all of them, but she seems to be something special. In some ways I feel that she has helped us to stay together through the hard times, that this child is a bond between us that holds us together. I'm sure that this isn't the thing for all stepfamilies, but as a stepfather I really enjoy this child."

Another stepfather talked about the difference he noticed in his stepson since the arrival of his half siblings. "He's really been much more into helping out around the house," this stepfather said, "because his mother and I need the help now. And he really loves the little ones. He's proud of them. He's their big brother."

With all of these positive experiences, it's important to note that, just as in a biological family, the addition of a new child can also cause sibling rivalry in a stepfamily. One stepfather who felt that he had a close bond with his stepdaughter reported that she pulled away from him almost completely as she entered her teens—just at the time he and his partner had a baby. Since then, though, he and his stepdaughter have begun the process of growing closer.

ADJUSTMENTS WITH PARTNERS

The amount of agreement between a stepfather and his partner about their roles within the family is a strong determinant of a man's experience of stepfathering. It is also an influential factor in determining how long and how stormy the adjustment period is.

In the best of cases there is as close to total agreement as possible between husband and wife, and in facing the challenge of creating your own relationship with the child, you have the mother's support. Even with this kind of agreement and support from Cynthia, it took, as I mentioned, about three years for Kevin's overt rejection of me to cease and for us to begin building the strong bond we have today, a bond which began deepening considerably when he went off to college. Because Timothy was more open to me from the beginning and Cynthia supported our closeness, we had already begun to form a bond within my first year as a stepfather. Though, as I said, it took many years after that until I would say that my own period of adjustment to stepfathering was over, even in regard to Timothy.

Without Cynthia's support, it would have taken far longer to develop bonds with my stepchildren and to establish the role I sought in our stepfamily. Another stepfather, whose partner is less cooperative with his goals in forming relationships with her children, commented, "What makes our adjustment so hard is that my wife is not going to let go. She has a desire to control. She is Mrs. Mother."

Even when the children's mother is intellectually prepared to accept the stepfather as a meaningful presence in the household, it may still take her some time to make the emotional adjustments to live up to her intellectual assent. "I would say that theoretically my wife and I had the same view of what my relationship to the children should be from the beginning," another stepfather told me. "But in a practical sense there were some problems. My wife had run the household herself for five years. And she, I felt, also had a hard time letting loose a little bit, because she had been used to running the household with three small children in it by herself. So I think if you had asked me what my role was with the children, we'd all agree, we would all check the same boxes. But when it came down to practical realities—who is going to make the decision as to what school one of the kids is going to go to—she took a while to adjust to having another person to share the decision-making with her. And also I think because of going through the trauma of her first husband dying, sometimes I think it was kind of hard for her to relax and accept the fact that somebody else might be around for a while. She was very protective of the kids."

Another stepfather commented, "There was a tremendous

period of adjustment in the beginning in terms of Cheryl adjusting to me as her daughter's stepfather. I think it took probably the first ten years, with three or four years being the most dramatic. It covered a considerable period of time. The problem is you have so many conflicting loyalties and things going on when you have a divorce situation. The primary one for us was guilt in terms of Cheryl taking the daughter away from the father, and even though the father didn't play that much of a role in his daughter's life after that, Cheryl didn't really allow me full rein to take over as the new stepfather."

Adjustments with the Children's Biological Father

Like many of the factors we have been looking at in this chapter, the subject of the children's biological father will be explored in a chapter of its own (Chapter Eight, "The Other Father"). Here, in order to suggest the outer limits of the kinds of adjustments stepfathers may have to make regarding their stepchildren's fathers, I'm going to present only one example. This is an extreme case, in which a biological father, intensely angered by the divorce, created enormous obstacles for his children, his ex-wife and her new partner making a new family life together. As you'll see, the stepfather's attitude in adjusting to the situation helped create an environment in which even these obstacles were not insurmountable.

"My older stepson had been going through a hard time when his parents were having problems, but what happened after the divorce certainly exacerbated that," this stepfather told me. "His father was obviously extremely angry and hurt, and basically sort of threatened to completely shut off the kids from their mother. Although this influenced the other children somewhat, for some reason my older son was affected more deeply, and he was caught right in the middle between his father and mother. So for a period of time he basically had no contact with us. It took probably three years for that to really sort of regenerate in any kind of regular fashion.

"The most painful thing I have seen someone have to go

through was what my wife went through when he was not here, because they had always been so emotionally connected. During those years, it was like losing a child. He would appear for awhile every three or four months, then he would go back to his father's. Years later he was able to tell us that coming into our house he would feel very welcome, very sort of 'held,' and then very conflicted because the loyalty bind to his father would get in the way. He told us he often felt he wanted to live here, but that if he did, he thought he would be deserting his father.

"I think the main ingredient in dealing with circumstances like these is patience: patience with the father, patience with the children, patience in satisfying your own desires. My wife made it clear to her ex-husband how much she wanted to see her son. And I stayed in the background when she talked to the kids' father, because I was obviously a sore point with him. I never pushed him in any way. We also never tried to push my involvement with the kids and say, 'You've got to treat me as a father. You've got to do everything I say instantly.' It had more of a sense of 'It takes a while,' and that I need to be patient, and let my older stepson and my other stepchildren get used to me.

"With the kids, it feels like it was essentially a matter of having had to learn to respect each other—in the timetable in which that could happen, which was very influenced by their father and their relationship with him—and after that the love could develop between us. As the love has grown, it's become easier and easier for them to see me as someone who is parental, too, and who can be there both in a supportive way for them and in a disciplining and limit-setting role when they are here.

"But the key to getting where we are now, as I say, was not trying to push quickly. The less I pushed, the less anxious the children felt about deserting their father and the more they began to feel free about taking charge of the time they spent in both our houses, and their forming closer relationships with me."

STEPFATHERS' NEEDS

The experience of the stepfather I just quoted is another example of how flexibility is an indispensable quality in coping with the adjustments intrinsic to stepfathering. At the same time, one of the most critical adjustments many stepfathers have to make is learning how to balance flexibility with a knowledge and a communication of their own basic needs. It's crucial that, as a result of our desire to form relationships with our stepchildren quickly, we don't in the face of their resistance continually give so much to them that we feel cheated.

As one stepfather observed: "Besides the difficulty of having to put up with my stepson's ambivalence toward me, on another level becoming a stepfather was very interesting because it forced me to be a little more assertive about my needs. Whereas if you're interacting with your wife, there's obviously an adult form of communication, with a child you have to use authority, which had not been the way I interacted with people, not having interacted with kids before I became a stepfather."

It's important to note that this is the same stepfather who commented, "I think in some ways I'm willing to put out now to build a foundation with my stepson. I know that the time I spend—if I can do it without really being upset, 'cause that's a separate case—is something that's worthwhile."

Just as in the getting-acquainted stage of dating and courtship it's crucial that we don't try to buy our prospective stepchildren with presents, at no time in our relationships with them should we attempt to buy them with words or actions that don't jibe with our own emotional integrity or that are at an emotional expense to us that we truly don't want to sustain.

As this stepfather explained to me, characterizing the adjustments that have taken place thus far in his two years as a stepfather: "I think the theme that really defined the early stage in making adjustments to each other was learning to respect my own needs; learning not to do everything he wanted; learning to do the things that were harmonious with me;

learning how to express my disinclination in certain things. So in many ways it was learning not to treat a child as much as a child as another person who had needs of his own which I may or may not have wanted to fulfill.

"In the beginning he also whined a lot and had frequent temper tantrums. Stomping out, shouting for his mother. Eventually I learned to say, when I would be possessed of my faculties, 'I don't want to hear you yelling that loudly. If you have something to say to your mother, call her in your room.' I learned to communicate things like that very clearly.

"When I wanted not to relate, just because I needed some time to myself in our small apartment, I would just concentrate on the paper, and he would respect that. When he had no interest in talking, initially I tried to engage him. I felt degraded. 'He doesn't want to talk to me,' I said to myself. 'Fine, let him not talk to me.' I took it very personally. Like, 'Shit, I wanted to be friendly, and here's this kid truculent and belligerent. Let him do it to his father.' But eventually the key was not trying to engage him. Because I don't want to engage socially with someone who's angry—it can be a kid, it can be an adult. If that's how I feel when he acts that way, then I'm not going to talk to him—which was a big help."

Turning Points

Whether stepfathers feel there is an actual period of adjustment in stepfamily relationships or that adjustments are part of a continual and never-ending process, looking back on their experiences, many stepfathers see certain moments or events as turning points in their stepchildren's adjustment to and acknowledgment of them.

These turning points are occurrences in the life of the stepfather and stepchild that seem to symbolize to the stepfather that a new stage of acceptance has been reached. As one stepfather said: "There's one time that stuck out in my mind that was very meaningful for me. Sandy and I rode our bicycles in the rain to work. And I felt like it would have been a long time before that might have happened, so it really stuck out as something we were really doing together. I can remember looking behind me at him; we were drenched; it was a downpour rain; the road was flat; and there were no cars. It was a beautiful ride. But I look back on that and I think, 'Hey, that was a good thing, because we did it.' We could have turned around; we were a lot less than halfway there. But we went out of the yard on our bikes anyway, and we just kept right on going. That was good."

Sometimes these turning points occur because of an emergency situation. "I think the moment that I see as solidifying the whole relationship was when Alexandra had an accident and had to be taken to the hospital to have her leg sewn up," another stepfather told me. "There was a point during that whole process of making phone calls and deciding which hospital to go to and getting her there when I carried her, and she accepted that and did not act as if I shouldn't. Usually if anybody was going to carry her it had to be Mom. But during this particular incident somehow or other it was all right; I was accepted. I think from that point on, her dissatisfaction with me decreased quite rapidly."

Other times turning points are helped along by a change in the life of the biological father. As the stepfather I just quoted observed, reflecting the experiences of other stepfathers I interviewed as well as his own: "Another thing that we found made a tremendous difference was when her father started dating seriously. Somehow she didn't feel she had to be so protective of him anymore and she could be closer to me."

In looking for turning points in my relationships with Kevin or Timothy, I see points at which I had to affirm my commitment to them, points at which I had to be firm about the boundaries I was drawing for them, points at which they were firm about the boundaries they were drawing for me and for their mother. But more than these, I, like most stepfathers I interviewed, remember many ordinary moments and events, either stressful or enjoyable ones, that brought us closer to our stepchildren and seemed to reaffirm the observation of the stepfather I quoted who said that "it's through the mundane daily aspects of everyday life" that, with time, we and our stepchildren adjust to each other.

Does It Ever Really End?

After talking about the adjustments he and his stepson have both made, Sandy's stepfather concluded, "I wouldn't describe what's been happening in the last two years as a period of adjustment. I'd leave out 'period' and just say 'adjustment.' It's an ongoing process I see, not a limited period that you adjust."

It's possible that after ten or fifteen or twenty or more years of stepfathering, this stepfather will look back on his experience and say that there was a period of adjustment. It's also possible that he might not. Stepfathers agree that adjustments are necessary. They also agree that these adjustments take time, and many agree that emotionally they are very difficult to make. Beyond this there is a great variety of opinion—backed up by stepfathers' experiences—of how much time these adjustments take. While a handful of stepfathers told me they had adjusted to relationships with their stepchildren within a year, others agreed emphatically with the stepfather who said it takes a *mimimum* of two to three years to develop trust; and only after that can love come (if in fact it ever will). Other stepfathers after ten years still agreed with Sandy's stepfather that they'd "leave out the 'period' and just say 'adjustment.' "

As one longtime stepfather of four stepchildren observed: "After thirteen years as a stepfather, I wouldn't say there was *a* point where I hit my stride and until that point it seemed more rocky. There were problems in the beginning that were resolved, and then there were new problems which emerged that still have to be resolved, and so forth. I don't think there's been a particularly steady evolution in that regard.

"Within the relationship of surrogate father that I've played to my stepchildren, since their own father has just been marginally in the picture since my wife's divorce, there have been peaks and troughs, as it were. I've noted that each of them has gone through a period of rebellion or rejection of me which has later been resolved in a higher stage of relatedness and acceptance. Sometimes they've rebelled against me as a father figure, sometimes as a stepfather. I think the rejection of me as a surrogate father, as it were, moving into their lives, came earlier. Sometimes the early pushing of my buttons was involved with the issue of accepting me as a family member; sometimes it was just sheer provocation, to push my buttons— children just being children. And then the type of natural process of separation that occurs with biological parents, too, has manifested itself as they have matured in the natural course of adolescent development."

As stepfathers, we must continually keep in mind that try as we might, we cannot *control* our relationships with our stepchildren by our own actions. We can make our adjustments to our stepchildren, but they have to make theirs to us as well— and so do their mothers and their biological fathers. Thus, whether the stepfather who said, "Nobody is so crazily complex that you can't figure them out in a year and a half or so," is right or wrong, it's not just a question of figuring out our stepchildren. Getting a sense of who our stepchildren are as individuals is certainly important; it helps us in forming relationships with them because it helps us to key our words and behaviors to their particular personalities, needs, and attitudes. And *still* it is not entirely up to us. This is why the length of time it takes to "figure out" our stepchildren—if we ever do—is not necessarily the time it takes to form relationships with them. It is also why stepfathers, depending on their experiences within their own stepfamilies, do vary in their descriptions of how long the period of adjustment lasts and whether it ends at all.

CHAPTER FOUR

Yours, Mine, and Ours
COMBINING STEPFAMILIES

U<small>P TO NOW WE'VE HEARD</small> stepfathers stress how important it is to know up front that television programs that portray combined stepfamilies as "one big happy family" from the word "go" are oversimplified fantasies. The question remains, however: What is life really like in a family made up of the husband's biological children and the wife's biological children?

Clearly, the process of forming a combined stepfamily is even more complex than the process of forming a stepfamily where only one of the partners has biological children. In a combined stepfamily, not one but two sets of biological children have to form relationships with two stepparents (and vice versa) and with each other as well. Given the challenge of forming any stepfamily, it's remarkable that many stepfathers living in combined stepfamilies reported that, despite the problems of integrating the two separate parent and children family groupings into one family, with time it can be rewarding for adults and children.

A stepfather of almost seven years, whose two biological children (ages ten and twelve) and three stepchildren (ages twelve, thirteen, and fifteen) live full time with him and his partner, is one of the stepfathers in a combined stepfamily who feels well rewarded for his efforts. Indeed, his view is a completely positive one. "I don't think the relationships in our family would have been any different had they all been ours, Mary's and my natural children, really," he told me. "Each kid has his own personality. They are very distinctive. You're going to have that whether it's a stepfamily or whether it's a nuclear family. So I can't say that it would have been different."

At the opposite extreme is the stepfather of three and a half years whose three "juvenile delinquent" stepsons and step-daughter in their early twenties live on their own, and whose four biological children (ages eight through fourteen) live part time with him and his partner. "I feel close to my kids. They are great kids—respectful, honest, kind, industrious. Whereas my stepkids, I feel, are like in-laws whom you hope don't come to visit. If my wife died, the last time I'd probably see my stepkids is at the funeral."

Between both extremes, and representing the view of the majority of combined family stepfathers I interviewed, is the perspective expressed by a stepfather of six years, with two biological children (ages seventeen and fourteen) and two step-children (ages seventeen and nine). He said that although, with time, there are very clear benefits to combining families, the problems persist as well. Because his view is the majority view, it's worth looking at in some detail. "Debby and I have been in what's called a blended family group for six years, and I think one thing that I've seen with myself (and I've seen with other people who have gone through the same process) is that blending is more difficult to achieve. Maybe it's a salad bowl rather than a mixer or something. The bloodlines stay there in a sense; they don't go away. Not that I felt they would go away, but I didn't think they would be as distinct as they are. I see it with myself in terms of my stepchildren and I see it with my own kids in terms of Debby, too. When it comes to the crunch at times, it's sort of this group here and this group there. There isn't always a sharp line, but it's almost instinctive in a way.

"Part of it may be because our exes live so nearby [the children split their time between the households]. And I think it's also a history—a history that was there before whatever blending has taken place began to occur. I think it's that as much as anything. And it's difficult at times for me to resist that instinctive pull.

"I know Debby and I both end up being defensive of our own kids. I can get upset with my kids, and the next day I can work it through and come back and sort of put it on the back shelf. It's harder, for example, with my stepdaughter. I don't know whether it's not being willing to go the extra foot or mile or whatever with stepchildren. But there is something there. It's not that I don't have very close feelings toward my stepson, and some of the time toward my stepdaughter. But there is still some difference, and sometimes I feel guilty about that. I feel like I'm not feeling the way I should, or there's something wrong with me for feeling the way I do.

"The kids get along okay. They always have, really."

This stepfather's comments bring up the major issues confronting all divorced parents who bring their children into combined stepfamilies. For a stepfather the issues raised in the combining of families translate into the questions: What kind of a bond will he be able to form with his partner's children, especially given the full-time or part-time presence of his own children? Will fairness and favoritism be problems? How well will his partner function as a stepmother to his children? How well will the children get along? Let's examine these issues one by one.

A Father's Bond to Biological Children and Stepchildren

"My own children will always have a much stronger bond than anything I could forge with my stepsons, who have a very active and involved father," said one stepfather about his bond to his children and his partner's two children. Another stepfather, whose stepson and biological son both live with him and his partner part time, remarked, "I feel closer, more involved and needed and loved by my son than by my stepson."

Echoing this, a stepfather of five years with one older stepchild who has moved out on his own and three biological children, one of whom lives full time with him and his partner, commented, "There is a common bond between my own children and me. This is only natural. You must work very hard in most cases to achieve any kind of love for stepchildren, especially if you get them in their teens or older [his stepson was twenty when the marriage took place]."

A stepfather of four years with one full-time resident stepchild, two older stepchildren who are out on their own, and one biological child for whom he has joint custody, remarked, "Toward my son I feel warm, loving, frustrated when he goofs up, angry when he lies or blatantly disobeys; toward my stepson I feel ready to throw up my hands and walk away, disenfranchise myself from him."

Attempting to quantify his feelings, a stepfather of two years, with one stepchild who lives full time with him and his partner and two biological children who are in their midtwenties and out on their own, said, "On a closeness scale from one to ten, I would say the closeness I feel toward my stepson is five and to my biological children, eight to ten."

Like these stepfathers, the large majority of stepfathers in combined families say they feel closer to their biological children than they do to their stepchildren and that they have to "work hard" to achieve a bond with their stepchildren. Many reported feeling this way even when their stepchildren live with them full time and their biological children do not.

Some stepfathers expressed an entirely different perspective, however. They feel there is no real point in comparing their feelings toward their biological and stepchildren and that the work it takes to achieve a bond with their stepchildren creates a special relationship with them. As one stepfather of sixteen years with two stepchildren and three biological children said: "I feel very close to my stepchildren. My feelings toward my biological children are quite different. I feel I've *earned* the good feelings toward my stepkids through what we've been through together. They feel good about me and where they are in life, so I feel I've succeeded. *We* survived—*we* succeeded."

This stepfather also expressed the view that living full time with his stepchildren and only part time with his biological children produced a greater closeness with the former and a greater distance with the latter. And although the majority of stepfathers I interviewed did not feel this way, there was a very vocal minority who did. As one stepfather of two years with five stepchildren and two biological children explained: "Time has been an influence. Whereas it's helped with my stepkids because they're here, it's kind of changed with my kids because they're not here. I feel disattached, I guess, to my children."

Another point about which most stepfathers in combined stepfamilies agreed is that they tend to have more physically affectionate relationships with their biological children than with their stepchildren. As one stepfather put it: "In terms of my relationships with my biological children and my stepdaughter, my relationship with Wendy [his stepdaughter, who is eleven] is much less physical. For some reason we never got to the stage where I could kiss her goodnight or anything. We're both comfortable with that." A minority of stepfathers reported that their relationships with their biological children and stepchildren are equally physically close. One stepfather in a combined stepfamily told me, "My stepchildren's father is rather distant physically and I'm not. So my stepchildren and I have a warm, affectionate physical relationship with each other, as I do with my son and daughter, and that's new for my stepchildren."

It's important to keep in mind that a stepfather's bond with his stepchildren and his biological children is affected by all of the factors we've discussed in previous chapters, starting with the personality and attitude of each child. Some stepfathers, while admitting the difficulties they have with their own children, feel that these difficulties pale by comparison to those they experience with their stepchildren. As one stepfather of four years, with one stepchild and one biological child, explained: "My son knows that I love him, my stepson feels a loyalty conflict not just involving his father and me but also his mother and me. My son will usually do what I ask—my stepson usually ignores my requests. My son wants to spend time with me—soccer, playing games, playing catch, or going on outings. My stepson will interact with me for 'fun time'—Disneyland, miniature golf, and so forth. My son will help me in the yard, my stepson only after his mother gets on his case."

Relationships between a stepfather and his biological and stepchildren are not always such a simple contrast. Stepfathers in combined stepfamilies, as they kept reminding me, have different relationships with *each* stepchild and *each* biological child. One stepfather said of his three biological children, "I have three categories of daughters. I feel close to my oldest daughter, less close to my middle daughter, and I hardly know my youngest. One of the things that's affected my relationship with my youngest two daughters—and especially the youngest—is that they were younger when I divorced their mother, and she tried to color their feelings against me."

Another stepfather in a combined stepfamily said about his stepchildren, "I feel closer right now to the older one. She will come to me with problems and feelings, and we can really grow and develop in these times. Up to now the younger one has seen me as an intruder who has brought more people and discipline into her life. In her eyes, her dad is infallible. But I think we're beginning a relationship." Another stepfather in a combined stepfamily told me, "Two of the three stepchildren I get along very well with. The third doesn't get along with anybody. I think he's probably still stuck in one of the early stages of divorce, and that's the denial or the angry stage."

One of the factors that strongly influences a stepfather's relationship with his stepchildren is his own personality and attitude. In Chapter Two, "The Stepfather's Role," I mentioned that just as stepchildren may feel a conflict of loyalty between their biological fathers and stepfathers, stepfathers who have biological children may feel a conflict of loyalty between their biological children and their stepchildren. If their children live with them only part time, these stepfathers may carry a parental torch for them that interferes with their closeness with stepchildren. As one stepfather explained: "It's hard for me to genuinely say that I love Nicole, and the reason why it's a problem is because I know that the feelings are different toward my son, even though he's not here often, than they are toward Nicole. And she's a neat kid and I feel a certain sense of pride and all of that, but there's just not that bond. I suspect part of it is feeling that if I love her I'm being disloyal to my son. It's like I have a certain space that is there to be occupied but I'm saving it for my own child rather than allowing Nicole to move into that space."

This stepfather sees the consequences of his attitude—and his far greater identification with his son than his stepdaughter—manifesting in several important ways. "To begin with, in my child's absence I idealize what it is to be a father," he told me. "For example, Nicole has no concept of hanging up her clothes, even though these days they have to be designer label. My feeling is you don't buy designer label clothes and drop them in a heap, but she does. And I say, 'Well, my child would have more sense.' And then Orin comes here, and after three days his room's a chaos, and his expensive clothes and sneakers are lying in a pile just like hers, and so I realize I do idealize. It's healthy to have him here to restore the balance, because I also immediately realize that a lot of the frustrations I feel about Nicole are not because she's my stepchild but because she's a child that I live with, and I get the same frustrations with Orin.

"But I also get a lot more pride from Orin. Last year, for example, my stepdaughter played in a soccer match and I went to it and felt a certain sense of pride in her. When something like that happens, I say, 'This kid's all right, you know, and I'm not sorry that I'm part of her life.' But then two days later that feeling can be completely gone and then you don't want to be a part of their life at all right then. The ambiguity gets puzzling sometimes. I fantasize that if she were my biological child I would just naturally want to be involved in everything, that all of her successes would be my successes and I would feel that she were acting out my fantasies more as my child. I don't think I place the expectations and fantasies on her as a stepchild that I do put on my son. When he gets a glowing report card, I glow inside in a way that I don't quite with Nicole. I congratulate Nicole and I'm pleased she's doing well, but I don't feel any personal sense of pride in her really. Whereas when Orin comes in with a report card that he's very proud of, I feel vicarious victory or something.

"Conversely, some of Nicole's defeats, I just don't feel deeply. I heard about a few of Orin's and I really felt the pain, probably even more than if I were actually there where I could be involved in it. When he calls me up because something very upsetting happened, I just get tied in knots because I feel the pain and I'm fifteen hundred miles away and there's nothing I can do."

Stepfathers whose biological children and stepchildren live with them full time are not confronted with the difficulty of this physical separation, but they face other tests. As another stepfather, whose full-time combined stepfamily includes his two children and his wife's one, told me, "Sometimes I wish my stepdaughter would live with her biological father, but I get equally annoyed at times with my own children, who also live with us. Sometimes I wish my biological children would live with their mother. My saving grace is that at no time have both myself and Eileen been so angry that we're willing to admit to that together. So I can take a time out while she smooths things over or vice versa. And that's the only way you can work it. If we both felt the same way at the same time, we never would be here today, never. People do it, but those people are always going through enormous problems."

On the subject of forming a bond with his stepdaughter, this stepfather told me, "I guess you kind of have to love your own children, and you have to work at it to love your stepchild. There's a point where you as a stepfather can say, 'I can just live with my stepchild and not have to deal with the deeper part of my feelings. I can just keep everything as polite as possible.' You really have to work at loving, because you don't know what the child is thinking about you and how you fit into her life. So I guess for me the goal is making it the best relationship I can. The point I'm making is that I have had a choice really if I was the kind of a person who would treat my stepdaughter in a certain more distant way than I would my own biological children. But I didn't want that type of relationship.

"When you're creating a stepfamily with your children and your wife's," he continued, "my advice is to do a lot of serious talking with your spouse about where you expect to go with the relationships with the children. You can do basically anything you want about it, only you have to work on it."

FAIRNESS AND FAVORITISM

In combined stepfamilies the issue that seems to require the most work on the part of stepfathers and their partners is that of fairness and favoritism. As a stepfather of two stepchildren and two biological children said: "There is now and always has been the issue of fairness. There is a characteristic tendency to be more lenient with one's own children and harsher with stepchildren."

Different stepfathers react differently to this tendency. This particular stepfather told me, "I believe there are times when I overcompensated and was more lenient with my stepsons." Another stepfather felt that because he identifies more with his own children he may also be harder on them. As he put it: "I think the same things will annoy you with your stepchildren as with your biologicals, maybe even more so if they are your biologicals." Many other stepfathers, however, say that on the contrary they show a definite favoritism toward their own children. Some stepfathers feel this is entirely appropriate;

others feel they should be "treating all the children equally." For some stepfathers, the goal of equal treatment for all the children is one they take on in the early life of their stepfamily but eventually feel is unrealistic for them. For other stepfathers, it is a continuing goal.

Stepfathers whose stepchildren live with them full time and biological children only part time seem particularly drawn to favoring their own children. On those occasions when their children are with them stepfathers frequently feel compelled to make up for lost time. For many stepfathers this causes great conflict between them and their partners. A stepfather with one stepchild and three biological children told me, "My wife accuses me of showing favoritism toward my own kids. Somehow I seem to be oblivious to my kids' shortcomings but not to my stepson's. If my kids need money, it's no problem for me to take care of them. My wife accuses me of not being so free with her son."

Expanding on this theme, a stepfather with two full-time stepchildren and one biological child who is in the household part time said, "The problems I have with fairness mostly occur because my wife feels I give my son more attention than her two. So I would say there's what *I* would call a jealousy factor, although she wouldn't say that. She would simply say, 'Why do you do things for your son that you won't do for my two?'

"She always claims that I buy steak when my boy is coming for a visit, whereas for her boys I'll get hot dogs or I manage to hit the food stores and get snacks. But her boys live with us full time; my boy visits twice a week. I tell her I'm paying him extra attention because I'm trying to make up for not being with him all the time. But of course she says her boys see me give the extra attention and they're going to feel bad. I said, 'Wait a second. They go see their dad every other weekend, and I'm not sitting around criticizing what he does for them, measuring it.'

"So I'm going to treat my son a little bit better or give him a little bit more attention than I'm going to give my wife's two sons. It's a deliberate choice I'm making. And I don't feel guilty about it. Because, as I say, they have a father, and he can do whatever he wants to do. An example the other way: He took them away on a vacation. I've never done that with my son. That's very nice. He can afford that; I can't. I've never taken my son really anywhere.

"I like both my stepsons. But it's always difficult when the three are together. Because if they get into a scrap in any way it's almost like second nature to me to try and side with mine. And you're never there when they have their fight. They come in and say, 'I didn't do this, well Seth did that, and so forth.' She springs to their defense and I spring to mine's defense, and that's where you get your little scenes going on.

"But they're not the ones who are upset about my spending extra time with my son; it's my wife who's upset."

The major factor supporting this stepfather's attitude that there is nothing wrong with showing extra attention to his own child when he visits is that his stepchildren's father also spends special time with them. This is true for the many other stepfathers in similar situations who hold the same point of view. One stepfather told me a particularly interesting story along these lines. He was attending a Little League game in which his stepson's team was playing his biological son's team for the League pennant. His wife asked him who he was going to root for, and he said, "My son's team, of course." I was very surprised when he told me this, until he added that his stepson's biological father was there, too, rooting for his son.

While, as in the combined stepfamilies I've just described, the primary problem in regard to fairness and favoritism is between husband and wife, to one degree or another children are affected by the issue, too. Sometimes one or more of the stepfather's biological children will have a problem with it. As one stepfather told me: "There was some jealousy at first with my biological son being jealous of my stepchildren." Other times it's the stepchildren who have the problem.

"I have a daughter about the same age as my stepchildren, and the area they tested most was about her role in the household and my relationship toward her," said another stepfather with three full-time stepchildren and a daughter who only visits the household. "I tended to favor her. The real question is how much on the one hand you want to communicate to your own daughter because she has a special place. On the other hand, you don't want to do it in a way that's threatening to the other children. That balance, or when the kids test you about it, it's tough, it's tricky."

In regard to how he handles his own children's visits, a stepfather of three full-time stepchildren commented, "There are certainly different feelings about your stepchildren and your own children when they visit and everyone's in the same house. You've got to understand that you tend to be protective about your own children and maybe even competitive in the beginning, and looking out that your children get a fair shake in the house of your stepchildren. One of the things you should do is have a room or place for them, the visiting children, to have their own toys, their own clothes, so they feel it's their home, too, that they're not intruders."

Some stepfathers, acknowledging their desire to favor their visiting biological children over their stepchildren, still feel that when the children are together they want to treat them equally. "It's a definite choice to treat Sara and my son equally when we're all living together as a family, even if I do feel closer to my son," a stepfather with a full-time stepdaughter and a son who visits only on school vacations told me. "I have special talks with him, and sometimes we do spend time, just the two of us, but when we're all together, we're all together."

Having the continuing goal of treating all the children equally is far more common among stepfathers of full-time combined stepfamilies than among stepfathers in other living situations. As a stepfather of seven years with two full-time biological children and three stepchildren said: "If you're going to buy something for one child, you don't think, 'Is it my child or her child? Are they going to get something somewhere else?' You just throw that out. You're all in one family now."

Achieving this goal isn't always easy, however. One stepfather with two biological children and one stepchild, all of

whom live with him and his partner full time, sees resolving
the issue of fairness and favoritism as part of the "work" he has
to do to form a bond with his stepchild, and that it's very much
a matter of personal choice. "I wanted all the kids to be
treated equally with my affections," he said, "even though it
does require work on my part."

This stepfather emphasized that his wife works equally hard
at treating his children equally. Their method of resolving any
contentions between them about fairness and favoritism (or
any other issue of stepfamily life) is "constant communication." As he explained it, the context for this communication is
a spirit of cooperation. "My wife and I review the day with
each other, we talk about whatever problems each of us is
having, and we see what we can each do to work it out. We
don't accuse each other. The point is to resolve things. And if
we're having a problem with what the other is saying to the
children, we might even call the other person out of the room
to confer and see if we can modify what's happening right at
that moment. Part of it is that we came from such non-com-
municative marriages that we're not going to let problems
arise from non-communication again. And we do want a family in which all the children feel loved."

YOUR PARTNER AS STEPMOTHER

The stepfathers I interviewed felt that the same issues confronting them as stepfathers also confronted their partners as
stepmothers. Just as stepfathers have to work to form bonds
with their wives' children, stepmothers have to work to form
bonds with their husbands'. They have to deal with the same
kinds of resistance from the children and depend on the same
kinds of support from the children's fathers.

The same variables that influence a man's role as stepfather
and his experience in that role influence his partner's role and
experience as a stepmother: the age, number, attitudes, and
gender of her stepchildren, the children's relationships with
their biological mother; the stepmother's attitude toward her
role and her ability to communicate and be flexible; the chil-

dren's father's attitude toward what his partner's role should be and his ability to communicate and be flexible; and how the stepmother's feelings about her own children affect her feelings about her stepchildren.

Since, in most cases, children are in the custody of their mothers, most stepfathers reported that their partners are only part-time stepmothers to their children. The majority of stepfathers with only part-time custody of their children felt that by and large their partners were doing a good job of forming a relationship with the children, especially given the limited amount of time they had together and the challenges confronting each of them.

A stepfather in this situation shed some light on the special difficulties confronting the many women who, like his partner, are stepmothers to children who live with them only on weekends and school vacations, if that often. "In terms of my attitude toward becoming Sara's stepfather and Ann's attitude about becoming David's stepmother, it's always been a little lopsided in that it's never been an option for David to be a full-time member of our family, whereas it was always a given that Sara would be. And I guess we just early-on took that as part of the ground rules.

"Generally speaking, Ann gets along with David well. She has never had to spend a great deal of time with him, and David I guess maybe shares this with his mother, but he draws pretty sharp boundaries. He's not going to let his loyalties get blurred. So that he will be very warm and open to Ann for a period of time, and then all of a sudden a wall will come down. It's almost like all of a sudden he feels he's violated the trust his mother has in him or something and he will say something to shut Ann off. Sara doesn't really do that with me. She and I don't always have a harmonious relationship, but at least we totally accept the fact that we're each here and we have to make do with each other, whereas David still acts on occasion as though he just wishes Ann would disappear. And this has been a source of pain for Ann on more than one occasion, and it's led me to have talks with David, which usually don't go very far. We will have two or three really nice days as a family, and he'll be hugging Ann, and then all of a sudden the wall comes down and he says, 'That's enough,' and then Ann feels very hurt. But it's been better recently, and I anticipate that it will be getting better and better."

This stepfather also told me what almost every other stepfather with full-time custody of his stepchildren and only part-time custody of his own children told me: that the more time his partner spends as a stepmother to his child the better she understands what he is going through as a stepfather to her child. "When David would visit for a longer period of time—a week or two weeks—sometimes some of the same feelings I was having about Sara intruding on my relationship with Ann, Ann would start to feel about David. And I always felt a certain sense of vindication or that it was a good experience that she would have those feelings, too."

Along the same lines, a stepfather with one biological child and one stepchild commented that his partner's recently increased participation as a stepmother is altering her view of his role as a stepfather. "I don't believe my wife has had the same view as I do about what my function as a stepfather should be," he told me, "but it's changing now that my son lives with us, because she is now a full-time stepparent—no longer an alternating-weekend adult in his life."

Not unexpectedly the area where many stepfathers fault their partners as stepmothers is in tending to be overprotective of their own children, sometimes at the expense of their stepchildren. As a stepfather with one biological son and one stepson told me: "Most of the time I'm happy with the support I get from my wife. However, if I am addressing a problem involving my stepson, Jake, she wants to either shift the situation to my son or involve my son, Steve, in the situation. For example, she'll ask, 'Are the boys ready?' And I'll answer, 'Jake is eating and reading—no he isn't ready. Steve's in his room putting on his shoes.' And she'll say, 'Steve isn't ready.' "

Whether the problems confronting husband and wife in a combined stepfamily have to do with favoritism or any other issue of stepfamily life, the foundation for resolving them is constant and open communication. In addressing the unique challenge facing partners in combined stepfamilies to form relationships with each other's children, a stepfather with one biological child and one stepchild advised, "Expect tensions, don't try in advance to define where they'll be, just try to be perceptive enough to pick them up, honest enough to recognize them, and confident that they will prove to be manageable. Know that it may be a struggle all the way. Stepfamily relationships demand a high level of maturity; they require an ability to step back and say, 'Now what is going on here?' in the midst of the pain or frustration or anything."

RELATIONSHIPS AMONG CHILDREN

I've left the issue of how children get along with each other for last because most stepfathers reported that their biological children and stepchildren either got along fairly well or that even if they didn't this wasn't a major problem for the stepfamily or the stepfathers themselves.

Stepfathers, as I mentioned earlier, most frequently reported that having their own children when their partners have children was actually a plus during the early stages of their dating because the children became playmates for each other. As one stepfather said: "Sara and David hit it off pretty well together quite early on, and I think that broke ice in a lot of ways. They were very close in age, and Sara saw him as another playmate for her. The kids themselves still get along quite well," he added.

While this father's son and stepdaughter became friends quickly and have remained so, other stepfathers have reported that their children and stepchildren's relationships have needed time to evolve. One father with two biological children and two stepchildren commented, "In the beginning they were jealous of each other. After about two years they have become very close. Especially my daughter, who is as close to both stepchildren as any sister. They call each other brother and sister."

Another stepfather with two biological children and one stepchild described the evolution of his children's and stepchild's relationships with each other this way: "During the first nine months sometimes my stepdaughter would get into fights with my son. Her defense was that her fingernails were long enough and she knew how to scratch him, and he would kick her. These fights happened rarely, but when they happened we had to pull them apart and sometimes take them to separate rooms and talk it over. Now we have very few problems, very, very few. We were honest with them always about how we saw their behavior."

In the initial months of the life of his combined stepfamily, this stepfather and his partner noticed a pattern common to the early life of most stepfamilies: that whenever the children came back from the homes of their other parents, they would be particularly difficult with each other and with their parent and stepparent. "We would call that the re-entry period," he told me, "and that night the children returned—and the next day—would be hell for various reasons." Coping with this was one of the biggest adjustments they all had to make, but eventually they did make it.

"That has evened out over time," he reported. "Part of it because my wife and I have worked out, let's say, better relationships with our ex-spouses, so that we are able to say, 'Could you get them back here a little bit earlier Sunday night, and maybe stick around while they get into bed and see if they're off to sleep?' What we ended up doing was really smoothing the transition, which helped the kids' relationships with each other and with us."

In addition to agreeing about the difficulty of the "re-entry period"—a subject we will look at in greater detail in Chapter Eight, "The Other Father"—stepfathers in combined stepfamilies with several biological children and stepchildren stressed that each child has his or her own relationship with the other, and that these change over time.

Some stepfathers felt that a large age difference between children is a positive factor in lessening potential problems between their children and stepchildren. "The age difference makes it easier," one stepfather told me. "Mine are twenty-four and twenty-seven, hers is thirteen. However, each set thinks the other is weird." The stepfather with the two step-sons and one stepdaughter he described as "juvenile delin-quents" sees the big difference in age between them and his three biological children as something he is extremely thankful for: "My kids are very young and hers are young adults, so we've never had a problem in dealing with them together, be-cause they've never lived together."

I think the reason the majority of the stepfathers I talked to did not say that conflicts among the children were a major problem is that as parents they have already learned to allow their children to form their own relationships. As one stepfa-ther with two biological children and one stepchild com-mented: "You can't force the relationship between your kids and your stepkids. It's just like I can't force my child to go across the street and become friendly with one of the neigh-bors. It won't work. They will or they won't." Time and again, stepfathers repeated the importance of keeping this in mind. Another stepfather, with two biological children and two stepchildren, told me, "I think one piece of advice would be not to force things. I think this works with all the relationships within the group. Particularly among the kids, let them try to work out their relationships; don't interfere too much. But I guess within the limits of what one is capable of doing emo-tionally, try to be supportive and helpful and caring, without making too many demands on the kids."

Although no stepfather I interviewed said that his children and stepchildren had developed a romantic interest in each other, two stepfathers emphasized the inappropriateness of this for stepsiblings. Even though a romantic relationship be-tween stepsiblings is not technically considered incest, they felt stepfathers and stepmothers should be aware that as step-siblings enter adolescence this issue might arise.

HAVING A NEW BABY

Some stepfathers whose stepfamilies begin with their part-ners' children from previous marriages, and perhaps children from their own previous marriages, eventually include children of their new union. Thus a combined stepfamily once made up of "hers" and perhaps "his" is now also made up of "theirs." Some stepfathers reported that a new baby has a unifying effect on the stepfamily. "Besides the pleasure our child has brought to my wife and me, it's also had an impact on the other children," said one stepfather. "It seems to be a thread of commonality between everybody—this natural child between Sherry and I—it relates the other children by blood and it seems to have a positive effect on them."

Of course, having a new baby doesn't solve fundamental problems between a stepfather and his partner. As one stepfather told me: "I love my new daughter, and so does my wife and my stepchildren, but my wife and I still can't get along. We love each other, but we have a lot of trouble communicating. We're both in therapy now, individually and together, and I'm hopeful now for the first time in a long time."

Many stepfathers report that the closer bond they feel with their new biological children creates a much closer relationship with them than they have with their stepchildren. Often this seems to be supported by the children's mother, and it doesn't necessarily create a problem between the children. One stepfather who has a stepson and a biological daughter from his current marriage observed, "There's a stronger bond in my relationship with my daughter, since it started at birth. So I feel more responsible for her problems. I personalize things with her and I am more objective with my stepson; my wife seems to be more comfortable with my parenting 'our' child, so I feel more comfortable, too."

From the interviews I conducted with stepfathers who have new children with their partners, it seems that the most critical factor to consider in deciding to have a new child is whether both the husband and wife want one. Obviously, this is no different from a nuclear family, where mutual consent about a new baby is far more conducive to harmonious family life—and to a happy child—than either spouse giving in to the pressure of his or her partner. Like all the challenges presented by stepfamily life, the challenges of supporting all the children in a combined family—whether his, hers, or theirs—are best met when both partners are sensitive to each other's needs as well as to the children's, and when they support each other in their goals as parents and as stepparents.

Although this chapter focused specifically on stepfathering in combined stepfamilies, I feel it provides valuable information even if you don't have biological children in your stepfamily or potential stepfamily. For me it was illuminating to find out in which ways having children of your own affects the experience of stepfathering and in which ways the experience of stepfathering is the same. It was also enlightening to hear stepfathers whose biological children live only part time with them express how painful this arrangement is. Not being in this situation myself, it was the first time I looked at stepfamily life from another perspective: the perspective of the stepchildren's father, who because of divorce suddenly gets to see his children only as visitors in his home while they live full time with their mother and her new husband. Along with this new perspective came an increased empathy that has added to my appreciation and respect for my stepchildren's biological father.

CHAPTER FIVE

Whose Kids Are They?
DISCIPLINE AND AUTHORITY

"MY WIFE DOESN'T WANT to talk about my role in disciplining the children or exercising any authority over them," a stepfather of two stepchildren told me. "She doesn't really want to talk about discipline or authority. So that has made it rough for all of us, I think."

"The issue of authority in the stepfamily seems to be a major one," a stepfather with one stepchild and two biological children said. "Authority, discipline, all those things that go together in handling children, seem to rest best with the parent who is the natural parent of the child rather than the stepparent.

"Men tend to have to play the role of being the authority in the family and the mother the role of being the nurturer. Children who aren't biological children of the stepfather haven't been there with him all the time, so when it comes to taking authority and discipline from him, they fight back, they rebel; this creates tremendous problems. It's the biggest problem of our stepfamily."

"My wife and I share authority over her son," another step-father reported. "Most of the time, our views of stepparenting coincide, and that's very significant to my functioning effectively with my stepson. My wife is mostly supportive of my efforts, but sometimes there is an unconscious resistance. When I'm unhappy, we talk about it."

"Basically Nell and I agree about discipline," a stepfather with one stepchild and two biological children from his current marriage said. "We share responsibility for child-rearing and disciplining as equally as we can. Sometimes it's 60/40, sometimes it's 85/25, sometimes it's 25/75, but we try it all the time, try to be as even-steven about it as possible. It's a wicked chore, and you want to make sure that it's done, because it's important."

Within the first year or two of stepfamily life, some stepfathers find solutions to conflicts over discipline and authority within their stepfamilies. Many stepfathers, however, find themselves with discipline and authority being the major problems in their family life, and solutions nowhere in sight. Some stepfathers said the primary conflicts in these areas are between themselves and their stepchildren; most said the greatest difficulties with these issues were between themselves and their partners.

Of course, conflicts about discipline and authority are not confined to stepfamilies. As a friend of mine who is a father in a nuclear family told me, discipline and authority are major items of contention in his own family and among all his married friends with children. As he put it, next to money and sex, this is the thorniest issue between husband and wife.

Traditionally, there seems to be a biological division between fathers and mothers on the subject of how much authority parents should have in the raising of their children and what kinds of rules they should make. Fathers tend to think that mothers are too soft on the children and don't take enough power in their relationships with them, and mothers think fathers are too harsh and inclined to be too authoritarian. Judging from my interviews, many stepfathers and their partners are similarly divided along gender lines. Those of us stepfathers who disagree with our partners about these issues tend to think that until we came along our stepchildren were getting away with murder, and that it's our job to right the situation—if our partners will let us. And therein lies the problem: Our partners don't always let us, because they don't always agree with us.

But when there's disagreement over these issues in our stepfamilies, again we may find ourselves contending with an issue that doesn't exist within nuclear families—the issue of who actually *should* have authority over the children. In a nuclear family, husband and wife may argue over who is being too strict and who isn't being strict enough, but as the children's biological parents they each have equal authority over them and an equal right to bring them up their way. So when there is disagreement between the parents, there is an indisputable basis for negotiation. Since they are both the parents of the children whom they are bringing up, *both* their views deserve to be considered.

In a stepfamily the issue of whose views deserve to be considered—or whose views deserve most weight—becomes much murkier. It depends on how stepparents and their partners answer the question "Whose kids are they?" For stepfamilies this question has many answers, depending on whether it's being answered from the biological, legal, and/or the practical day-to-day perspective. Different parents and stepparents put more or less emphasis on each of these viewpoints, and the answers they come up with vary accordingly.

Where in a nuclear family the answer is limited to two people (the children are *definitely* under the jurisdiction of the mother and the father who engendered them), in a stepfamily the answer to "Whose kids are they?" can be as few as one person (if the children and their mother have no contact with the children's biological father anymore, the mother may feel they are her children) and as many as four (if both the children's biological parents have remarried, the mother and biological father may feel the children are the responsibility of both of them and both their new partners).

Of the stepfathers I interviewed, those who felt most satisfied about the way authority and discipline were handled in their homes were those whose partners shared their authority over the children with them equally and those whose partners exercised more of the authority over their children than the stepfathers did, but did so with the stepfathers' input and approval. "From day one my wife and I blundered into doing the right thing: sharing authority and backing each other up," a stepfather with two stepchildren and two biological children reported. "Authority and discipline for my stepchildren, except in emergencies, are basically in the hands of my stepchildren's mother and biological father, which is entirely appropriate, since the father is very active, and my wife does listen to my needs, too," explained another stepfather with two stepchildren and three biological children. These are two very different approaches, but, depending on the stepfathers and their stepfamilies, both can work.

More than half the stepfathers I interviewed were critical of their partners' attitudes toward authority and discipline, their partners' lack of respect for their viewpoint and lack of support for their taking a more active role as a disciplinarian and authority figure for the child. "For years my wife wouldn't share her authority with me over her daughter," one stepfather told me. "She enjoys authority and power more than I do, and she had gotten used to it being a single mother."

Many times, it's not the enjoyment of authority over their children that makes mothers tend to exclude stepfathers from sharing the responsibilities of authority and discipline, it's the mother's own tendency to be protective of her children. Stepfathers who have biological children often find themselves experiencing the same emotions, and protecting their children from the intervention of the children's stepmothers. As one stepfather with two stepchildren and two biological children explained: "In terms of child-rearing, I think what gets in the way of resolution sometimes between my wife and me is where we come to defend our kids from the other adult. I think that's where the friction comes in."

This stepfather said that he and his partner "talk about

these issues and resolve them when they come up." Stepfathers who felt frustrated about their partners excluding them from exercising authority and enforcing discipline with their children told me they responded to their situations in one of two ways. Either they communicated their feelings, needs, and observations to their partners and worked together toward a resolution or they kept silent and inwardly stewed. "We are constantly struggling with our expectations of support," one stepfather reported, "and sometimes I withdraw." Stepfathers themselves are the first to say that communication is the only path that leads out of the thicket of conflict between parents and stepparents over authority and discipline of the children.

Of course there's also another group within the stepfamily that has strong feelings about these issues: the children. Children in a stepfamily have their own particular slant on these issues that makes their views and responses somewhat different from those of children in a nuclear family. But as in any family, the child's goals are to get what he or she needs and to try to get away with as much as he or she can. The parent's (or parent figure's) job is to give the child what he or she needs, to give way to those demands that will not harm the child's development, and to draw the line when the child wants something that could be injurious or when the request is for something the adult cannot manage.

In a stepfamily, children have far more ammunition for not listening to their stepfather than they have for not listening to their biological father. They also have many more impulses leading them to resist the stepfather's authority and efforts at discipline than children in a nuclear family do. The age-old stepchild response "You're not my father!" (a subject we will discuss later in this chapter) may be prompted as much by the child's feelings of conflict of loyalty to his biological father if he allows his stepfather to significantly shape his life as it may be prompted by his desire to avoid restrictions or the consequences of misbehaving or breaking agreements. Other factors may influence the child as well. As a result of the divorce and of the marriage situation that led to the divorce, the child may be generally resistant to authority. If he or she has been living alone with the mother for any length of time, and the mother has had a problem asserting authority or being consistent about it, this may exacerbate problems for both the child and the stepfather when he comes in. There is a further confusion for children in a stepfamily as well: With the entrance of a stepfather, there is a whole new set of standards being brought into play, and it may well be in conflict with the standards the children are used to from the nuclear family from which they have come or the family unit they formed with their mother after the divorce.

As one stepfather in a combined stepfamily, with one step-child and two biological children, explained: "The main problem is that they come from two different family lifestyles, two different styles of discipline—how you did things in each family—and the children are not really willing to change those styles. They don't want to. So when you're trying to form them into a new lifestyle that's foreign to them, they rebel, and they give you a hard time of it.

"Your own natural children have been with you from the beginning, and they adjust to you incrementally all through their lives. The stepchildren have to do it all at once. And it just creates a great deal of unhappiness, disruption, frustration, and anger for the parent and the child both."

The primary reason most stepfathers are so emphatic in their view that their partners should be in agreement with them about authority and discipline is that they are keenly aware of their stepchildren's resistance to them as influences over their lives. Stepfathers whose partners don't agree with them about their functions in discipline and authority are unanimously frustrated and upset. As a stepfather of almost five years with two stepchildren and two biological children told me: "The children's mother doesn't have the same view I do about my place in the family. I feel that I should have a more authoritative position, a well-defined role with backing from her. I'm a stronger disciplinarian. Because I don't get her backing, the children play one against the other to their disadvantage. In my opinion, there should be general agreement that both adults will play a parenting role, but that the stepparent's role is not in conflict with the natural parent. In my case, my wife often gets caught in the middle between conflicting demands by me and the children." This stepfather also said that "things are getting better after a slow, undefined start." In order to improve the situation, he and his partner have been involved in "counseling, open discussion, and comparison with others in similar positions."

WHAT'S OUR STAKE IN HAVING OUR WAY?

As we look at the issues of authority and discipline in our own stepfamilies, it's critical to realize that, as our partners may have already told us, our views on these matters are not always as entirely objective as we may think they are. We may be right or wrong about whether our partners are exercising their authority and disciplining our stepchildren properly. We also may be right or wrong about wanting more of a share in authority and discipline. Aside from our being human, which in itself leaves us open to the same errors of judgment as everyone else on the planet, another reason we may not be entirely objective about authority and discipline as they apply to our stepchildren is that, as stepfathers, these are loaded issues for us.

As we've discussed in previous chapters, we come into our stepchildren's lives when they are to one degree or another already formed. Since their biological father is one of the influences that has led them to become who they are, we may express our competitive feelings toward him through conflicts with our partners and stepchildren about discipline and authority. A stepfather who is also a therapist, observed, "There are definitely many men who feel threatened by the biological father, feel that if his wife is going to have a relationship with the biological father it's a threat or it's a rejection of him, so they try to exercise control by getting their philosophy put in there, getting their discipline laws adhered to by the stepchild.

But I think if they would really look at it, they could really see it's not a discipline issue, it's an insecurity issue with them."

Thus, in resolving problems that may arise in your stepfamily regarding authority and discipline, it's necessary to see that the problems have many components, including your own very personal needs and desires to establish your place within the family. As you'll see from stepfathers' comments, the best way to approach conflicts is to step back and see the needs and desires of each family member, including yourself, to see why these needs and desires are currently not being fulfilled, and through communication and negotiation to make whatever changes you can to satisfy your own and your other family members' needs and appropriate desires more fully. Since it is extremely difficult to step back from situations as emotionally involving as these, many stepfathers and their partners find support for this process in therapy or counseling or in attending stepfamily groups, like the Stepfamily Association of America, and hearing the experiences of others.

PROBLEMS IN INDIVIDUAL STEPFAMILIES

Let's look at the kinds of situations various stepfathers find themselves in, and those which make so many say that discipline and authority are the major problems in their households.

Stepfathers' problems with discipline and authority fall predominantly into one of three categories: those having to do with their stepchildren's resistance to their exercising authority; those having to do with their partners' resistance to them functioning in these areas (or to the manner in which the stepfathers attempt to function in these areas); and resistance from *both* partner and stepchildren. As I mentioned before, most stepfathers who experienced conflicts over these issues spoke primarily about their partners' resistance being the problem, but many felt that the problem began with their stepchildren's behavior and then showed itself in their partners' defense of their children—the urge toward protectiveness that time and again came up in stepfathers' descriptions of their problems with these issues.

An example of resistance from both stepchild and partner is contained in the comments of one stepfather who observed: "Leslie, my stepdaughter [age fourteen], presented the situation rather quickly as to what my challenges were going to be in regard to my being any kind of authority figure or disciplinarian with her. So I kind of backed off to give her time to get used to there not being as much room for her as there used to be. I guess that was what it amounted to. I think that was a big thing for her. She had been the big cog; and all of a sudden when I moved in she wasn't as important anymore. She really felt that with respect to her relationship with her mother, so I didn't exercise a lot of authority right away. The first time I really did, she was being ridiculous, and I decided to hold my ground, and I guess it caught my wife off guard and she got a little protective of her daughter. If I were advising her from what I know now, I would tell her that's not the most prudent thing to do. It makes it a little hard on our relationships—Leslie's and mine as well as my wife's and mine—when you do that."

As this stepfather's comment suggests, no stepfather can walk in on the first day of living with his stepchildren and expect to exercise authority and enforce discipline. In the best of situations, and with each stepfamily member having the best of dispositions, a stepfather needs time to develop relationships with his stepchildren. As one stepfather pointed out: "You don't have authority unless the child grants it to you, and the stepchild isn't willing to grant it to you until you've established a bond, and that takes years of time." That's part of what the period of adjustment is all about. A stepfather also needs time to develop his relationship with his partner in regard to her children. That's another part of the process of adjusting. And all the parts take place simultaneously. "The period of adjustment was my wife and I coming to share the view of what my authority is as a stepfather," a stepfather explained. "It was me, my wife, and my stepson adjusting to what my role as 'parent,' 'father,' and 'person' was all about and including that in the family my wife and stepson had formed before I came along."

Given that it does take time to make these adjustments, it's appropriate to expect some amount of difficulty with the issues of authority and discipline, at least at the beginning of step-family life. The more elements of difference between the step-father's point of view and his partner's, the more difficult it will be and the more time it will take to make the necessary adjustments.

For Leslie's stepfather, whom I quoted at the beginning of this section, the problem of authority and discipline had two dimensions. Both Leslie and her mother resisted his exercising authority in Leslie's life. Children can resist for years; in fact, as we know from some stepfathers' comments in extreme cases, they may *never* accept their stepfather's authority—or love. But when a stepfather finds himself fighting with his partner as well as her children about his functioning in these areas, he is bound to feel he has no basis on which to reach any kind of resolution with his stepchildren. Just as he needs their mother's support to develop closeness with them, he also needs her support to function effectively in terms of authority and discipline.

That's why so many stepfathers said that agreement between the stepfather and his partner about what his role should be is essential, even if they disagree about the specifics of discipline or other areas of child-rearing. In the words of a stepfather of four and a half years, with two full-time stepchildren whose resistance to him makes his relationships with them "very difficult": "It's absolutely crucial that you and your wife have the same views about your authority in the stepfamily. Without the support of the biological parent, the stepparent will never be able to influence or play a parental role to the stepchildren. If children do not give the stepfather the respect an adult member of the family deserves, then the stepfather feels isolated and at a loss. And if he has biological children, as I do, his stepchildren's treatment of him also exaggerates his feelings of loss on being separated from his biological children."

Stepfathers who were critical of their partners' reluctance or downright refusal to share authority with them over stepchildren, or to have an equal say in the disciplining of the children, reported various reasons for their partners' attitudes.

A stepfather who felt he didn't get his partner's support in these areas explained his partner's protective attitude toward the child in terms of her continuing guilt over divorcing the child's father. "I felt at times—and for a very long time—there was an overindulgence of Jenny by her mother," he said. "I'd say I was able to make that go more in the direction I wanted over the years, but I still think that always remains somewhat of a block to the stepfather, the way the mother feels about leaving her first husband. I don't think that's ever totally cleared, even if number one is a horrible bounder."

Another stepfather, who felt he was blocked at every turn from having authority over his stepson, felt his partner used her authority over her child to wield more power in the marriage. "I never felt respected in that marriage for a second, either by Jason or by my wife, Bobbi," he told me, "ever, from the word go." After nine years of marriage, this stepfather and his partner divorced. Since stepfather and stepson had begun their relationship when the boy was an infant, and the child's biological father had been absent since his birth, stepfather and stepson maintained a close though problematic relationship with each other. During this period they sought counseling together to work out the child's extreme problems with discipline and authority in regard to his stepfather and to school. "Dr. Larson referred to Jason as Bobbi's unguided missile," this stepfather told me, relating what he and his stepson had learned. "That's a real danger, when the mother uses the child as her unguided missile. It makes it impossible or extremely difficult, unless you have enormous wisdom."

Another stepfather told me that his partner Laurie's difficulty exercising authority over her son, Matt, and her difficulty in allowing her new husband as a stepfather to exercise authority over her child, have contributed to Matt's having extremely serious problems in school. This in turn has produced a crisis in the stepfamily, creating problems in the stepfather's relationships with Laurie as well as with Matt.

In resolving disputes such as this one about authority and discipline, outside feedback is often necessary. When a stepfather and his partner continue to fight about whether he has the right to exercise authority over his stepchildren, or whether he has the right to discipline or not to discipline them in the way he sees fit, both he and his wife become so emotionally entrenched in their own points of view that they need to hear voices other than their own. They need an objective eye—or the eyes of other parents and stepparents who have been in similar circumstances—to help them to see the underlying dynamics of their problems and how they may look at their situation differently. In addition to insight, they often need encouragement in the process of working things out.

The Effects of Your Own Background

Frequently, a key step in the process of resolving differences about authority and discipline is recognizing how many of our heartfelt (and gut-felt) opinions about these matters are a result of our own backgrounds.

This brings us back to our discussion about how our personalities and attitudes affect our conceptions and our experiences of our roles as stepfathers. Obviously our feelings and thoughts about how much or how little authority parents or parent figures should exercise over children, and how much or how little children should be disciplined by them, are determined at least in part by how we ourselves were raised. We may agree or disagree with the way our parents brought us up, but nevertheless many of our visceral responses to child-rearing come from how we were treated by them. In talking about the differences between themselves and their partners in regard to discipline and authority, many stepfathers stressed the differences in their backgrounds. Many also said that once they and their partners grasped how much they were products of their own upbringing, they could consider each other's points of views and be open to changing their minds. Some stepfathers reported that once they could see clearly where their prejudices about child-rearing came from—and they could see that they were prejudices rather than objective facts—they could even learn from their stepchildren.

One stepfather, describing the changes he had experienced in these areas during the first five years of his stepfamily, said, "Alice and I came from widely divergent child-rearing backgrounds and approaches. My background has been influenced very heavily by European values. It's a very subordinating kind of thing in regard to children. Alice is the other way around. She would go to extraordinary lengths to satisfy the kids. There was lots of stuff that we had to go through: elbows on the table, what they may and what they may not do. I was a lot tougher.

"I think typically those kinds of things were minor annoyances that were aggravated by any kind of disagreement between Alice and myself. Any time there was bad stuff going on between us, the kids seemed to catch it. They were also used as the political football in that sense.

"In handling these disagreements, most of the time Alice and I try to discuss it on our own, though quite often these kinds of discussions open up when we're all sitting at the dinner table.

"In terms of child-rearing styles, it's been a matter of compromise; we each listen to the other's point of view and then integrate some kind of agreement. I think I have learned much more and I have accepted much more. I have come much further from where I started out than Alice has. So we sort of started out at opposite poles and we've met, but we've met much further up toward her end. I've learned a tremendous amount. It's almost sad when I think back on the terrible things I did to my kids that I've learned now were really quite terrible and that I'm not doing to my stepchildren. There are occasionally twinges of guilt when my kids come to visit and they sort of see that, and they remember what it was like when they were that age.

"We talk about it, and they tell my stepson and stepdaughter, too. You know, 'Hey, Dad, you remember how you used to . . . ?' and my stepson says to me, 'You did that?' It's usually nice. I have learned a *tremendous* amount.

"One of the areas of growth for me has been the idea of children's rights. That never occurred to me the first time around. 'What do you mean, kids have rights? Get out of here!' When my kids were small, I don't think that I even recognized their needs. So there was a lot of growing. Yes, I've learned a whole lot in there from my wife and stepchildren."

Many stepfathers reported similar adjustments to the ones this stepfather experienced regarding how they saw children and the value of what children had to say to them. Many also felt that a significant area of departure from their own backgrounds was learning to admit to their stepchildren when they were wrong about matters of discipline and authority. Often this produced breakthroughs in their relationships with the children, too. As one stepfather told me: "The first time that I was able to say to my stepdaughter, 'I was wrong, I overreacted,' the effect was absolutely amazing. It took a while for me to get to that. The first time it was like the air cleared. You know, 'Look, I'm sorry. I shouldn't have done that.' It made a great deal of difference."

"I've learned to reverse a position I took when I see that I was mistaken," another stepfather said. "I hate to, it hurts. And I have done it. In fact, some of the better, more touching breakthroughs with Sara have come in the wake of her doing something that really was out of line and my coming down much too heavy, and then that leads to a big blowup, and then after tears and all that we realize we have to reach some understanding. Then we try and talk it out, and draw all this back together somewhat. Wrenching experiences. Ultimately very good. Because we're both overcoming our egos at that moment. A very painful thing to do."

Along the same lines, a stepfather of a teenager reported,

"Living with my stepson has made me more flexible. I've gotten to see that if he wanted to do things, it wasn't any problem even though at first I may have thought it was. I learned pretty quickly to just say, 'Yeah, it had to be, that was the way it was, and that was the best way to deal with it,' and I would just basically have to adjust my attitude rather than try to adjust him."

For some stepfathers, learning to have another perspective on discipline and the use of authority is crucial to the well-being of the children in their lives. One stepfather, for example, who because of his own upbringing had always believed in physical punishments for children, commented, "An area where I've changed my mind in terms of disciplining the kids [he has two biological children and three stepchildren] is about spanking. When my own children were a little younger, I would spank them. As they grew up a little more, it was forget the spanking. I'd try to talk with them more, reason with them. Some of this has come about because of the kids' growing up. Another part has been because of Mary's involvement with children and child-abuse programs. It's made me more aware. Mary's taught me about the research, which shows that physical punishment of any kind isn't good for children. I love my kids, all of the kids. I wouldn't want to do anything to hurt them. I keep thinking, 'Is what I'm going to do here going to be good for the child? How is this going to affect the child?' Not right this moment so much, but later on in their life. I don't want the kids to grow up warped over something that I have done that I could have handled differently. So you have to think about your discipline and find other ways of doing it."

"YOU'RE NOT MY FATHER!"

One very provocative situation involving discipline in which most stepfathers eventually find themselves is with a stepchild who says, "You can't tell me what to do; you're not my father!" Strangely enough, I didn't hear these words from either of my stepchildren until Timothy was about fourteen years old and he screamed that at me when I was reprimanding him about something. I had already been his stepfather for years by that point, and our relationship was in most ways a fairly close one, but there were certain areas where sparks still flew. One of them was in the area of my telling him what to do. I tended to be sarcastic and judgmental, and he tended to hate being told what to do, whether by me, his mother, or anyone else, including teachers at school. I think his yelling, "You can't tell me what to do; you're not my father!" was part of the earliest stage of his teenage rebelliousness, an attempt to pre-empt any criticism.

When he answered me as he did, I remember dropping my sarcasm, becoming much more real and serious, and telling him very firmly but without any superciliousness or judgment that I very well could tell him, and would tell him, what to do in certain areas of his life where I felt he needed to be told what to do. I added that this is because he lived with his mother and me most of the time, and together we shared responsibility for him during that time. He became silent at that point and listened.

Another stepfather, with one stepchild and two biological children, reported; "At first if the kids said 'You can't tell me what to do, you're not my father/mother,' we responded that we can tell them what to do because we're adults, and when they are adults they can do what they want. They don't use the line anymore, because they see it doesn't work."

Most stepfathers said their stepchildren responding to them by saying they weren't their fathers was just a phase in the early stages of stepfamily life. After almost five years of stepfathering, one stepfather of two children under age ten commented, "As to my stepchildren accepting my authority, I don't think there's a problem there. There were occasional problems where they would come back with responses like 'You don't get to tell me that. You're not my dad.' Alice and I are the authority figures, and since we agree most of the time, there's no problem."

A stepchild may resort to the response "You're not my father" for several reasons: because he or she is rebelling against your entrance into the family or is testing your commitment; because he or she is feeling a conflict of loyalty between you and the biological father; because you as a stepfather are being too severe, too assertive, or because in some other way your manner is offensive; because the child is picking up signals from his or her mother that resisting your authority is all right; because the child is rebelling as part of adolescence by pulling away from those adults he or she is close to; or simply as a way of trying not to have restraints put on his or her behavior and seeing just what limits you really mean to impose.

Recognizing the tendency of this response to come up some time or other in the interaction between stepfathers and step-children, a stepfather of four years observed, "The same situation holds for the woman when she tries to assert authority over a stepchild as it does for a man. The stepchild can say, 'No, I don't have to listen to you, you're not my parent.' And even if you're strong enough to beat the child down verbally or intimidate him physically, they'll find ways to rebel against it. They'll find ways to disrupt the family, they'll find ways to get you back. And that's just not going to work too well. Intimidation isn't the answer. The thing to do is to find solutions: ways to deal with the authority issue, the discipline."

DIFFERENT CHOICES, DIFFERENT STEPFAMILIES

It may be useful to see the variety of ways in which authority and discipline are handled in the homes of stepfathers who feel they and their partners are successfully meeting the challenges these issues present.

One way was well expressed by the stepfather who said, "Authority for my stepchildren is basically in the hands of my wife and her ex-husband." There are times when the exact manner in which they are bringing up the children is in conflict with the stepfather's own ideas, but he accepts this because, as he said, "I don't see why the children's biological father's views shouldn't impact on their lives just because he isn't living with them. He sees them a lot, and he cares. His philosophy, as well as the children's mother's, should be the primary influence on their growing up. My philosophy and my ex-wife's are the primary influence on my children, so why shouldn't my stepchildren's parents have the same prerogative about their philosophy?

"Now remember I talked about philosophy," he continued. "I didn't talk about the kids setting fire to the drapes. There's a difference. If the kids are going to have bad behavior right in front of me, I'm not going to wait till my wife is there."

Regarding how he expresses his own ideas about disciplining his stepchildren, he said, "My discipline, other than if there's a major emergency going on, like they're setting fire to the drapes, is handled through my wife. I really discuss my needs with her, tell her what I like, tell her what I don't like, and have her be the disciplinarian, the authority on that. I generally don't involve myself and set up my own rules for the kids without conferring with her. She would say to them, 'Larry would like you not to such-and-such.' My reason for not presenting it to them myself, and I don't know if it's valid or not, is that I feel there might be more resistance to my request if I presented it than if she presented it. And also my wife might not be pleased about how I presented it. So I avoid the problem that way, too. If she presents my issue, it's done and taken care of her way."

Another stepfather who also used this method for handling discipline in his combined stepfamily commented, "Our original approach was to have a united front, the way you would do in a nuclear family. That didn't work. What we eventually evolved to as our approach, after reading a pamphlet by Elizabeth Einstein,* is that we split up the discipline. I discipline my biological children, my wife disciplines her biological children, and when we're absent we pass on the discipline function to the stepparent in charge, and we make it plain to the

* *Dealing with Discipline,* co-authored by Linda Albert, published by Elizabeth Einstein, and available through the Stepfamily Association of America, 28 Allegheny Avenue, Suite 1307, Baltimore, MD 21204.

children that we're going to do this, that it's the way we're going to handle things. And it's really relieved a lot of problems, a lot of stress in the family. The children seem to accept it a lot better."

Another stepfather, who has two stepchildren and two biological children, made a distinction between how authority and discipline were split in his family. "Authority in the household over the kids is shared between Debby and me," he said. "I think we just both wanted that. It was not verbalized, but we both knew that we wanted it and we'd do it, and that's what came naturally to us. It's the cause of some friction, too, because we both for a few years had run our own households as single parents. We're still fighting some of those battles.

"As for discipline, the stepfather's role in discipline and child-rearing is different from the biological father's role. At least I think so in the sense that as a stepfather I probably don't take as much direct action or get as directly involved in a number of situations as I would have were I the biological father of my stepchildren. Sometimes I do when Debby isn't here, but more often when she's here she'll deal with it. The same holds true the other way, in terms of my kids."

Although the three stepfathers I just quoted all have combined stepfamilies of biological children and stepchildren, some stepfathers who have no children of their own also leave the disciplining of their stepchildren primarily up to the mothers. "I think the key thing to why it works to have my wife take the lead role in disciplining," one such stepfather told me, "is that she respects my rights and doesn't overrespect my stepson's. And since there are very few rules in the house at all—we're a very liberal family in terms of people being authoritarian; rules aren't a big part on an absolute level—the few rules there are are easily obeyed by my stepson, since he's so heavily connected to his mother and doesn't rebel against her at all. He more or less regulates himself; he doesn't like to break rules."

Despite his partner's taking the primary responsibility with her son regarding authority and discipline, this stepfather found that in many daily situations he had to learn to use his authority as an adult in ways he had never used it before becoming a stepfather and living with a child. As he explained it: "In my interacting with my stepson, I've learned to use authority in terms of getting to do something I want to do, like if I want to watch TV, for example, and he's watching it. I've learned sometimes just to say, 'I'm going to watch TV now,' interacting in a little more authoritarian way than I would ever act with adults. But that's necessary, as long as underneath there's a reasonable basis for doing it. Obviously, if I say I want to watch TV the whole day, it wouldn't be. But where it's reasonable, and given that he's a child, and yet old enough to perceive that it's reasonable, I'm going to do it. If he's angry and stomps out of the room, that's his responsibility. If he's unhappy at that moment, well then he'll be unhappy.

"I talk to him about my feelings when he does something, and he'll talk to me. He'll say he wishes I wouldn't do something and so on. It's a process."

Many stepfathers, like myself, who have no children of their own and whose stepchildren live with them full time, eventually share authority over their stepchildren with their partners, and also share the responsibility of disciplining the children during the time they are living with them. With Cynthia and myself, the decision to do this was mutual. She wanted me to share authority and the responsibility of disciplining Kevin and Timothy, and I was willing to take these responsibilities on. Their father and stepmother had full responsibility when they lived in their household during summers and other school vacations. We also communicated with their father on issues involving their education or problems he should be aware of when they were on their way to visit with him.

Like other stepfathers I've quoted, my experience was that even with Cynthia's agreement and support for my sharing with her the authority and responsibility of disciplining Kevin and Timothy, it still took time for me to be accepted by the boys in these aspects of my role. Until my relationships with each child developed to the point where they trusted me, I only handled those issues of behavior myself that had to be dealt with immediately. Anything that could wait till later I handled through Cynthia. Because Timothy was younger, and because my relationship with him got off to a better start, I was able to function with him more quickly as a disciplinarian than I was with Kevin. But even Timothy's acceptance of me in this capacity developed incrementally.

Judging from my own experience and the experiences of other stepfathers I interviewed, it seems that the younger the children, the easier it is to be accepted by them as a disciplinarian. Since teenagers are pulling away from authority figures in general, including their biological parents, a child's adolescence is a particularly difficult time for a stepfather to come along and attempt to function as an authority figure and disciplinarian. With time, however, many stepfathers find that children whom they met as adolescents come to look up to them as authority figures and to seek advice and guidance from them.

Also on the subject of adolescents and discipline, I found that although Kevin was initially so much more resistant to me than Timothy was, by the time he reached adolescence he often accepted me more readily as an authority figure and disciplinarian than Timothy did when he was a teenager. Of course, Timothy was also more inclined to reject his mother, his biological father and stepmother as authority figures and disciplinarians. This supports the observation of other stepfathers that some teenagers need to take a stand for their own identities more than others do, and when a teenager shows signs of this, he or she seldom singles out a stepfather for cruel and unusual punishment but tends to include the biological parents, and other stepparent, if there is one, as well.

Despite Cynthia and me agreeing from the start about sharing the responsibilities of authority and discipline in our household, like most husbands and wives we sometimes disagreed about exactly what should be done in any given situation. Following our biological stereotypes, I tended to be more strict with the boys and she more lenient. Since, however, we did agree that the responsibility of child-rearing should be shared, we weren't fighting about my right to have or express my point of view, but only about which point of view should prevail. As a consequence, we've always argued as more-or-less equals, with me acknowledging her undisputably greater stakes in the matter as the boys' mother. It seems to me that it's because we've always addressed child-rearing issues within the context of being co-parents that we've always been able to talk over—or shout over—our differences. What happens is that one of us persuades the other that he or she is right or we both change our minds and reach a compromise decision. We have also been affected by what Kevin and Timothy have said in response to our decisions and disciplinary procedures, and both my stepsons have always been quite verbal if they felt we were being unjust.

I haven't hesitated to change my mind if I felt they were right, although, as one of the stepfathers I quoted earlier pointed out, changing my mind and apologizing has often been very painful for me. However, as other stepfathers stressed, the rewards of doing this in terms of my relationships with my stepsons have been more than worth the effort to admit that there's egg on my face.

Many stepfathers in combined stepfamilies also share with the children's mothers authority over and the responsibility of disciplining their stepchildren. As one stepfather with two biological children and two stepchildren who live with him full time explained: "We're all one family now as far as discipline. Once we got married, they didn't look only to their mother if they wanted something; they'd have to expect to ask me or expect discipline from me if it was justified."

Talking about how he and his partner share authority, enforce discipline, and encourage cooperation among the children in their home, a stepfather with two stepchildren (ages thirteen and fifteen), and two biological children (ages ten and twelve), all living full time in the household, said, "To keep in touch with what people in our family are thinking and feeling we have informal talks. At times after dinner we'll sit around the table and talk. Or sometimes on a Saturday evening we'll all be watching TV or something and somebody will bring something up and we'll all talk.

"To set up rules, we'll tell the kids, 'Hey, you shouldn't be doing this,' 'I would rather you did it this way,' 'Don't do it this way,' whatever. Then if they break a rule, we'll tell them, 'Because you have broken the rules that we have set out here you're going to lose your TV or your radio or another privilege for a certain number of days.'

"At one time we even tried holding court with the kids. If one of the kids did something wrong, we would sit down, the kid would give his side of it, and the other three kids would listen, and then would announce their decision, if they thought it warranted this or that, and then would sentence the child. It worked really well. I can't remember why we ever got away from it. It would be hard with just two; with the four here, you'll see sometimes how reluctant they are to punish this child, because this child's going to be sitting in judgment of them someday. So it's touch and go either way. It's just something a parent tries."

The basic elements of the discipline process described by this stepfather are part of the process described by many stepfathers who felt they and their partners had systems that worked at least reasonably well. These elements include an atmosphere of open communication with the children; a clear expression of what the rules are; and a loss of privileges as a consequence of breaking the rules.

Reflecting this, a long time stepfather with six stepchildren who are now in their teens and early twenties commented, "We've always fallen back on the traditional modes of punishment: sending the children to their room; trying to correlate particular punishments for deprivations with particular acts; no TV; docking them from going out; discreetly taking away from them some things they may have wanted. But I hope that we would always resort beforehand to warnings and make very clear what the consequences would be, so that we would avoid a type of arbitrariness. Of course we tried to be consistent. But if you live in a household with eight people, six of them children, you're always going to make mistakes. I guess in that way families have to allow for mistakes, too; you can't run it as you would an army barracks. It can't be that tight of a ship. You try to avoid arbitrariness—although I should say parenthetically that children are masters at making their parents feel as if they are acting very arbitary."

Obviously, the age of the children affects how parents and stepparents must treat them. A stepfather with two biological children and one stepchild, all under twelve years old, commented, "In terms of discipline, we both dislike having to hit the children and consequently we don't. As for the punishment, we found if you make it short and you make it fast enough so they remember why they're being punished, and you make it swift so that it's fifteen minutes in their room and then they're calm enough to talk to, that works out very well."

A stepfather of a stepdaughter almost thirteen years old reported, "Punishments in our home are usually a loss of privileges of one sort or another. My stepdaughter is a little too big to get sent to her room, but she has to stay home on a Friday night when she wants to go roller skating or to a movie if we're really upset about something. Often I defer to her mother in terms of disciplining. In calmer moments, I consult with my wife before I discipline. But the reality is that on more than a few occasions I just say, 'This is enough and this is what's going to happen.' "

His advice is "I really think one has to think very clearly what discipline is appropriate for children and how you handle it, because that so easily winds up being abusive. That may be the lowest common denominator approach, but I really think the question of how to discipline a child who is not biologically yours is something you have to think about very carefully."

A stepfather of three stepchildren, ages fourteen, twenty, and twenty-two, finds that he and his partner depend almost entirely on discussions rather than a loss of privileges to keep things running smoothly in their household. He also finds that having as few rules as possible is a good idea, especially with older children. "We don't have a lot of discipline," he commented. "We talk. When agreements are broken, again we talk. I don't think we've ever grounded anybody. When Zack was smaller, we'd tell him he'd better shape up or do it better, do it right next time.

"Once the kids were in their teens, one of Renée's big things has always been to tell them 'If you're going out, let us know when you're going to be back. Leave notes or call.' The same went for all the kids. I remember talking with them and saying, 'Let's work out a plan. What feels fair to you?' When they stayed out too late we'd say, 'This is not working and it's not fair to us to have us worrying. And it might seem silly to you that we worry, but we do, so we have to come up with a plan that feels fair.'

"With my stepdaughter we ended up with a plan that for each minute she was later than she said, and she didn't let us know about it with a phone call or something, then the following day it would be that much earlier that she had to come in. I remember one summer we worked that out, and it sort of semi-worked. Usually we'd end up fudging it after a while, because the main thing was to get the message across. But the main thing, I think, and Zack's been real good about this for the most part, is saying, 'Let us know what your plans are and call.' If he doesn't, we get angry, and he says, 'I'm sorry' or 'I forgot' or 'I tried.' He's generally been pretty responsible about it. But if he isn't, we really don't have any big discipline plan about it. It's more talking about it."

WHEN YOUR WAY ISN'T WORKING

Many stepfathers who found that discipline and authority were problems within their stepfamilies reported that they and their partners—sometimes with the support of a therapist, counselor, or stepfamily group—were able to re-evaluate what they were doing and to come up with a strategy that worked better. For example, one stepfather said, "I mistakenly figured I could be a father right away. I found out by attitude that my stepson did not want me. He was older, and his real dad is still alive. I had to step back or lose him totally. Even after my realization, he expressed verbally that I did not step back far enough so I had to go even further in not pushing my ideas on him."

Given the complexities of forming a stepfamily, it's not surprising that a workable solution to any problem in an individual stepfamily, is so often discovered through a process of trial and error. We keep coming back to the point that forming a stepfamily is a *process;* it's not a *fait accompli* that occurs at the time of the marriage. And given that it is a process, it's heartening to realize that one can learn from mistakes and then correct them.

One stepfather recounted how not only he but his stepchildren's mother, started off in the wrong direction entirely and had to make a 180-degree turnaround in their approach to authority and discipline with his stepchildren. "In the beginning," he told me, "my wife worked very long hours and I became the authority figure. We see now that this was not good. I brought different rules, views, and ideals with me into their—my wife and her children's—domain. She now takes a more active role in the authority. It is now shared, and many times it's discussed with the children.

"I was not happy in becoming the instant boss. She was not happy in being put into the middle many times. After many discussions we realized the situation was out of hand. Before we sought counseling, there was no way that I could begin to realize the goals that I had as a stepfather—to earn my stepchildren's love and respect and to be treated as a second dad and not as an enemy that has invaded their domain. Now I am generally happy with the support my wife gives me. The counseling we went through helped us all very much."

Another stepfather also initially found himself as the primary authority figure and disciplinarian—and he also found it didn't work. "There was a period for whatever reason or set of reasons, I became the major disciplinarian. Then we had a moment when I got fed up with it, because I thought Emily was abdicating her responsibility for Jacqueline, which I think she was. Which I can understand, because you've had this tough, ornery kid for a long period of time. Emily and I talked about it, and I said, 'Look, we've got to do this together. If we don't do this together, this is early adolescence, we're going to have trouble, because she needs more of a unified voice.'

"I think Jacqueline was playing both of us, one against the other. That's obviously the classic thing that happens in any child-parent relationship, playing one parent off the other, playing complicated games. It's more likely to be feasible in a stepparent relationship, and I think we fell into that. Emily abdicated. I took over for certain things, and Jacqueline was playing both ends against the middle. After we talked, Emily realized that that was indeed what had happened, and that we could do better together."

The stepfather whose three stepchildren are "juvenile delinquents" said he and his wife have had a history of stormy arguments over them because, as he put it, "My wife has been brokenhearted but she has defended them too often when I told it like it was." He wanted to exercise what's sometimes called "tough love" with them: enforcing very stringent requirements that they display responsible behavior if they want to come into the household, even as guests. But their mother kept giving in to them, regardless of their behavior. Finally the stepfather confronted the issue with his partner head on. "A few months ago I wrote her a long letter and in essence said that things must improve, because our marriage was being shattered. After several weeks of tension, she apologized to me for all the pain she'd caused me by her severe criticism for the way in which I related to her kids. Now she supports me most of the time."

The stepfather I quoted earlier whose stepson, Matt, was having serious problems with school, and whose partner, Laurie, was having difficulty exercising authority over Matt and also having difficulty letting the stepfather exercise authority over him, is also a wonderful example of a stepfamily triumphing over difficulties. At the time of our interview, the stepfather told me I should check back with him in six months to see what would transpire as a result of the family going into therapy together. Six months later he reported, "Matt is doing beautifully in school now. I had wanted to send him to a school with a very structured curriculum, one that made a lot of demands on him, and that had a highly disciplined, traditional atmosphere. I thought that was what he needed. I also had wanted to give him a structure at home and to be consistent about what our—Laurie's and my—demands were on him. Laurie had a lot of trouble with that. In the course of therapy, she could see that her attitude really wasn't helping Matt, and that I wasn't attacking Matt by suggesting that we make demands on him. The way it's turning out, Matt likes his new school very much. I've never seen him so happy."

A Final Word Where There Is No Final Word

While, of course, children have different strengths and weaknesses, and vary in their ability and willingness to live up to their mothers' and stepfathers' demands and expectations, stepfathers are bound to be frustrated and upset when the way to handle their stepchildren's behavior becomes a battleground in their marriage to fight out the larger battle of who should have authority in the house. Matt's stepfather was pleased that through therapy he and Laurie were actually able to focus on what strategy would be best to help Matt in school, and Laurie was willing to reconsider her point of view. She saw that her own problems with being a disciplinarian and an authority figure, as well as her problems with sharing authority over Matt with her new husband, were having a detrimental effect on Matt as well as on her marriage.

In my own stepfamily, I've learned over the years that whether you're fighting with your partner or your stepchildren, it's pointless to fight endlessly over the same issues. Persistent fighting over any issue may be symptomatic of larger issues that are being ignored and that must be resolved for the family to function with any degree of fulfillment for any of its members. The first step in solving continuing conflicts over discipline and authority is to see if the issue you are fighting over is really a mask for a deeper issue about your marital relationship, relationships with your stepchildren or the dynamics of your stepfamily. If it is, then that's the issue to address.

Persistent fighting with children over any single issue or set of issues may indicate a lack of a realistic perspective on the part of the stepfather, the mother, or the child. While Matt's stepfather proved to be right in demanding more of his stepson, there are other cases in which persistent fighting with children over something may signal that there are too many demands being made on the children, at least for that particular period of their lives. If you find yourself in this situation, ask yourself if what you're fighting about is truly important for the children's growth or for your sanity. Ask yourself if the way you're going about solving whatever problem you and your stepchildren are having is the only way to go about it. See if there's another strategy that might work better.

During Kevin's adolescence, for example, he so consistently ignored his household responsibilities, and we so consistently got annoyed that he did, that both Cynthia's and my relationships with him were reduced to our becoming nags and his throwing us excuses on his way out the door. Finally, as a result of some very good feedback from my therapist, I realized that the thing to do was to eliminate his chores entirely and to tell him he had to earn some pocket money in an after school job, since I tended to think of him as a freeloader if he wasn't going to do anything at home. After Kevin's initial shock at being told he must get a part-time job, he went out and got a job he very much enjoyed, our relationship began a steady improvement that has continued to this day—and he began to develop the sense of responsibility for himself and the sense of cooperation that I felt were so important.

Some stepfathers suggested that we "don't set many rules." Whether we're talking about household chores or any other area of discipline or authority in stepfamily life, I think the cardinal rule is to set only those rules that are necessary either for the children's safety and development or for your peace of mind; the fewer and the less arbitrary the rules, the more the children will feel respected and the more they will respect you and the rules that you do give them. This is important to keep in mind, especially as your children grow older.

CHAPTER SIX

Time Alone with Kids

IN CHAPTER THREE we examined how the members of our stepfamilies adjusted to living as a family unit. Now I'd like to explore an element of stepfather-stepchild interaction that I found tremendously helpful in building my relationships with stepchildren: spending time alone with each stepchild.

I've found that any time I spent alone with Kevin or Timothy or both together increased the intimacy and the quality of our relationships with each other. Fifteen years ago, when we started living together as a stepfamily, it was easier for me to be alone with Timothy because he was so much more open to me than Kevin was. But when I dared to be alone with Kevin, or when I had to be, for example, to take him on an errand when Cynthia couldn't, there was a feeling of something being shared between us, even if it was just a car ride. Even if we didn't speak much—and if what we said was superficial—I felt good about being able to do something for Kevin, and I felt good about it even if he didn't acknowledge me in words for doing it.

It was my way of making a statement to him that at the time

I couldn't verbalize but that I very much wanted to. Taking the example of a car ride, for instance, just sitting side by side in the front seat listening to the radio—to the stations that Kevin wanted to listen to—and driving to Kevin's destination, whether to the house of a friend or to the store to get something he needed, was an affirmation of our connection, of our belonging to the same family. I was making the silent statement "I'm doing this for you, and I'm pleased to do it." Kevin's silent statement might very well have been "I'm letting you do this for me—and I'm noticing that you are doing it." We felt awkward with each other, but we were both willing to be there feeling awkward, and in time that willingness to be together without Cynthia helped us to feel less and less awkward with each other. I see now, looking back, that those times prepared the foundation for what has become today a very positive and enjoyable relationship for both of us.

With Timothy, there was no such thing as a quiet car ride or a quiet anything else for that matter. Whether we were driving, taking a walk, cooking together, or playing in the backyard, he was always chattering about something—usually people he had met or an adventure he had had at school or with friends after school—and I was always chattering back. Sometimes he asked me questions of a philosophical nature—about God or why we have nuclear weapons—and other times he told me jokes or asked me questions about my writing, and then advised me if I had a problem.

To this day, spending time alone with Kevin or Timothy—and spending time alone with both of them—is very special. In some ways it's even more special today, because they are older; and because we have become so close, we always have a lot to talk about. But in the early months and years, the time I spent alone with each of them and both of them was invaluable.

Although spending time alone with children is important for biological fathers (and mothers, too, of course), it has a unique importance for us as stepfathers. While biological parents need to continue the bonding that began with their children's birth, we stepfathers need to make up for lost time in a sense and begin forming bonds with children whom we didn't even know at birth. With the need to do this so pressing, we are compelled to take advantage of every opportunity that can possibly lead to developing trust and affection. And as I and many other stepfathers have discovered, being alone with our stepchildren in the absence of our partners tends to create a new environment in which closer relationships are often the result.

One way to look at why this is so is that the very absence of our stepchildren's mother forces our stepchildren and us to relate to each other rather than to her or through her.

In my experience and in the experience of many stepfathers, children actually tend to be freer with us when they are alone with us. This may be because when they are alone with us they can't be involved in attempting to play parent against stepparent or in trying to read their mothers' signals about how they should act toward us, or perhaps because when their mothers aren't there as reminders of their family history, our stepchildren feel less compelled to withhold their attention from us as a way of upholding the place of their biological fathers. Also when they are alone with us they are not caught up in their sometimes very complex relationships with their mothers.

We're often freer with the children when our partners are absent, because we're less self-conscious about doing "the right thing" with the children and we have no one to compete with for the children's attention. Also, when it's just us and the children, we don't have to compete with the children for our partners' attention.

The Benefits of Time Alone

Let's see what other stepfathers said about what they've gained from spending time alone with their stepchildren.

"Some years ago, when my wife started commuting long distances to work and being away two or three days at a time, I discovered something really extraordinary," said the stepfather of a stepdaughter who is now seventeen, and who had a very difficult time with the girl when she was a young child. "What I discovered is, I think, something people don't ordinarily have the opportunity to discover, which was that when Emily wasn't around Jacqueline and I got along without friction or with very little friction—or when there was friction it could be very easily overcome. Jacqueline would be guarded, sometimes silent, sometimes petulant, sometimes not there at all in the psychic sense when all of us were together. I always presumed that Emily and Jacqueline had some kind of thing that they do, which I can't. But when Emily was not around, Jacqueline would talk to me. We had conversations.

"When Jacqueline and I were alone, at first I used to cook dinner for her when Emily was away. I discovered very quickly that it was much better to take her out to have junk food or something like that, because we just could talk. It was worth a small amount of money. I found things would flow very easily when Emily wasn't there. I don't think there was a hell of a lot of nasty negotiating going on. Then when Emily would come back, things would get tenser, because of their relationship. But I was not being forced to be involved in it as much. In fact, I was becoming somebody who was clearly being accepted by Jacqueline as somebody who was not caught up in the craziness of her relationship with her mother. She was in some instinctive way able to recognize that there were boundaries to that.

"When her mother was around there was always complicated negotiation between them; there was a whole lot of ego stuff. Then, after two years, that lessened, too. They began to reach an equilibrium of a certain kind—then adolescence; I mean, adolescence, that's another story altogether.

"When Emily is commuting what Jacqueline and I do most now that she's an adolescent is we eat in different restaurants. That's my favorite activity with her, because we actually talk.

"Jacqueline talks to me about her school and social life in a way that she simply doesn't talk to her mother. She's more frank, I think, which I'm astounded by, because she talks to me about things that I would never have talked over with my own parents. I think she still keeps a lot of things in reserve, but she's not afraid. I think she likes to shock me in some ways. It's part of the permissive child-rearing; nothing ever shocks anybody, so you can go out to the frontier. Part of it's a little bit flirtatious, too, I think. She is a woman growing up. I see it, and it doesn't make me uncomfortable. Our boundaries are clear."

A stepfather of a stepson age ten and a stepdaughter age seven observed, "There's something very special about having the two of them to myself. They are much more acquiescent in anything. Hurrying them along is not necessary when I'm alone with them, whereas when it's the four of us it's always a 'Let's keep things going, guys' attitude from me. That just doesn't happen when we're alone; on the contrary we always have much more time than we really need. It's always a very special time of one kind or another. And we do a lot of very special talking."

A stepfather with two stepchildren ages nine and seventeen and two biological children ages fourteen and seventeen said that, for reasons that vary with the personality and age of each stepchild, the time he spends alone with each of them gives him a chance for a type of interaction that simply doesn't take place with their mother present. The time he spends alone with his stepdaughter, age nine, gives them a chance to relate without the tension that so often characterizes his relationship with her when his partner is there and the child so overtly favors her over him. "With my stepdaughter Rachel," he said, "I've taken her a few places, to get ice cream cones or whatever, and I've driven her on a couple or three field trips for the school. And every once in a while when Debby has a meeting I'll be here with Rachel. It's not so much having dinner alone, but we'll talk in the living room or something; I'll talk to her a little bit before she goes to bed. Those, I think, are some of the nicer times."

The time he spends alone with his stepson, age seventeen, gives them an opportunity to talk about things that are an issue of conflict between the boy and his mother. "With Hank, I guess, the time we spend alone has mainly been when he's watching television or something and I'll sit and chat with him, or talk to him about what he's doing in school, things like that. At times when Hank and I are alone, he talks to me more than his mother about grades. Because with Debby there's sure to be that automatic reaction when he doesn't do well. I think the issue of his dress and appearance, that's also something I could talk to him about a little bit. Because I don't tell him 'I don't like what you're doing' or 'I don't like the way you look.' His dressing has been a red flag for Debby, but not for me, so that was an area where Hank and I could talk to each other."

As the comments of the stepfathers I've quoted thus far suggest, one of the things that makes stepfather-stepchild time alone together so special is when stepchildren confide in you about their lives. I know that spending time alone with Kevin and Timothy gave them the opportunity to discuss things with me that were on their minds and which they felt self-conscious about bringing up with their mother. It also gave them the opportunity to ask for feedback about things that were bothering them in their relationships with her. One especially memorable issue they raised was that Cynthia never discussed her career with them (she is an actress). So they had no sense of her goals, her frustrations, or her progress. I told her what they said, and since then she has opened up to them about her professional life, and they have been enthusiastic and strong supporters.

Another stepfather, who has two stepsons and one stepdaughter, talked about the differences with each child and the different areas about which each of them will confide when alone with him. "Zack [age fourteen] is the one that I've had in some ways the most influence on, that I've played the most parenting role. We have this whole thing that my wife, Renee, and I call our sex talks. Usually on the way to one of his baseball games, where he and I are in the car together. It felt relatively easy for me to talk about, and he was willing to listen to me. But it felt like I really was the one who sort of took him through his puberty in some way and told him what was going on. One of the things that always feels good to me is that sometimes just the unconscious comes through, and the kids would come in and say to me, 'Hey, Mom,' and there's sort of this sense of it doesn't really matter who you are talking to, it's the same function, the same role.

"With Julie [age twenty-two] it just feels like throughout the last five or six years of her life, even though of course she talks with both of us, I've been the one she'll come and talk to about a lot of stuff. She's come to me to talk about what to do with college; about studying and high school and the struggles she'd have about that; a lot of stuff with her boyfriends. There was a period of time when she was in a relationship with a guy that was really painful to see because he was not treating her really well—she sort of kept getting back into it, and Renee got to the point where she couldn't talk about it at all with Julie. Renee got so upset about it that she'd just get furious as soon as it started coming up again. So Julie would talk to me about how upset she was and what should she do, and I'd be there for her in that way."

MAKING TIME ALONE A PRIORITY

As you can see from my experiences and the experiences other stepfathers shared with me, there is often another dimension to the interaction that takes place between us and our stepchildren when we spend time alone with them. Whether we're going on outings or playing games or sports together, going on car rides, eating meals, watching television, doing chores, or just sitting and talking—even talking on the telephone—there is an increased opportunity for getting to know each other as individual people.

For a while after both boys had gone off to college, I regretted that because of my own lack of interest in athletics I had spent so little time participating in sports with them when they were younger. That certainly would have been a great opportunity for a stepfather to spend time alone with his stepchildren, I would say to myself—going with them to and from games and meets, practicing with them, coaching them. Today it's clear to me that the activities I did share with them as they grew up helped us first to become acquainted and then to become close to each other. The better we got to know each other, the more trust there was between us and the more comfortable we felt with each other generally. The more trust we had for each other and the better we felt with each other, the better I could function as a stepfather, even in problem areas, because as stepfathers our ability to enforce discipline with our stepchildren is so dependent on their trusting us. Also, the more they trust us the more they are willing to confide in us, even about those aspects of our relationships with them where we are doing something that upsets them.

We may be unaware of the impression we are making on our stepchildren during these times alone with them. But I realized it when Kevin was in college, entertaining an audience of 1,500 at a charity fund raiser sponsored by his fraternity, and he sang the songs I had taught him when he was eleven and twelve years old and I had accompanied him on the piano when nobody else was around.

Whatever your interests and abilities and whatever the interests and abilities of your stepchildren, there are always things you can do together. The most critical thing is the interaction that takes place between you. And the first requirement for that interaction to take place is that you set aside the time to be with them.

A stepfather of two young stepchildren told me, "I enjoy almost every activity alone with the kids. And I do make an effort to go off and do something with an individual kid from time to time. That gets to be hard, because that time is hard to find. But every now and then one of them will have a play date, so I'll try and take the other one off and do something or other. I can see a difference since we first got married. Then if the kids had a play date, Alice would take care of them. Often she would stay with one kid in the neighborhood of the other's play date so she could then pick the other one up after the play date was over, instead of having to keep going back and forth from one side of town to the other. I suddenly realized that Alice got to see the kids much more than I did, and so I was missing out on all of that. When I began to do it, I began to see what a treat it was for me; it's just wonderful! Now if I know that one of the kids has a play date after school, I'll encourage Alice to take the other one home, and when I'm through with work I'll go and get the one from the play date, just so we can spend some time together."

A longtime stepfather of six stepchildren reported, "From the beginning, I spent time alone with the kids, more so when they were younger than now. Now they're at the age [they are all in their teens and early twenties] where they're virtually independent in terms of organizing their own social lives and so forth, their own activities.

"Spending time alone with them is something I set out to do. It was deliberate, and I think the time I spent with them alone was crucial in establishing my relationships with them. I have the type of job that permitted me to get home, to have flexible hours. Although I worked long hours, basically they were hours of my own choosing. So when they were younger, I would ensure, for instance, that virtually every day I would be home at three when they got home from school. I was the one who primarily prepared meals for them, particularly during the week. Then after dinner very often I would have to go back to work and my wife could be home. So I did spend a lot of time with them. In fact, in the time we've been a stepfamily, their mother and I have spent a more or less equal amount of time.

"I should say that I was probably more socially involved, even when they were younger, with the boys than I was with the girls. Generally when I did things with the girls, it was also in the company of their mother—jaunts to the zoo or going to the movies. But there were things I did alone with the boys that were very enjoyable. For instance, when they were younger and I was younger, I was a motorcyclist. Some of the most important experiences I had with my stepsons was taking them on extended motorcycling camping trips, which I also did from time to time with the girls. But there was a type of bonding I think through those excursions that was more pronounced with the boys than the girls."

Another stepfather of a stepson and a stepdaughter, both in their teens, had a different experience. "Initially I would say, two years ago, I was feeling that I was doing too many things with my stepson and not enough with my stepdaughter," he told me. "All we were doing was going to computer shows together, little things like that. But as it works out now, I seem to be doing more activities with my stepdaughter than my stepson. Initially I said, 'What am I going to do with a girl? I didn't have sisters, I don't like dolls. I don't know what she likes.' But she talks more with me. That makes it easier. I find it doesn't matter what the activity is, I just enjoy talking with her as well as with my stepson."

A stepfather with two biological children and one stepchild, all under twelve years old, said, "I suppose my favorite shared activities with the children are doing whatever they like to do. My personality is not heavily sports oriented. If they want to sit down and write a computer game or something like that, I help them do that. I'd make a good mother. I enjoy just interacting—fixing something that is broken, repairing a notebook, whatever."

A stepfather with a stepson age thirteen, a stepdaughter age fifteen, and two biological stepdaughters ages twelve and ten told me, "The easiest thing to do with the kids is just sit around and watch TV, but I'm not much on TV. I get the kids out to play. All of them like to play ball. The oldest is not much for playing ball, but the others are. So we play softball. Also they just like to get out, get away from the house, so we go downtown shopping or whatever."

A non-married stepfather who has lived with his partner and her two children—a boy age fourteen and a girl fifteen and a half—for almost five years said that the time he spends with the two of them alone has been very important, and that often they seek him out. "My two stepchildren come to me for specific needs," he said, "like homework, rides, and so forth, as well as for strokes and support."

A stepfather of a stepson age ten observed, "I think the main thing I've learned is if you want to do something with a kid, do it. And if you don't want to do something with him but can do it anyway in a relatively comfortable way, do it. But if you really don't want to do something and you can't get over that feeling, then don't do it. Because you're going to hurt yourself, you're going to hurt him. He'll pick up on it."

IS IT ALWAYS SO EASY?

Not all stepfathers have an easy time talking to their stepchildren, even when they spend a lot of time alone with them. As one stepfather explained: "It's not uncommon for me to be home before Ann is, so frequently there'll be an hour or two hours in the late afternoon, early evening, where I'm with Sara and Ann isn't here. That happens fairly frequently. And I have been typically the one to take Sara to her swimming lessons, for example. I get drawn into things that parents get drawn into. We tend to spend a lot of time together doing errands. She shares things with me, little things that are going on in school and whatnot.

"But for me there's never been a feeling of real spontaneity about spending time alone with her. I always have felt a little uneasy about it, like not knowing quite what to talk about. When we are going to an activity or have come from an activity, that focuses what we'll talk about. When I became the coach of her hockey team, we had a lot of fairly good times around that. I guess what I'm trying to say is it works to spend time with her when there is a mutual activity, but just unstructured sharing time often becomes quiet time."

While this stepfather often feels somewhat awkward spending time alone with his stepdaughter, the situation is considerably more unpleasant when a stepchild is continually hostile and rejecting. One stepfather in this circumstance reported, "My stepson, who is now a teenager, is so angry that we have very little in common now. I hope when he comes out of this mood he'll talk more to me again. Until then I've told him what I think of his behavior, I've told him I'm available to see him and talk with him and spend time with him the way we used to if he would like, and I'm pretty much staying out of his way—and asking him to stay out of mine—until he gets less angry."

For most stepfathers, however, spending time alone with a stepchild, even a reticent one, tends to parallel my experience with Kevin: The awkwardness tends to decrease the more time stepfather and stepchild spend alone in each other's company. As a stepfather for two and a half years explained about his stepson, now almost fourteen years old: "At first when I would go to pick him up in my car from an activity or something, he had the attitude 'Hey, who's this? Where's Mom?' There was not a lot of talking or acknowledgment. Now he's gradually softened, and he's glad to see me; he even acts kind of proud to his friends when I show up, and we talk pretty much freely on the way home."

When we spend time alone with our stepchildren, suddenly we are, at least temporarily, going beyond a definition of our relationships with them that centers on our partners being their mothers. Suddenly the "triangle" element that some stepfathers referred to is not present, and neither is the ability to avoid each other by focusing on her. During these times we are getting to know each other as people; hopefully, we are also getting used to each other; at the very least we are coming face-to-face with the problems we have with each other. Spending time alone with stepchildren may not work magic, but as far as I can see, it's a necessary ingredient for evolving any degree of real closeness with them.

CHAPTER SEVEN

Private Time with Your Partner

WHEN KEVIN AND TIMOTHY were growing up and living with us full time except for summers and holiday vacations, after a while I began to notice two consistent qualities in my own behavior and responses. The first was that I wanted very often to be alone with Cynthia—a desire which, thank goodness, she also felt; the second was that sometimes I found myself disapproving of and annoyed by how Cynthia related to the boys and the boys related to her. I sometimes even resented how much time she spent with them. These feelings were not something Cynthia shared or supported. At times I didn't feel too good about them myself.

Part of my desire to be alone with Cynthia was the desire husbands and wives generally feel to be alone together amidst the pressures of family life—pressures that are even greater in stepfamilies. Part of my desire to monopolize her, as well as to criticize her relationships with Kevin and Timothy, came from a competitiveness. In time I recognized that these feelings of competitiveness I felt with the children for Cynthia's attention and affection added to my desire to spend time alone with her. When she and I were alone, I could avoid the discomfort of feeling disapproved of, resentful, and competitive. When these feelings came up and I couldn't be alone with Cynthia, often, to escape, I would isolate myself from her and the boys. Recognizing this same tendency in himself, another stepfather observed, "Sometimes I resent my wife for the time she spends with my stepdaughter, the things she does to care for her. Sometimes I don't handle these feelings too well. Sometimes I go off on my own and say, 'Well, I have to go back to my office,' and I really don't, but I'll go down there. I'll remove myself from that situation. That's probably my major way of dealing with it."

Once I acknowledged these feelings of competitiveness and resentment in myself, I also realized that I had to make an adjustment; I had to learn to distinguish between the legitimate need for time alone with my partner—which she or I might have to assert quite firmly in order to get—and what might well be termed a childish desire to have her for myself.

Many stepfathers have similar feelings and have reached similar conclusions about working out these feelings; most are also emphatic about the importance of spending private time with their partners. We've learned that it's essential to become aware of the childish side of our feelings and also to make sure that we *do* have enough private time with our partner to fulfill the needs of our relationship. While this is obviously true in nuclear families, too, in stepfamilies the children are there from day one of the relationship and are likely to have at least some degree of resistance to it. This makes private time with our partners even more crucial and frequently harder to get.

If our needs for intimacy and affection are not being satisfied in our relationships with our partners, we are far more likely to be resentful of the time, attention, and affection our partners are giving our stepchildren. We are also more likely to resent the time, attention, and emotional energy our stepchildren may be demanding from us or that our partners may be demanding from us on behalf of their children. We may even resent our own expectations of what we *should* be giving to our stepchildren.

If we continue feeling this way, we are going to be unhappy in our stepfamilies, and our negativity will hinder us from resolving our stepchildren's competitive and/or resentful feelings toward us. On the other hand, if, in the midst of the children's ambivalence or downright hostility we and our partners are nourishing our own relationship and communicating about how we can solve stepfamily problems together, then we feel nourished ourselves. We are then better able to take on the challenges of stepfathering. We are also better motivated to take on these challenges, because, as we well know, our love for our partners motivates and inspires us in relation to their children.

THE CHALLENGES OF INSTANT FAMILY LIFE

How does being in an instant family affect a husband and wife? A stepfather with one stepchild and two biological children said, "When you marry a woman with children and you become an instant family, there isn't time to form a complete bond with your spouse. There isn't the time it takes to be together alone for a long period of time, a year or two, to form the bond that needs to be formed between parents. So you have an additional difficulty to overcome. I think that has created a lot of problems between Gretchen and me. We really don't know each other that well, and it's been hard for us to find the time to form that bond that I think would carry us through. And that adds an additional burden.

"Both of us are great problem-solvers, and I think it's served us well, but we still need to form this bond of trust and understanding and supportiveness so that we're closer. Just the demands of having instant children, the interference and disruption of kids, and always trying to solve problems centering on kids, have not really given us time to know each other well and to be together, to grow together in that direction. We do well with the children, but in other areas we haven't done that well.

"I know both of us recognize that, and we are trying to make attempts. I think it's really important that stepparents actually take more time to be together without their children, focusing on themselves and their relationships, rather than how they relate to their kids and their family. That's a big job, but it shouldn't be one that consumes every minute of your time by yourself or with your spouse. And I find it's kind of frightening, because there'll be a day when the children won't be there, and what happens then? You'll be married to somebody you don't know, and that's going to be tough."

His suggestion to prevent this from happening: "My advice is that you and your wife do find time to be alone to be together and to grow together. And I mean a significant amount of time. Time each week. And time even on vacation."

From the beginning, Cynthia and I felt the truth of this stepfather's observations. The dilemma was immediately clear to us: We were in an intensely romantic time in our own relationship while simultaneously having to commit ourselves to the children and to the adjustments we all had to make in forming a stepfamily. Following Cynthia's and my two-day honeymoon, we never had a chance to be alone together, even for the minimum of nine months, without the presence of children. As one stepfather observed: "The kids are interfering with your honeymoon. You're more sexual in the beginning, and you have to hide that because there are kids around. So that's a problem, competing for time."

Cynthia and I discovered that we had to do our extended honeymooning around the children—either by waiting until they went to bed to be alone, by going off together to our room when they were still up, or by going out and hiring a baby-sitter.

Also, apart from the honeymoon aspects of private time, there was a second very real need for private time for Cynthia and myself. We needed to discuss our points of view about my role as stepfather, what kinds of support I felt I needed from Cynthia, and what kinds of support Cynthia felt she needed from me. Too, we needed time alone with each other for our ongoing discussion about Kevin and Timothy, any issues that might be going on with either of them at any given time and what each of us thought was the best way to handle whatever they might have been going through.

As a stepfather with one stepchild and two biological children explained: "I think if you're going to do the necessary groundwork and talking that produces that groundwork, you cannot make those kinds of decisions in front of children. As a matter of fact, that is a very serious trap to get into. If you start debating on who's right and wrong over some point in front of a child and you don't think they know what's going on, you're wrong. They are very, very smart in these matters. So you're best getting those feelings out about how you would perceive a particular point when you are alone to interact with your spouse. Otherwise you are looking for trouble. Once in a while you have to do it. But the kids have to be removed from the picture, because they'll play games—divide and conquer."

STEPFATHERS' RESENTFUL FEELINGS

There were times I thought Cynthia was being overindulgent with Kevin and Timothy. At those times I also thought I was being objective. Eventually I realized that much of my criticism of Cynthia stemmed from feelings of wanting to be indulged myself left over from my own childhood. Many stepfathers reported a similar experience. In the words of one of them: "Becoming a stepfather was very interesting in terms of helping me to see who I am psychologically and where I am in my own development. It certainly stimulated a lot of my own more genetic-type material in terms of infantile needs, sibling rivalry, resentment of my stepson taking attention away from me to him."

For a stepfather like myself, who has never had any significant contact with children prior to having stepchildren, these feelings may be very intense and equally surprising. At times biological fathers, too, may feel a jealousy, resentment or competitiveness over their partner's attention to their children. They may also feel judgmental about her ways of interacting with them. But it seems that with stepfathers—especially those who've never had biological children—these feelings are more pronounced.

One stepfather who found himself in this situation and whose feelings parallel those of others I interviewed explained, "Once we got married and were all living together, and I saw Adam getting gratified as a child, my more needy feelings—those unresolved feelings from my own childhood—began coming out, and they were more a surprise than the enraged feelings. I think Josie felt caught in the middle sometimes, because I'd be obsessing about him or angry at him.

"This was quite a difference from before we were married, when Josie and I were friends and she got a tremendous amount of assistance and support from me about Adam. When we got married, suddenly because of my reactions she's had to monitor what she says, I think, in some ways when we're all together. I'm complaining to her about Adam, Adam is complaining to her about me, or at least he is disgruntled, stuff like that. So she's caught in a situation with two people she loves, both of whom are complaining about the other. It really reduced the amount of support she had.

"For instance, I became preoccupied with certain things Adam did that bugged me. I think it was related to my own needs at the time. He has sleep problems, for example, so he has to call his mother into his room a number of times in the night. I'd say, 'Why don't you let him alone?'—stuff like that, really nasty feelings. In other words, 'Don't take care of him; take care of me.' 'Why should she give so much attention to him?' type of stuff is what I was constantly bringing up; whining type of stuff. I would stomp out sometimes, acting out.

"My feelings were basically that on some level I saw him as me as a child, and so I felt, If I'm him and I didn't get much gratification as a child from my parents, or nurturing from them, and he's getting a lot, somehow I'm transferring my negative feelings toward my parents onto this situation. I think I experienced a lot of anger at him, but I think in some ways I may have been angry at Josie.

"It's safer to get angry at Adam, because if I'm angry at Josie that's going to cause major problems. And also being angry at a mother figure is much more difficult. So he got the brunt of it—not too much actually delivered at him—but at least in my own mind. And I'm sure he picked up on it. I think in a lot of ways we both picked up on each other."

The way this stepfather now handles these types of feelings about the time his partner spends with her son and the way they relate with each other is to look carefully at how he feels and conduct an inner dialogue to balance out his childish feelings with more mature observations. "Now that I know I have these feelings and that I see when I'm resenting him I'm really resenting unfulfilled needs of my own, that helps calm me down," he said. "When I communicate the feelings to Josie, I think it's very difficult for her. If I talk about those feelings and having them, it's fine; if I sort of have an angry tone at him as an object, then she gets upset.

"What helps Josie's and my relationship," he added, "is that we do have a lot of private time together, because Adam spends time with his dad. The problem is, if Josie and I have a kid, who's going to take him Wednesday, Thursday, and Sunday? I think we'd have to hire a stepfather. That's the horrifying thing, the thought of having a biological kid and not having anyone to give the kid to for a few days."

STEPFATHERS' FEELINGS ABOUT MOTHER-CHILD TIME

Perhaps the primary reason we may feel overly critical about how our partners are relating to our stepchildren or how much time they spend together is that in the most fundamental way the children are not *ours*. Lacking the genetic link and the resulting identification and ego gratification that come from that link, we are bound to feel far more separate from our stepchildren than biological fathers feel from their children. Consequently we may be more likely to put a priority on our own needs and desires over the children's and to have less sympathy for their mother's interaction with them—especially if these very same children are testing us to our limits simply because we are their stepfathers.

I know in my own case that my seeing my stepchildren as

separate from me rather than as extensions of myself made me much more hard-nosed in my attitude about what appropriate child-rearing consisted of—heightening the tendency that fathers generally have to be stricter with children than mothers are. Sometimes Cynthia's being what she would describe as "motherly" made her seem like a total pushover to me, and I would become furious. Whether I was correct or incorrect in specific instances, the overall intensity of my reactions in this area was fueled by what the stepfather I just quoted called "unresolved feelings from childhood." As a stepfather, I felt more of a right to indulge these feelings. After all, since they weren't *my* children, why should I have to act maturely and postpone gratifying myself for them?

There are a variety of other factors, all rooted in the circumstances of being stepfathers rather than biological fathers, that also contribute to our being more critical of the time our partners spend with our stepchildren. To begin with, since most often we haven't had the opportunity to grow up with our stepchildren from their birth, we don't have a chance to begin working out our jealous feelings during the children's infancy and early childhood. Instead of having the opportunity to adjust to our feelings about children needing their mothers more than we would wish when the children are tiny and helpless, we stepfathers suddenly find ourselves in relationships with older children who already have defined relationships with their mother that include some amount of dependency, and we must begin to deal with our jealous feelings at that point. Since our stepchildren's dependency on their mothers is a pre-established component of the new family arrangement in which we are attempting to create a place for ourselves, we may perceive it as a threat to our ability to do this. We may also see the children's dependency on their mothers as an obstacle to our continuing to build our relationship with her as our marriage partner. In fact, in some cases we may be right in our perceptions, and our stepchildren's dependency on their mothers may be an obstacle to our creating a place for ourselves in relationship to our partners.

Biological fathers also have the opportunity to gain a better perspective on children's dependency on their mothers than most stepfathers do. Since biological fathers are involved from the beginning, they get to see that this dependency decreases as the children grow older. Too, through their interaction with their children from the children's infancy, biological fathers have the opportunity to gain an understanding of the uniqueness and value of the mother-child relationship and also of the uniqueness and value of their own relationships with their children. As stepfathers, we generally can't have the perspective to appreciate that our stepchildren's relationships with their mothers are gradually evolving toward less dependency (even if for a time the children do become more dependent on their mothers than they had been prior to the divorce). We also can't have the same sense of security in our value to our stepchildren that biological fathers generally have, because that value just isn't there, especially in the beginning. These differences tend to make many of us less tolerant of our stepchildren's actual needs, and this may make us critical of their dependency on their mothers, even though their behavior may be entirely appropriate to their age and to their feelings about the divorce and their mother's remarriage to us.

Our ability to accept our stepchildren's needs is tried even further, because while we as well as our partners are attempting to give them the support they need to adjust to stepfamily life, we are also attempting to get our own needs satisfied. Rightly or wrongly, we may feel we need the love and support from our partners at least as much as our stepchildren do. And to one degree or another, at least in the early stages of our stepfamily, we are likely to find our stepchildren (and our biological children, if we have them) interfering with our ability to get all that we feel we need emotionally from our partners.

Often, the problem is simply that the children are present and have needs about which they can be vocal. "When we were living together but before we got married," one stepfather recalled, "even though we sort of knew we'd get married from the moment we got the house, still it was a sort of courtship and testing period, and there were times I needed to have Ann to myself because I needed to talk something out. But I couldn't get that time alone with her. Sara wouldn't go to bed. She'd wake up, keep wandering in, something like that. So those were the conflicts and I'm sure they were worse for Ann than for me, because she always felt that she was being pulled in two separate directions."

In fact, our stepchildren may be more demanding of their mothers' time and attention than biological children are in a nuclear family because they do resent our presence and because they are testing our commitment. They may try to interfere with our intimacy with our partners either by direct intervention or manipulation. Some stepfathers said their stepchildren were so intent on driving a wedge between them and their partners that the children tried to pry them apart physically. One stepfather described his stepson's subversionary tactics this way: "Tess and I are real physical with each other. And Lee literally would try to get between us the first couple of times we were all together. So there was that dynamic, which we dealt with right away, right up front. My reaction was 'Hey, man, she's my girlfriend, okay? I'm hugging her; you can hug her, too, but let's try to keep it as separate as possible unless we all decide we all want to hug.'"

Many times such interactions take place on a non-verbal level. "Sometimes Sandy used to resent the time I took to be with Leah as much as I used to resent the time that he would take her away from me when we first got to know each other," another stepfather told me. "For me, at that time, it was kind of a situation where you'd try to figure out 'What is he doing now? What is he doing now about me? What's going on? How come I'm not included in this situation?' We're getting a lot better at it; it's improved a million times."

Children may also be even more competitive with us for their mother's attention than they would be in a nuclear family, because their mothers may also have become increasingly dependent on them after divorce. Explaining his view of why stepfathers often feel their stepchildren are overstepping the boundaries in their protectiveness of their mother, a stepfather of two stepsons remarked, "In a lot of cases the child has become a surrogate spouse to the wife and has been a caretaker, and so now suddenly there's another man there displacing that child, and the child is very resentful. That's an issue that comes up quite often. Also, stepchildren tend to be very protective of the absent father, with an attitude of 'Who is this stranger intruding?' and things like that."

Commenting on how all the factors I've described have influenced his feelings toward his partner's interaction with his stepchildren, and the whole issue of private time, a stepfather with two full-time stepsons said, "There have been problems of, well, seeing my wife as pushed around by her kids and feeling that when I call her attention to it she takes their side rather than seeing what I'm seeing. So I guess I can label that problem as competitiveness for my wife with my stepchildren. I think that's a very common thing. She wants to be a mother, maybe even more so because the biological father isn't there and she feels guilty having divorced and tries to make it up to the kids by giving them too much—too much time—and the new father, myself, moves into the house and it's really honeymoon time for the new husband and wife but there's the intrusion of kids, and you resent that, and I think that's a big part of it. I don't think that's just at the beginning, though. I think that's an ongoing problem."

PROBLEMS WITH PRIVATE TIME

The stepfathers who reported the most difficulty in getting enough private time with their partners were those whose stepchildren's father were no longer living or were not active participants in the children's lives. But among stepfathers whose stepchildren live with them full time—even some whose stepchildren's fathers were active and available—many said they didn't have enough private time with their partners. This is either because their children were so present and demanding when they were there that the stepfathers felt they needed more private time to regroup and recuperate, or because they and their partners didn't make private time enough of a priority to make the arrangements to get it. Some stepfathers said that even when their stepchildren's fathers took the children for the day or the weekend, they or their partners didn't use the time free of children as private time together but instead allowed the demands of taking care of home or business to come first, though they felt their marriage would have benefited from spending that time with their partners without busying themselves.

Some stepfathers in combined stepfamilies said it was particularly hard for them to get enough private time with their partners because they had logistical problems for both sets of children in addition to all the other personal and professional demands being made on them. A stepfather with two stepchildren and two biological children observed, "I think the stepfamily is very busy, much busier than the nuclear family. There are all kinds of plans to make. If you've got biological kids they may be coming to visit when your stepkids are going off to their father, and you get robbed of time with your spouse. So you have to pay particular attention to spending time with your wife and really set aside the time. Make it a priority or else the marriage suffers. There's a very bad statistic about remarriages, especially when there are stepchildren involved. There's a big failure rate, and I think it's because the children are there and create problems, or maybe what I mean is that the children are there and the adults don't take their full power and don't make private time a priority."

In some cases, stepfathers felt that although they and their partners had enough private time together their partners didn't use the time the way they wanted. For example, some stepfathers whose children were old enough not to need constant parental guidance felt their wives were too sensitive about making love while their children were awake because of guilt over the divorce or overinvolvement with the children. These stepfathers were upset by their partners' lack of willingness to work on this area together.

How Stepfathers and Their Partners Manage Private Time

As I mentioned, most stepfathers reported that when the biological father is an active one, then finding time that could be spent with their partners is not the problem. In a combined stepfamily, the more active the other biological parents, the more private time you and your partner may have together. As a stepfather whose two stepchildren live with him and his partner half the week explained: "Split custody may be good, since we don't see the kids every day. It does give us a breather, and it makes us appreciate the kids."

For stepfathers like myself, whose stepchildren live with them and their partners full time for most of the year, other arrangements must be made for parent and stepparent to have "a breather." When Kevin and Timothy were growing up, since we lived on the opposite side of the country from their father, they didn't have the opportunity to visit with him every weekend, so Cynthia and I didn't have regular weekly breaks. Instead, whenever we wanted to be on our own, we would hire a baby-sitter and go out for dinner, to a movie, or to visit friends.

When Kevin became old enough to watch himself and Timothy, we would make sure the two of them had a good dinner, discuss any homework or other agenda that had to be taken care of on the evening we were going out, and then we'd go off on our own for a date. A few times we went off for weekend vacations during the school year. On two or three anniversaries we stayed at a beautiful hotel only several miles from our house, just so we could be alone and uninterrupted. Twice we had close friends move into the house to care for Kevin and Timothy so we could take ten-day vacations. But most of the time we didn't go away overnight when the kids were home because we fulfilled our own need to be together by going out on weekday or weekend evenings. Also, when we stayed home, we would sometimes go to our room early in the evenings, or, on weekends, we would spend our mornings there and would not emerge until noon, when the boys would knock on our door and then sit on our bed, telling us about their morning adventures.

By having our need for private time taken care of in these ways, the petty jealousies and resentments that I had felt at first gradually dissolved. As this happened, I became more and more able to enjoy the loving and close relationships that Cynthia had with her sons, which, in time, helped me to develop my own loving and close relationships with them.

One stepfather I talked to, whose two stepchildren, ages ten and seven, live full time with him and his partner and visit one or two days a week with their biological father, told me that by and large he preferred to stay home, rather than going out and hiring a baby-sitter when the children were home. But in order for him and his partner to get the time they needed to be alone together when the children are in the house, they have had to institute some policies that are new to the children.

"To be alone during the evening, occasionally Alice and I go into the bedroom," he explained, "because it's the only place in our house where we have some privacy. During the first year or so, the kids would sort of line up in front of the door, and would sing, yell, bang, pretend that the cat was throwing up. They weren't used to a room being off-limits—especially their mother's room. Now it's become fairly easy to keep the kids out. And they respect that. I mean, a closed door really doesn't keep children out anymore; they're much too big for that. But they do stay out. And even if we sleep late on a weekend morning or something, they'll knock before they come in, or they'll sort of call from the outside. They're real good. They're very respectful.

"Also, we've established bedtimes for the kids so that Alice and I can be alone. And I don't feel any guilt about demanding that. Their bedtime is about eight-thirty, and fairly quickly after eight-thirty I would like to have my time with Alice or alone. I think they've accepted that."

A stepfather with one stepchild and two biological children living in the house also supplements the breather he and his partner get every two weeks, when the children spend time with their other biological parents, with a "closed-door policy" when the children are home. "Eileen and I make time to be together," he told me. "Sometime between the point when we finish eating and the dishes start to get done, usually an hour has elapsed, and we go to our room, close the door, read the paper, and chat. This is our closed-door policy. The kids are allowed to come to the room, ask questions and get directions and help in schoolwork. But unless there's an emergency, we have this period of time for ourselves."

For another stepfather with two stepchildren and two biological children living full time with him and his partner, occasional nights out with his partner provide some private time, but the bulk of it comes during the summer when they have over two months to themselves. The other biological parents live a long plane ride away. "Occasionally my wife and I'll go out for dinner or to a movie or something and leave the kids alone. Our oldest is fifteen, so that's no problem," he explained. "And they seem to enjoy it. We leave something for them to do here. As far as taking a little vacation and leaving the kids, we don't do that. We don't have someone that we would want to leave all the children with here. So we save our vacation time to be alone until all the kids are gone for the summer. This is something we worked out last year, and it's given us more flexibility to plan for our vacation."

Another stepfather, whose stepdaughter lives full time with him and his partner and visits her biological father only on school holidays, characterized his and his partner's need for private time and their solution for how they get it this way: "The broadest description I can give about our need for privacy is that Ann and I seem to have a need to get reacquainted with each other on a fairly frequent basis. We need a free weekend or something like that. We talk about each other's work a lot during the week, but the more personal or the deeper issues somehow get glossed over until they build to a point where we sense a tension in the air or something like that.

"When Ann and I are making arrangements to have twenty-four or forty-eight hours to be together, Sara registers disapproval or disappointment when she first hears about it, but all in all she accepts it. We usually try to set it up in the context of her spending an overnight with a friend. Sometimes it's a trade-off: we need this time, so you are going to go do so and so, but next weekend we'll all do something together. So it's not been a big issue."

His advice: "Make it clear to the children that you need the time together—it's important for children to understand that. Because they're going to be adults, too, and they have to know that although they as children are very important, so are we. The world just doesn't revolve around them so totally that our needs don't count. They have to learn that we have these needs that may not be visible to them. You have a right to private time with your wife or wife-to-be, and you'd better take it. You have to negotiate how much time is available. It's clearly not something you do every weekend—it's a balance. You do have to be also involved in the life of the children. But if you don't take that private time, you have a rocky road ahead."

When stepfathers and their partners disagree about making private time a priority or about how to spend private time when they do have it, it frequently indicates a deeper problem in their marriage. In these situations, stepfathers and their partners often seek outside feedback. For the stepfathers I interviewed who found themselves with deeper problems, outside feedback came in the form of individual therapy, couple therapy, and/or family therapy, as well as from joining a local stepfamily group.

CHAPTER EIGHT

The Other Father

"You know the lesson I suppose that's hardest to learn?" one stepfather said to me. "You never escape the stepchild's other biological parent. You just never do. I guess it's better to be open and up front about that and try as best as possible to keep the channel open to the other parent."

This stepfather is certainly right that we never escape our stepchildren's father, whether or not he is right that this is the hardest lesson we have to learn. As we know, our stepchildren's biological fathers are a significant influence on our stepfamily life and on our roles as stepfathers. This stepfather also chose the right word to describe the impulse many stepfathers feel regarding their partners' ex-husbands—"escape." The reason it can be so hard to learn that we can't escape them is that our desire to do so is so strong. Generally, we would like to escape the fact that they were important relationships in our partners' past and that they engendered their children. We may even wish that they did not still have relationships with and influence over our stepchildren. More than this, we may wish that as part of their role as fathers they did not also have to be involved in our partners' lives today. Most of all, we may wish to escape the fact that, regardless of how little or how much contact we have with our stepchildren's fathers, they are a continuing part of our lives, too.

Although this chapter focuses on stepfathers' relationships with and feelings about their stepchildren's fathers, for the most part if we are in combined stepfamilies the same observations apply to our partners' relationships with the mothers of our children from previous marriages.

Stepfathers' tendency to want to escape the biological father is especially evident in the experiences of men who marry widows or women whose ex-husbands have broken off contact, or have extremely limited contact, with them and their children prior to the remarriage. Many stepfathers who entered these situations said they initially tried to deny the existence or at least the importance of the children's biological fathers, only to learn that present or not the biological father must be accounted for.

As one stepfather who married a widow with three children told me: "I didn't have a live father to deal with, just a dead one." Another stepfather, who married a widow with two children, explained how he had totally discounted the importance of his stepchildren's late father when he married their mother, only to learn that his stepdaughter was assuming the burden of keeping his memory alive for both herself and her younger brother. "She was always organizing pictures of her father, subtle things like that that I didn't think anything about," this stepfather said. "I wasn't aware of her concern about her brother never knowing her father and her taking on the challenge to rectify that. When her mother and I got married, I thought everything would be like it was supposed to be—perfectly normal in all respects."

Clearly, a parent who has died can be a presence in the life of a child for the child's entire life. A parent who has abandoned a child and whom the child has never seen can be an unresolved question that hangs over the child's head. A parent who lives far away may be in the child's thoughts daily even if the child doesn't speak to him or about him. As the stepfather

I just quoted eventually discovered from his stepdaughter's behavior, a child can experience a conflict of loyalty to a stepfather regardless of whether her biological father is alive. So when a stepfather imagines a picture of his stepfamily without drawing in the absent biological father (or the mother of his children, if he has any), he is drawing only a partial picture of the family.

Most of the stepfathers I interviewed told me their stepchildren had living and active fathers whom they saw holidays or summers at the very least. Many said their stepchildren saw their fathers once or even twice a week. Most stepfathers also expressed a desire to avoid having contact with their stepchildren's fathers, because they are uncomfortable with them or because they disapprove of them. In a minority of cases this prompts stepfathers and their partners to make it hard for the children to see their fathers. Most times, however, stepfathers and their partners tolerate the differences of opinions and styles, and they and the children's biological father declare or attempt to declare some kind of a truce.

Sometimes this truce is superficial and covers resentment on both sides. Stepfathers may find themselves feeling jealous and competitive when they have to deal with their partners' ex-husbands, and biological fathers may feel the same way when they have to deal with us. Women are often caught in the middle of this and have to learn to cope with two men whose agendas may well make it impossible for the women not to offend one by being sensitive to the other.

Besides the kinds of extreme negative factors that may influence stepfather–biological father relationships—such as the stepfather having met his partner while she was still married to her ex-husband or the remarriage having followed a particularly bitter or ambivalent divorce—one of the strongest influences on almost every stepfather's relationship with his partner's ex-husband is the tendency to take on the point of view of someone you love about someone you don't know who has upset or hurt her. By the time stepfathers meet their partners' ex-husbands, most often they have preformed opinions of them based on the stories they've heard from their partners.

This means that stepfathers tend to inherit their partners' biases.

This kind of foundation is not likely to produce an open feeling in the stepfather toward the biological father. As one stepfather told me about his partner's ex-husband: "I don't particularly like him. I didn't like him even before my wife and I started living together. Maybe in a way that was unfortunate, because I got to know him through my wife in a club we belonged to, which is where she and I met each other. Much of what she talked about was her problems with Sam, so I sort of got the bad side of him before I got a chance to see anything nice about him."

If a stepfather's partner is too bitter about her previous husband, her bile may pollute the stepfamily. As one stepfather who is also a therapist observed: "I find the reason that some stepfamilies don't work is because there's not a letting-go by one of the spouses of the old relationship. There's an anger and a hatred that permeates everything. But if you can let go, if you can find a way to release and say goodbye and just deal with your ex-spouse about your own children's issues and forget the anger and the animosity, then it can work. I mean if you hold hatred in your heart and your body for somebody, there isn't really enough room to love the new people anyway. It blocks you up. What you really want is to be fully actualized and be able to fully love."

All this means realizing that, despite our competitive feelings and our stepchildren's father's competitive feelings, the less competition there is between stepfather and biological father (and, in a combined stepfamily, between stepmother and biological mother) and the more peaceful, communicative coexistence, the better for all concerned.

LOOKING AT THE RE-ENTRY PERIOD

One of the times when it's most important—and perhaps most difficult—to remember that the father-stepfather relationship is not inherently a competition is when children are being shuttled between their father's and stepfather's house.

The actual exchange of the children is the time when the children's mothers and, at least potentially, their stepfathers, have the most direct contact with the children's biological fathers, and many stepfathers said that, especially in the beginning, this created tension for all concerned. The time immediately following stepchildren's return to their stepfather's household was imaginatively described by one stepfather as "the re-entry period." Almost all stepfathers reported experiencing difficulty with their stepchildren during the re-entry period, at least in the first year or two of stepfamily life and sometimes longer than that.

Let's first get an overview of why children may behave as they do during the re-entry period and then look at what we and our partners can do to make the transition from one household to another easier on all of us.

One stepfather described the evolution of what went on in his household this way: "At first when they get back from visiting their dad they have trouble getting into the swing of things. They come back and just sort of hang around, sort of being at loose ends, to the point of bothering us, sort of hanging on to Alice or not wanting to be in their room on their own.

"After the visit they are usually very angry. They're usually very angry beforehand, too. They manifest their anger in every possible way. Doing things to irritate. When we say no, slamming around, leaving clothes around, doing things that they know we don't like done, being argumentative. I think part of it is the anger or the anticipation of going then coming back. I think it's just the change. Like some people getting anxious before a vacation; they just get angry. Maybe they don't know another way to handle it."

This stepfather reported that as he approached the fifth year of his marriage his stepchildren's behavior during re-entry had shown some improvement. "Sometimes now they sort of come home and dump their stuff, go racing in to turn on the radio or play records or tear the pages off their calendar or whatever it is. It's just back to normal life," he said.

When the children do act angry or in an irritating manner

before going to or after coming back from their father's, this stepfather and his partner talk very directly to them about it. "We try to bring this behavior to their attention. 'It feels like you're angry because you're going to see your dad,' we might say. Or, 'It feels like you're angry because you just came back. Maybe you should stay by yourself for a while and work it out.' I guess that's all a person can do. You can say to the children, 'This is what I'm feeling or seeing, and maybe you should think about it.'"

Even when children, out of a sense of loyalty to both parents and out of a desire to avoid conflict, keep their lives in each household very separate, it's clear from my interviews with stepfathers that stepfathers and their partners have a sense of what transpires in the other parents' homes. They sense that stepchildren's experiences in their other parents' homes are very different from what they experience in their households, and that difficult behavior on the part of stepchildren during the re-entry period may result from more than the basic conflicts of loyalty children are bound to feel, especially in the early stages following their parents' divorce and/or the formation of a stepfamily. It may also result from going from one kind of an environment to another.

Most typically, stepfathers whose stepchildren lived with them and their partners most of the time depicted the environments of the biological fathers' homes as like summer or winter camp compared to theirs, which they felt was necessarily more structured. In the words of one stepfather: "The other parent's home is more a fantasy for them. They go there, it's a party; I don't mean a party, but they go out to dinner, and the attitude is 'Let's have a good time—let's go to the beach that's around here.' There's no school, of course, because they are away from school in order to go there. So they sleep late in the morning, stay up late at night, have what they want to eat, and they don't have to do this, they don't have to do that. And when they come back here it's back into the routine. Get up at six and get ready for school, the same drudgery and evening chores to do. So the other is really a holiday. I can understand how kids would enjoy it."

Stepfathers also say that difficult behavior when their step-children return to their house may result from the children having to switch very quickly from one lifestyle to another. Discussing his observations along these lines, one stepfather said, "The kids' father is much more rigid than my wife and I are. He strikes me as being much more of an elitist. . . . He has a big thing about clothes. He is occasionally quite upset at the sloppy way the kids dressed. We are much more casual about these things. And we have a much more open way of relating here—we talk more about our feelings and the relationships within the family. Maybe it's because we're so intent on making things work this time."

It might seem as if children whose father was rigid and demanding would feel nothing but unalloyed pleasure in returning to the more relaxed, nurturing home of their mother and stepfather. But as this stepfather reported, especially during the early stages of stepfamily life, children can be upset both before and after visits with their father because the obvious contrast—which no one spoke about—made them feel that much more conflicted in their loyalty. Children in this situation often experience the potential pleasure they could be getting in the stepfamily environment, and from their relationships with their stepfather, as an implicit criticism of their biological father.

Stepfathers reported that difficult behavior when the children make the transition from one household to another may also result from problems they are experiencing in one or both households. One stepfather, for example, said that his stepson and stepdaughter, both teenagers, felt great turmoil when they were with their father because he was an alcoholic and his behavior was so erratic. Their father's unpredictable conduct catalyzed a whole range of emotional reactions in the children before and after visits with him. Another stepfather, who has his own problems with his stepson because after two years the child is still very resistant to him, reported that the child also has a highly troubled relationship with his biological father. The father's emotional problems made it hard for him to be as supportive of the child as the child would like. Whenever the child returns from his father's home, this stepfather said, the child's behavior is particularly difficult. His father has generally been too preoccupied to focus productively on the child, because he is trying to deal with his own emotional life.

Although some of the stepfathers I interviewed reported situations as extreme as the two I just described, most stepfathers said their stepchildren had only "the normal problems" with their fathers and had at least moderately good relationships with them. Very often when children have a positive relationship with their biological father, they may want to use the re-entry period to integrate their lives in both households. Indeed, they may want to integrate both families. For little children this may take the form of a fantasy. One stepfather, for example, said his four-year-old stepdaughter had requested that instead of her having to go back and forth between her daddy's house and her mommy's and stepfather's house, why not have her mommy, stepfather, and herself move in with her biological father in the house she had lived in before the divorce?

Frequently, children simply want to see their biological fathers being accepted in the mother's and stepfather's household. As one stepfather said: "Frank has done things like visit Sara about once a year, and he will spend the night. Last year, we once stayed over at his house when we dropped Sara off there, because he lives so far away and we couldn't drive home. Sara has been instrumental sometimes in trying to engineer get-togethers where her mother and I and Frank and Shelley, her stepmom, will all get together, and we play along with it up to a point. We're all civil."

Many times stepfathers told me that at first—and sometimes longer than that—this civility to the children's father is hard to achieve. I was painfully self-conscious the first time I met Kevin and Timothy's father. I was at a complete loss at how to behave. As much as I lacked a role model for being a stepfather, I also lacked a role model for interacting with my partner's ex-husband in my home. This kept my communication brief, to the point—just logistics, time schedules, travel arrangements. For many years any chitchat was just that, entirely superficial and not meant to establish any real communication.

POSITIVE RE-ENTRY INTERACTION

Unlike Sara's stepfather, who has actually spent several nights under the same roof as her father, some stepfathers and biological fathers carry the desire to escape each other as far as they can within the bounds of what might be considered normal behavior. This may create difficulty for everyone when the children are being exchanged from one household to another. For instance, one stepfather said he always waits uncomfortably and impatiently in the car while his partner goes into her ex-husband's house to get the children at the end of their visit there. And the stepfather who said he didn't particularly like his stepchildren's father told me, "I don't think my stepchildren's father is terribly at ease in our house. I'm sure I am not when he's here. For the most part he won't come in, and that's fine with me. But he has been here several times. If he brings the kids back on a Sunday evening and it's Christmas or something, we invite him up for a drink or whatever, and that's quite all right. I think by and large we've done all right. We sort of pass each other as much as we can, but if we have to we're perfectly civil to each other."

The stepfather who coined the phrase "the re-entry period" and his partner have worked to establish more than an air of civility with both their ex-spouses when the children are brought back from a visit. Observing that in the past "that night the children returned would be hell for various reasons," this stepfather explained that he and his partner soon learned to brace themselves for what was going to happen. "We would come home from work and make a supper that was going to be easy for us to prepare so we could get our iron suits on quickly enough," he told me, "because the kids were really tired and they had schoolwork to do, and they were cranky, and they were being stuffed back into this mold that they probably needed but didn't like."

After some months of doing this, he and his partner embarked on a determined program to build better relationships with their ex-spouses and to get their cooperation in making re-entry a more pleasant, less jumbled and anxious period for all concerned. They began this program by asking the other parents to bring the children back an hour earlier than they had been and to make sure the children had eaten dinner before returning. Then they had the idea of making the children's other parents part of the re-entry process.

"Today we have very good relationships with our exes," this stepfather said. "I have the feeling that's one of the reasons the kids can live here and not tear each other's hair out. There are absolutely no negative feelings about the other parents—well, we may harbor them privately—that are transmitted toward the children. We invite our exes into the house; I think it's important for my kids to be with their mother and for my stepdaughter to be with her father. It seems to work.

"We have a situation Sunday nights where my ex and her husband will bring back the kids about eight, and they'll stay and have a glass of wine and chat for about two hours. The kids go to bed quietly. They're delighted. We have a good working relationship. We've gone to the extent where, let's say, my stepdaughter Wendy's dad was going somewhere so he couldn't have her on the weekend, and my ex and her husband have filled in and taken Wendy to allow us to have the weekend free. When my wife's ex-husband offered this, we almost fell off our chairs. So we have worked out a fantastic relationship. It shows up in the kids."

This stepfather's attitude and experience are the most positive of all the stepfathers I talked to, and they represent a goal toward which many other stepfathers say they and their partners are working: to have positive relationships with their stepchildren's fathers (and if the stepfathers have children from a previous marriage, with their children's mothers). As one stepfather with this goal reported: "The relationship between us and our former spouses is better than I think it's ever been. It's just that we have all accepted the situations that we're in and we're mature adults. It's for the benefit of the kids. We have a mutual goal, and that's raising the kids."

Let's look more closely at some of the factors that may stand in the way of making this a mutual goal.

Your Partner's Relationship with Her Ex-husband

Earlier in the chapter we saw how one stepfather felt that his partner's negative picture of her former husband predisposed him to have a negative picture of the man long before he met him. When our partners continue to have negative relationships with our stepchildren's fathers, it makes it harder for us to have positive relationships with them.

While in some cases negative relationships between our partners and their former husbands may result from our stepchildren's fathers not keeping their financial obligations or other agreements involving the children's health or wellbeing—and solving these problems may even lead to going to court—most often, stepfathers said, the problems between their partners and their ex-husbands arose out of continuing lifestyle differences and values. Frequently these are the differences that broke up the marriage, and even the divorce does not stop the conflict.

One stepfather explained how this manifests itself in his particular situation: "Debby and the children's father have had some real issues. There are enormous differences in style of child-rearing, discipline, and worldview. I don't know him that well, but from what I've seen over the years he is an extremely inflexible person. He's always setting schedules, for instance. He's very hard to deal with and very different from Debby in that regard. He's just extremely rigid, and everything sort of has to filter through that rigidity, and that's what causes the flare-ups between him and Debby."

This stepfather's advice for dealing with a fiery relationship between your partner and your stepchildren's biological father: "Don't try to get involved yourself in old issues between the biological father and your wife. Be supportive of your wife, but try not to insinuate yourself into old battles. The few times when I have tried to get involved, it really was the wrong thing to do."

If the stepchildren's mother feels she wants to punish her ex-husband, she may pressure the children's stepfather to help her keep their father out of their lives. This may cause severe problems for every member of the stepfamily. A stepfather who is also a therapist elucidated the complexities of this type of situation when he pointed out that if women out of hatred for their ex-spouses ask their new husbands to take over and block out the biological fathers completely, eventually "the kids are going to rebel. As a therapist," he said, "usually what happens in these families is you get a phone call saying 'There's something wrong with my kid, fix him.' And then when you get the kid in and you see it's a stepfamily situation, you know it's something the parents are doing and the kid's just reacting. So you bring the parent and stepparent in and you start to go through all the stepfamily counseling to try to straighten out the issues so the kid doesn't rebel and react to the negative things that are being thrust his way.

"What I say to a woman like that, generally, is 'If you continued to live with your first husband, that man, his philosophy, and your philosophy would both be impacting on your child, and that should not change now that you're divorced. You're angry at him, you may hate him, but that doesn't mean your kid should.' "

What many stepfathers told me they have learned, through trial and error, stepfamily groups, or counseling or therapy, is that there's a difference between being supportive to our partners in working out their feelings toward their ex-husbands and stepping in and taking on these feelings ourselves. The general consensus is definitely in agreement with the stepfather who advised others to stay out of their partners' "old issues" and "old battles." If stepfathers do this, they are at least not adding new knots in their relationships with each other.

COMMUNICATING WITH YOUR PARTNER'S EX

Although stepfathers' views vary widely on just how much direct communication should go on between stepfathers and biological fathers, there is a general consensus that if there are problems of logistics or other practical issues that necessitate a new agreement with the children's biological fathers, if possible, the stepfathers' role should be a supportive one to partners rather than a mouthpiece dictatorial one to their ex-husbands. While input to and support of our partners in working out issues and feelings are generally helpful, and sometimes being there with our partners when they discuss their suggestions or demands with the children's fathers may be helpful, many stepfathers say the latter course of action may create additional conflict. The conflict is especially prone to arise if we are the ones who state the demands and suggestions to the children's father or if we are too visible in our support of our partners and stepchildren with him.

In this regard, one stepfather told me, "I remove myself from any kind of potential conflict between him and other members of my stepfamily. Maybe I've stayed out a bit more than I could have, but I have stayed out, and it seems to be working. I think for your own peace of mind, stay out of the relationship with your wife's ex-spouse as much as possible. Just getting embroiled with that other person I think would harm your relationship with your stepchildren."

A sizable minority of stepfathers felt that it was their job to intervene in situations where their partners were unable to get across their demands to their ex-husbands. One stepfather said, "Usually I have minimal contact with Adam's father. My relationship with him consists of 'Hello,' things like that. Once we had a conflict when he kept switching times when he was going to take Adam. We asked him to come up and talk, and I said, 'What you're doing is very disruptive to our lives.' That was the one head-on talk we had. I said, 'We take care of him all the time. Your responsibility is to take him on these nights, and just take him on these nights.' On the surface he seemed to accept this and respond to it."

The stepfather who felt that the hardest lesson to learn is that "you never escape the stepchild's other biological parent" has also found himself having to behave in an assertive manner to his stepdaughter's father from time to time during his almost ten years of stepfathering, and at least one time he has had to communicate with more volume and less politeness than he would have wished. "The relationship hasn't always been civil between him and me," he recalled. "Usually when one or the other moves or faces a transition, there's a flare-up of some sort, usually over the issue of who's going to pay for the extra travel costs for the kid or something like that.

"There was one particularly hostile flare-up when Sara's father left our area and moved out of state and asked Ann to do certain things in terms of ferrying Sara back and forth that I felt were unfair. And I got quite directly involved because Ann and he got into a shouting match over the phone and Ann started to cry, and I just grabbed the phone and said, 'Look here, you mind your manners; you're talking to my woman.' And he said, 'Get off the line, you don't know, you're not involved in this,' and then he and I got in a shouting match. And it's good that it happened, because I think he is basically respectful of Ann since then, and we are civil to one another."

This stepfather feels that even when there are problems about which a stepfather must talk to the children's father directly, the stepfather's goal should be to deal with the problems and maintain as communicative a relationship as possible with him. "I guess it's better to be open and up front about never escaping the other parent," he observed, "and try as best as possible to keep the channel open to the other parent. At least you don't judge the other parent in front of the child—which has been a real chore on occasion, because Sara's father and I are deeply different—and also to try to see things from the other parent's point of view as much as possible so that you don't attack."

In fact, this stepfather has noticed a definite evolution in his relationship with his stepdaughter's father: "We've improved our relationship over the years; we've accepted the existence of the other and worked it out from there. When fairly recently I took a job a thousand miles from where we had been living, Sara's father called me up and he was very upset that I would do this to him, which could have led to a really bitter exchange, and I decided not to let it. I was really surprised that he would in effect tell me I had no right to take that job. That was the closest we could have come to a real confrontation, and I pride myself on having recognized that he was really upset that he was losing Sara, and I chose not to fight back, because I was leaving my son, too, who lived roughly in the same area as we had been living before the move. I said, 'I know what you're feeling, but we also have to live in the world and work and you know how hard it is to find jobs.' He eventually understood. And as it turns out, it worked out just fine, and Sara got to spend a lot of time visiting with him and his new family, although it couldn't be every weekend."

Fighting Your Partner's Battles

If you haven't followed the advice of some of the stepfathers and stayed out of your partner's old battles with her ex-husband and instead decided you're going to step in and fight them for your partner, whether or not she wants you to, it's going to be hard to have an open, empathic attitude toward your stepchildren's biological father and to work out problems. When stepfathers take on a combative role, rather than being open and in any way compassionate to their stepchildren's fathers, and communicating with them as equals, they frequently act in a severe "take it or leave it" manner and encourage their partners to act the same way.

In some extreme instances, severity may be the best tack—for example, if a biological father continually breaks his agreements about child support or any factors affecting the child's safety. But a stepfather's call for severity on his own part and the part of his wife based on past injustices may simply indicate his own insecurity. In such a case, if he pressures his partner to follow his suggestions, and if he acts severely himself with his stepchildren's father, instead of facilitating agreement and mutual understanding, he hampers the communication between himself, his partner, and the children's father. By doing this he potentially interferes with his stepchildren's relationships with both biological parents as well as with himself, just as the therapist stepfather I quoted earlier pointed out a mother may do by trying to cut off her ex-husband from continuing in his role as father.

KEEPING CHILDREN'S RELATIONSHIPS WITH THEIR FATHERS SEPARATE FROM THEIR RELATIONSHIPS WITH YOU

In addition to having our own emotional reasons for wanting to confront our stepchildren's fathers, or having real issues to confront with them, sometimes we stepfathers may be manipulated by our stepchildren into feeling we have issues to confront with their fathers. And their fathers may be just as manipulated by the children as we are. It takes some wisdom—generally gotten through experience—on our part to see these kinds of things transpiring and not get caught in a trap.

A perfect example of this was described to me by a stepfather who said, "Last week Joey misplaced a new drum set that we bought that cost over three hundred dollars. It was missing for over three weeks, and we had not known about it. We knew Joey had become a real grouch, but we didn't know why. He did not tell us. We knew that his grade dropped in band, and we couldn't understand why, and he could not tell us why. At the end of the week we overheard him talking to his dad on the phone about losing his drum set, and it shocked us. So then we got to the point where his dad must have said, 'Well, I'll rent it for you. I'll send you the money so you can rent it for the rest of the school year.'

"I felt like saying, 'Butt out,' but really thinking about it, I realized that's not an adult way to react to it. The thing to do was to think it out and work it out, because if I were to go off the handle and tell him to butt out, then animosity would start building from there. After that when there's anything at all involving the kids, the animosity could keep building and heavens knows what it could amount to. I knew I certainly didn't want to create any animosity in the kids toward their father. Why should they have that? Then I realized it was Joey who didn't tell us. It's not his father's fault at all. When Joey finally admitted it, within three days we had the drums back. They had been in a locked closet at school. The main issue was between Joey and us."

Clearly, one of our greatest challenges as stepfathers is to learn that we should not allow our even temporary annoyance or anger at our stepchildren to influence our relationships with their fathers or to allow our annoyance or anger at their fathers to influence our relationships with our stepchildren. While keeping communication lines open, we must also learn that our stepchildren have separate relationships with their fathers and with us, that we should not intervene and we should especially not communicate to the children negative feelings about their fathers. If this were as easily done as said, there would be fewer problems in stepfamily life.

One way some stepfathers allow their own and their partners' negative feelings about their stepchildren's fathers to influence their relationships with the children is by focusing negatively on a resemblance in appearance, personality, and behavior between the children and their fathers. Generally, stepfathers said, their partners are the ones who point out this resemblance, and frequently it is most in evidence during the re-entry period. Once stepfathers begin reacting to this perceived similarity, if they feel negatively toward their partners' ex-husbands, they may begin taking out these feelings on their stepchildren as if the children are miniature clones of the men.

"When Sandy gets back, Leah tells me he behaves just like his father," one stepfather reported. "He retreats and becomes more gruff and more sheltered, kind of cold. Then he pulls out of that after a while. But their personalities, from what I understand, are the same. That's what Leah tells me. Sort of hot-tempered and sort of rough-type people who fly off the handle in situations."

Rather than punishing his stepchild for being similar to how his partner sees her ex-husband, this stepfather is determined to encourage the child in his relationship with his father and also to give him his own input as the child's stepfather."He's getting a lot of different stuff from me that he has to deal with in our house," he said. "His father's attitude can influence him only when he's on the phone with him for a short period of time or when he visits with him. Other times he has to kind of deal with what's here. I'll support him in having his relationship with his father as long as he's happy. As far as his being hot-tempered goes, that can be dealt with, tempered easily. You can have a long-range effect on somebody who's like that if you choose to, if you know they're like that. You can do a lot with it. It's up to you."

Some stepfathers are irritated not by their stepchildren's bringing signs of their father's influence on them back into their households but by the adjustments the stepchildren may make in their behavior. If, for example, we and our partners have a very different style of dress or comportment from that of the children's father, we may find our stepchildren adapting to our style in our home and his style in his. Rather than seeing this as one of the mechanisms the children may be using to cope with complex feelings about being part of both households, we may perceive it as a form of hypocrisy and may become peeved at both the children and their father.

Feeling competitive with their father, we may be judgmental about his having different values from ours and resentful of the children for trying to live simultaneously in both worlds. As a result we may be tempted to criticize our stepchildren and either directly or indirectly to criticize their fathers through them. This is especially true if our stepchildren's ideas of what is appropriate in each household hurt us economically. When we spend more money on their clothes or toys when they live with us than their father has to spend when they live with him, because they feel it is inappropriate to ask him for money or things because of his financial situation or lifestyle, we may be critical of their feeling it's appropriate to ask us. If we feel their demands of us are inappropriate, then we have every right to speak up. However, if the children are actually assessing the situation correctly, our punishing them for their astuteness is just being petty.

COMMUNICATION BETWEEN THE TWO HOUSEHOLDS

While many children adapt to living in different households by bringing some traces of each home back to the other, some children lead two wholly separate lives with virtually no communication between households. This is frequently the case where the divorce between the stepchildren's parents has been acrimonious. It's challenging for a stepfather in this situation to remain neutral and to support his stepchildren in having relationships with their father.

One stepfather who secretly began dating his partner while she was married to the children's father and who was a party to their very heated divorce reported, "The only people who have contact with the father are the kids at this point. There have been rare occasions when my wife and he would need to talk, but he stopped that a long time ago. Basically now if they need to communicate about, let's say, a change in the schedule, they'll do it in a letter. We accept this situation; the kids' father isn't comfortable with it being any other way.

"There was probably a period of four years when he would not even drive on this street. So if the kids were at his house and had to come over here, which is just a few miles away, to get something, either someone else would have to drive them or they would be dropped on the next block and they'd have to walk here to get it. Now he's willing to drive into the driveway or at least sort of drive out front, which sort of feels sad to call progress, but it is progress."

Fortunately, such extreme situations are rare. Most often there seems to be some communication between households. Most often, too, stepfathers find that what works best for all concerned is being generally supportive of the children but not interfering in their relationships with their biological fathers. Stepfathers also find that not commenting to their stepchildren on conflicts between the children's biological fathers and mothers is best. As one stepfather commented about his own experience: "The kids have a close relationship with their father. I have avoided at almost all costs talking to my stepchildren on issues that relate between my wife and her ex-husband. I would feel uncomfortable doing that. I don't want to come across as her ally against their father or anything like that. My contact with the children's biological father is very little."

Many stepfathers have more contact with their stepchildren's father than I've had and many reported that the children discuss with their mothers and them what happens during the time they spend with their fathers. "The kids often talk about him with Alice and me," one stepfather told me. "My attitude? He's a different person; he lives his life and we live ours. I wouldn't comment on him to them. The kids feel close to him. I think they have problems with him like any kid has with a parent, but I don't think it has to do with them living here and not there. I've noticed now that they're more relaxed; they talk about home interchangeably, which is sort of interesting. It used to be either that they'd talk about each house in terms of its address, but now it's just home, and that can be either place."

Another stepfather, who, with his partner, has worked hard to create open communication with his children's mother and his stepchild's father and their new spouses, said his stepdaughter prefers to keep a silence about her relationship with her father, even though she is having some difficulties with it. Like other stepfathers whose stepchildren chose to keep their own counsel, he finds it best to let his stepdaughter set the level of communication about her father that she is comfortable with. "I would say her father has a very different style from mine. Non-interacting is the word that comes to mind. He's very closed. She doesn't talk to me about this; she deals with it. I think she's at a point where she knows she has to keep working on that relationship with her father, and that's part of the reason she goes to see him every two weeks to do that task. It's something she's got to live with for a long time. My wife and stepdaughter work on that together, so that my stepdaughter understands what that's like. My wife supports my stepdaughter. He's a nice man, her father, just hard to make contact with. That type of support has also been carried over to my stepdaughter through her father's new wife, because now she is in on this also. But it's not easy."

This stepfather reported an unexpected benefit of the communication and improving relationships among him, his partner, and his stepdaughter's biological father and new stepmother. "Actually it's from her stepmother that we get feedback about how my stepdaughter feels about living here," this stepfather told me. "And my wife talks with her and they work out problems together. Because she's trying to be a stepmother, and she cares."

A NEW WOMAN ON THE SCENE

Many stepfathers reported that when their partners' ex-husbands became involved on a steady basis with a new woman there was a definite shift in the dynamics of their stepfamily's life. Some children became jealous of the new woman and some experienced a conflict of loyalty, as if accepting her meant they were betraying their mother. For many other stepchildren—especially if the new woman was genuinely open to them and loving to their father—it was a very positive experience.

"Because of their father's involvement with his new lady friend and Alexandra's sort of awakening sexuality," one stepfather recounted, "it's been a very interesting experience for her, and it's caused a lot of discussion. She comes back and tells us that he and his lady friend lick each other's tongues, and what was that all about? Why do they lick each other's tongues? This type of thing leads to all kinds of questions on the children's part. They don't quite understand that aspect. It might also be quite a change for them. By and large their father has not been very physical, either with them or with their mother when he was married to her. So here there's a whole new physical aspect being introduced into their life in their old house when they visit their father, and naturally they want to talk about it. Scott is having a few problems in terms of adjusting to all this, but again that's talked about, too."

This stepfather, like others I spoke to, observed an improvement in his stepdaughter's relationship with him as a result of her father's becoming seriously involved with a new woman. "We found it's made a tremendous difference that her father started dating seriously," he told me. "As long as he had occasional lady friends, some of whom would sometimes stay over at his place, some of whom didn't, that didn't seem to make any difference to Alexandra's relationship to me. But as soon as he started dating one woman on a regular basis—and a woman that my stepdaughter is quite drawn to—all of a sudden it was almost as though she didn't have to take care of him anymore, which meant she could be friends with me.

"As for her father, there are occasional things at school that he comes to that I might be at, and there also I think it's made it easier between us now that he has a new lady friend. He doesn't feel as awkward with me."

Of course, a new woman in the life of the biological father isn't always viewed by stepfathers and their partners as a plus. Especially if the woman is aggressive about asserting her place in the children's lives—or if she does not get along with the children—her inclusion as an influence on the stepfamily may bring new problems and may add new fuel to fires of conflict between our partners and their ex-husbands.

THE STEPFATHERS' RELATIONSHIPS VS. THE BIOLOGICAL FATHERS' RELATIONSHIPS

Every stepfather I spoke to saw very clear differences between his stepchildren's relationships with him and their relationships with their biological father. One of the most common differences stepfathers noted was that their stepchildren were more physically affectionate with their biological fathers.

Many stepfathers also noted that their stepchildren felt more comfortable discussing certain subjects with them than with their biological fathers and vice versa or that they tended to participate in different activities with each of them. In this sense, stepfathers and fathers may complement each other, each giving to the children in different ways.

One stepfather of almost nine years observed, "My stepdaughter is more intimate with her father. They hug each other; they walk around arm in arm. They're just closer. I represent to her someone who knows a little bit more about how the world works. Her father is more of a kind of idealist, and he's managed to find ways to get by as such. She is starting to realize that he's a very loving person but there's a big world out there that he is kind of awkward in, and I'm doing better in that bigger world. So in that sense I represent to her, I suppose, someone who is a little more in touch with normal life, and she turns to me for insights into what the world is like out there. He is a very warm, loving person; he gives her a lot of support and they do things together. So he's very good in that regard."

The underlying fear many of us have is that if our stepchildren are really close to their fathers we won't have a place in their lives. As one stepfather said: "While I was supporting my stepdaughter to have a relationship with her father, I was also sort of nervous about what was going to happen to me, where was I going to fit in. Automatically, since he had the blood relationship, all he had to do was snap his fingers and it was there. Whereas I had to work for it. At times I would sort of feel, not necessarily rationally, just scared about what my place was."

The more a stepfather feels he is serving some purpose in his stepchild's life, the more satisfaction he is bound to get from his relationship with the child, and the easier it is for him to accept and support a close relationship between the child and her biological father. This stepfather observed, "I eventually realized that my stepdaughter and I have a rapport that defines our relationship—we feel very good about each other.

That's not going to change regardless of how good she would feel about her father. She and I can really talk to each other about very personal things, and we enjoy each other."

Another stepfather, whose combined stepfamily includes his two children as well as his partner's two children, told me, "I believe the kids' relationship with me is different from their relationship with their father. At times I feel my stepson is more comfortable with me. When he comes home, sometimes I think he's just comfortable to be back with me. My stepdaughter has a lot of respect for her father and the things he does and his position and so forth. She dearly loves her father. I will not try to take his place. This is something that we got started on right away. 'I'm going to be your stepfather not your father,' I told them. 'I will help you to grow up.' This was explained to him also. 'I'm going to be a part of raising the children. I'm not a replacement for you.' The kids understand that this is my viewpoint. It's not the way it necessarily has to be, I guess, for some people. But I think that kids should realize they do have a father who really cares for them, and I don't want to take anything away from that. I think somewhere along the line it would get back and hurt me in the long run."

Indeed, one stepfather who, with his partner's agreement, severed communication between his stepchildren and their father when the children were younger, told me he recently realized that his relationships with the children may have been jeopardized by that act. Now that his stepchildren have grown up and are re-establishing their relationships with their father, he is concerned about how close they will remain to him.

CHILDREN SWITCHING HOUSEHOLDS

The whole issue of our stepchildren's allegiance is brought out very strongly by the possibility of their changing households, a possibility that by definition simply doesn't exist for children in a nuclear family. If our stepchildren live full time with us and our partners, from time to time most of us certainly wish the arrangement could be switched and they would live full time with their fathers and only visit with us. However, if the children themselves consider doing this, we may suddenly find ourselves reacting ambivalently, especially if our partners are opposed to such a move.

We may also find that stepchildren themselves are more ambivalent than they at first appeared. Only a handful of stepfathers I interviewed said their stepchildren had actually switched their full-time residence from their household to that of their fathers, and in these cases the children were older adolescents. But several stepfathers said the possibility had come up at least once.

One stepfather explained: "After Jacqueline's summer visits to her father I always assumed that it was coming back to school that made her uncomfortable, but more than that was going on there. It was a different life there with her father. We live in a hectic, high-powered environment. We work a lot; we do a lot of stuff; we accomplish a lot; and there are a lot of other people in this community who are high achievers. It's a world of work, a world of achievement, and it's a world of nervousness about achievements. And her father lives a kind of provincial low-keyed life. The contrasts between those two settings were very difficult for Jacqueline to handle. I think basically she felt more comfortable in that other setting, and that life was easier there.

"There was a moment, it must have been three or four years ago, when she said she wanted to go back and go to school there. Emily completely rejected it and said, 'God, it's going to be horrible and hard if she does that.' We sort of warded it off for a year. Then subsequently there was a moment when she really was in a lot of personal trouble and gave us a lot of trouble. We seriously considered at that point letting her go to spend a year there with her father, which I thought in some ways might be good. She might discover that some of the issues that she thinks are our responsibility are in fact her responsibility because they'd come up when she had to really face her life. But when it became possible for her to think about the move, she had decided that she didn't want to do it anymore, and as it's turned out, a lot of those problems have been resolved right here."

Obviously, whether or not a child does switch households depends not only on the child but on the willingness of both biological parents to make such a change. If our stepchildren or one of their biological parents suggests this type of change, we stepfathers can act as sounding boards for our partners and our stepchildren and possibly encourage a thoughtfulness in the decision-making process that would result in the healthiest choice for all concerned. If we are instigators of this type of change, we must be open to investigate our own motivations and to have a counselor or therapist act as a sounding board and source of feedback so that we contribute to a responsible decision.

WHEN STEPFATHERS FEEL THEY HAVE HELPED RELATIONSHIPS BETWEEN FATHERS AND CHILDREN

Many stepfathers feel their stepchildren's relationships with their fathers have improved at least partially by the stepfather's being in the children's lives.

"The kids have come around a lot closer to their biological father since we've been married. I think I had a little to do with that, which I'm very pleased about. They were quite far apart, rarely talking, and now they see quite a bit of each other. The way I helped was just being supportive of him, I think. There was a lot of bad-mouthing going on before and I didn't like it at all. While I didn't like him personally and still don't, I was basically supportive of him. He never helped my wife out with any of the problems, but since our remarriage he's come across by seeing the kids," one stepfather said.

"Jacqueline sees her biological father every summer. And, in fact, since there is a certain amount of stability in her relationship with her mother and me, I think she is able to see him, and he is able to see her more. Oddly enough, I think the fact that there's stability here allows her relationship with her father, her half brother, and her stepmother to work better, and she gets to do things with them that she doesn't do here," another stepfather commented.

As stepfathers themselves pointed out to me, often this kind of improvement also results from the biological father's becoming a better father after the divorce. As one stepfather said: "Their father seems very tied to the children, very concerned. He's a much better father now than he ever was when they lived together. He really seems to go out of his way to plan to do things that will interest the children when they are with him. He seems to spend real special private time with them. He's also been quite willing to take advice—which is something he'd never do before—from the children's mother. He has sometimes even asked for it."

Most often, of course, it's a combination of many factors, including time and maturing, that produces an improvement in the relationships between stepchildren and their fathers. Some stepfathers reported that not only had they and their partners begun to see a therapist or counselor but so had their stepchildren's fathers. Given that stepfamilies are formed in the aftermath of divorce and emotional turmoil, this is a healthy and not unexpected reaction. One stepfather, for example, whose stepson's biological father has had continuing emotional problems, said, "I think fairly recently my wife's ex-husband realized a lot of his problems are his and that he's been acting them out toward his son. I think he has progressively become more involved in therapy in the last year and a half, and I think that's helped him with his son. I think his son getting older has helped. I think what I provided Adam has helped Adam to see that not all his needs for male identification have to be met through his father. It has enabled him to be more adapative to his father, and being more adaptive to his father and fighting with him less has enabled his father to feel warmer toward him."

Even in the stormiest of relationships between stepchildren and their biological fathers, stepfathers may feel they can—and should—exert a beneficial influence by supporting their stepchildren to have relationships with their fathers. Sometimes the problems between children and their fathers are just part of the children growing up, and some stepfathers find themselves in a unique position to observe this.

For instance, just as, especially in the early stages of stepfamily life, a stepfather may get short shrift from his stepchildren, a biological father may get short shrift from one or more of his children during their adolescence. As one stepfather said: "My stepdaughter is eighteen, and she's breaking away, and the first person she's breaking away from is her father. At one time he said, 'I understand, you're growing up and you're living a couple of hours away and if you don't want to come in and see me, you don't have to.' And she said, 'Okay.' "

When this happens, many stepfathers attempt to support their stepchildren in bridging the gap between the children and their fathers. As the stepfather I just quoted said, implying how he and his partner handle the situation: "We don't force her to come in and see him too often." Many stepfathers expressed a similar concern to see their stepchildren communicate with their fathers and voice to them their differences and their needs so the children could work out their relationships with them. Many stepfathers who take this approach do so because of the idea that if they didn't, as one of the stepfathers I quoted earlier observed, "It would get back and hurt me in the long run."

As we can see from the preceding examples, stepfathers generally break their own rule about non-intervention when it comes to encouraging the children to keep contact with their fathers. Many of us feel that the more supportive we are of our stepchildren in their relationships with their fathers, the better it is for our stepchildren's development and for their relationships with us. Thus, encouraging the relationships between our stepchildren and their fathers is self-serving; it's our best protection against our stepchildren feeling that we came between them and their fathers.

Along these lines, a stepfather I quoted earlier, whose stepchildren's father was so angry that for a while he tried to prevent his daughter from seeing her mother, only to have the child move in with her mother and stepfather full time, commented, "My role with my stepdaughter and my stepson, too, in regard to their father is basically one of encouraging them to keep at it. I would essentially say, 'You've got to understand his point of view, too. He's hurt, and so forth.' In some ways I would take a counseling role.

"It feels very clear to me, in my rational moments anyway, that the better the relationship with him the better off we all are, because I think that conflict with him essentially is just going to translate into internal conflicts with the kids. That's going to make things harder for them, and in some ways that would make them ultimately need to pull away from us because they would experience more conflicts.

"It always felt real important to me to have Julie reconnect with her father. I felt there was a period of time when in a way it was real nice for me, because I was clearly the good guy. But it feels like, in the long run, the better her relationship with him, the smoother she'll be able to go on into her life. Just thinking of her as an adult, and what issues are going to be left unresolved, I knew she'd be better off having a good relationship with him."

CREATING HARMONY

In looking at the relationship between a stepfather and a biological father, it's important to keep in mind that whatever competitive feelings may exist, the real challenge is to learn how to coexist, communicate, and cooperate. A stepfamily works best when we and our partners accept, rather than resist, the existence of the children's other parents and work out harmonious relationships with them. If your stepchildren's biological father has passed away, be aware that the children need to take time to go through mourning and that they need to remember the parent. As many stepfathers have observed to me, harmony in a stepfamily depends on our working on our attitudes so that when we hear about the other biological parent or parents and see their closeness with the children, we

don't perceive that closeness as a sign of distance from ourselves.

I mentioned previously that one of the most enlightening
parts of researching this book was interviewing stepfathers
who also have biological children. Although I sensed over the
years that Kevin and Timothy's father has felt very acutely the
loss of having them in his household, I, like most stepfathers,
have kept my distance from him, so I had never heard him talk
about the pain of this separation and how deeply it has influenced his life. Hearing stepfathers with biological children
talk about their feelings on this subject, I suddenly understood
what it would be like "to walk a mile in his shoes." I began to
see my stepchildren's father not just with the respect that I've
always had for him as a constant and caring father, but with
compassion for the long spans of separation from his sons that
he has had to endure.

This is one of those times when I can say that if I'd known
then what I know now, I'd have done things differently. In addition to supporting Kevin's and Timothy's relationships with
their father, which I was always committed to doing, I would
have made a commitment to opening up my home more to
him and his new partner and to improving communication between us. If there had been more communication and cooperation among myself and him and Cynthia and his partner—as
I've now seen taking place in some of the other stepfamilies I
talked about in this chapter—we would all have been more
comfortable in sharing the responsibilities of raising Kevin and
Timothy.

CHAPTER NINE

Money Matters

W<small>HEN</small> I <small>WORKED</small> at *Parents* magazine, one month our cover featured a picture of an infant with a headline that read, "Your $250,000 Baby." The story explained how the expenses for raising a child born in 1980 from birth through age eighteen add up to a quarter of a million dollars. After that, of course, the cost continues to rise sharply. College expenses at a state college cost upward of four thousand dollars a year and at private colleges well over ten thousand dollars and often over fifteen thousand. While cutting corners and college scholarships may reduce these figures somewhat, there's no doubt that the expenses of raising a child through age twenty-two are quite hefty. As stepfathers, how much of these expenses fall on our shoulders depends on how old the children are when we come into their lives, how much of the financial responsibility their father has agreed to take on (and whether or not he is keeping his agreement), how much our partners can take on, how much the children themselves contribute through part-time work and how much we ourselves agree to—or want to—take on.

For some stepfathers, money matters a great deal. Money can be a great source of friction within the stepfamily and with biological fathers. In such cases, the stepfathers almost always feel the biological fathers are not paying enough, and frequently they feel the biological fathers have the means to do so. For other stepfathers, money matters don't count very much at all. These stepfathers are very easygoing about the whole subject and feel that the biological father's contribution, whether adequate or inadequate, equal or unequal in absolute terms, is fine, and they are willing to make up the difference for what is needed to raise the children.

As you'll see, many times it's not so much a question of who has the money, who pays the money, and what the real expenses are. It's a question of attitude. What does the stepfather *feel* about the whole thing? It's a psychological truism that the two most loaded subjects are sex and money. The hot-tempered reactions of some stepfathers to how money matters are handled in their homes shows just how loaded a subject money can be.

In my own case Cynthia and her ex-husband split the expenses for raising Kevin and Timothy according to a formula arranged at the time of the divorce. Shortly after I joined the family, I, too, contributed to taking care of their expenses. When five years later Cynthia called it to the attention of the boys' father that, since the cost of living had risen considerably, it would help us if he could make a bigger contribution to their monthly expenses, he voluntarily raised the amount of his child-support payments as much as he could afford to. He also paid for their air fare when they came to visit him during holidays and summers. Later, when we moved back to New York City from California, he contributed additional money that he had put aside for Timothy's college education in order to help us make the tuition payments so that Timothy could go to a private high school. Timothy, too, contributed by getting a part-time job and taking care of many of his own clothing and entertainment expenses—just as Kevin had done when he was in high school and as he continued to do when he was in college.

In other words, we all did what we could. There was relatively little friction between us and the boys' father about money matters, and relatively little friction about money matters among us as a family (except in getting Kevin and Timothy over the hurdle of accepting the idea that they should use the money they earned from their jobs to pay not just for frills but for some things they considered necessities). Internally, however, I often experienced a lot of stress about money matters. At times, some of this was caused by the very real issue of how Cynthia and I would meet our share of the expenses. Some was caused by my own internal dialogue about money matters: What *should* I be paying? Were the boys doing enough around the house? Were they appreciative enough? Was I as a stepfather being taken advantage of?

Eventually I realized that much of my internal stress about money and my stepchildren came from stressful attitudes about money that I had had long before I met them. Through therapy I gradually learned to defuse this stress, and I became more relaxed about the flow of money in our household and more able to come up with strategies for handling real financial problems when they came up. It's helpful to keep in mind that there is a distinction between real financial problems and stress about money that is self-generated or comes from another problem in the relationships within the stepfamily.

FROM ONE EXTREME TO THE OTHER

One of the most interesting things I found out through my interviews is that child-support arrangements vary from one extreme to the other, as do the attitudes of stepfathers and their partners about these arrangements.

At the lower extreme on both counts is the situation of a stepfather of two full-time stepchildren, both approaching adolescence, who told me, "Is financial responsibility an issue to me? *Yes!* The children's father pays zero. What am I doing? Withdrawing all financial support effective immediately." At the other extreme is another stepfather of two full-time stepchildren, both in their adolescence, who said: "We are very fortunate in that the children's father has been very responsible financially. He really supports them totally."

Most of the stepfathers I spoke to find themselves somewhere between these two extremes in terms of child-support arrangements. Generally, the children's fathers and mothers share the responsibility. How much or little stepfathers themselves contribute to this package varies. One stepfather, for example, said, "My wife's ex-husband does what he committed to. I supply the rest along with my wife, who also works. No hassle." Another stepfather reported, "I have no financial responsibility. Their mother and father do now, and the mother and/or father will cover college along with the kids' savings, part-time jobs, and so forth."

In some stepfamilies there are different arrangements for each child. As a stepfather of two stepchildren told me: "The financial responsibility varies for both children. Their father has almost total financial responsibility for Hank. For Rachel he pays some and we do the rest." A stepfather with three stepchildren commented, "We have financial responsibility for Julie; Mike sort of does his own thing. He decided he wasn't going to go to college until he could pay for it himself, because he didn't want to borrow money from his father. He felt he wanted to be free from him. With Zack the arrangement was set up that he would be living half the time with each of us and that Carl would pay a certain amount of child support. Carl has arbitrarily—because that's his thing, just making decisions without discussing them—decided that even though we each buy things for Zack, any time he buys something for him he deducts half the cost of it from whatever he sends. We decided a long time ago that we were not going to fight that, that it's just not worth making an issue around, because it would just be lousy for Zack to have us fighting about anything."

Even when biological fathers take no financial responsibility for any of their children, some stepfathers accept the situation with relative equanimity. One stepfather told me, "My stepchildren's father still hasn't given my wife any of the support which the court had granted. My wife and I are supporting the kids pretty much on our own. It's okay with me. I think it was a bit of a problem at first because my wife kept wanting to take her ex back into court. 'He owes, he owes,' she used to say. I said, 'We'll make do on our own,' and I think that's pretty much the way it is. We've made do, we've struggled, and we will continue to struggle, but we'll work it out." Another stepfather reported, "My stepdaughter's father did not support her during her minority. When I married my wife, it was my intention to support her and her child."

The key word here is "intention." A stepfather's willingness or unwillingness to accept whatever degree of financial responsibility he is asked to carry—and to struggle if necessary to do it—depends in large measure on his ideas about what he plans for himself as husband and stepfather, how he envisions his roles. If he feels it is appropriate for husbands and wives to share their financial resources, whatever the need, then he is more likely to be willing to share his partner's financial responsibility for her children. The more responsibility for the children he wants to take in general, the more willing he will be to carry financial responsibility.

As one stepfather who shares complete financial responsibility for the children with his partner explained: "It was clear to me as part of my self-understanding as somebody who would play a surrogate father role, which is something I wanted, that that clearly meant responsibility for the finances. It was a burden I happily accepted. I think that helps to develop a legitimacy."

Another stepfather with a similar intention said, "I experience them as my kids, so I feel like I am financially responsible for them; anything they want that's reasonable that we can afford, I would do, just like I would for biological kids. It feels like the financial part is just part of parenting. So the attitudes would be the same thing. I think that has a lot to do with the marriage itself. When we got married, I basically felt my resources are my wife's resources and we are the parents to the kids, and anything that they need it was our duty to supply."

Another stepfather told me about how and why he restructured the child-support payments for his stepchildren when he married their mother: "I really preferred that the children's father cut out all financial support, but he didn't want it that way. He felt as long as he is contributing he could have more of an influence. He still has a finger in there somewhere, and we're not relieving him of everything. So we reached a compromise and reduced what he and Mary had worked out prior to their divorce. We lowered that considerably. I was willing to take on the financial responsibility. Hey, I'm not only marrying the woman; I'm marrying the children also."

Not all stepfathers have this attitude, of course. Witness the stepfather who told me, "A couple of things are really bothering me—they are almost entirely financial. I do not feel obliged to cover the expenses of a college education for the stepkids, for example, even though I can afford it. I do not think I should have to."

Another stepfather, whose stepchildren's father does cover the lion's share of the children's expenses, feels very acutely the implications of their father taking this responsibility when it comes to handling issues such as the selection of a college, where the father would like to make one choice for the children and he and his partner would like to make another. "It's a situation where you're sort of caught between a rock and a hard place," he explained. "Because he is the father, he does have some rights, apart from which he's paying. That sort of makes it difficult, as Alice's income is very low and his income is considerably higher than mine, probably two or three times if not more. That sort of gives him some prerogatives."

Besides the issue of money as power, another factor that necessarily influences stepfathers' reactions to child-support arrangements is how much money is actually available in their households. While, as you'll see later in this chapter, some stepfathers with very adequate finances still gripe about money matters in their families, most stepfathers, when the flow of money in their homes meets the need, are flexible about accepting whatever support the biological father can or will give. One stepfather, for example, reported, "Bill sends some child support. It's not a lot. He's quite faithful about it. He sends exactly the same amount he did when they first separated ten years ago. Then it was all right, and now it's a pittance, whereas my level of support for my son has gone up as my income has gone up. So there's a discrepancy. There's more going out than coming in, but fortunately we're not hurting for money, so it's not a big issue right now."

STEPFATHERS' GRIPES

Stepfathers' complaints about money matters cover a wide range of territory and arise from a variety of causes.

The most common complaint is that the stepchildren's biological fathers take too little responsibility for child support. One stepfather, for example, told me, "The father and his wife earn a significant income, maybe $45,000 a year. I object to the support order now of $270 per month. Last year he arbitrarily stopped paying support for the six weeks his son was with him. This year he voluntarily increased the support by twenty-five dollars per month but reduced the payments to eleven months, which gives a net annual increase of sixty dollars or five dollars per month. I'm not happy with the amount of financial responsibility my stepson's father is taking, but I'm not doing anything about it even though it is an issue to me."

This stepfather's comment is as common as stepfathers' complaints about the inequity of the arrangements. Stepfather after stepfather said (using the words of one stepfather), "He should pay more child support, but I'm not doing anything about my unhappiness."

Some stepfathers feel they've done as much as they can and they just have to accept the situation as it is for the sake of the marriage. "My stepson's father takes no financial responsibility, and it makes me angry," a stepfather of seven years explained. "I'm not doing anything about it, though, due to my wife's decision to raise her son alone and my decision to accept the circumstances before we married. I have the feeling nevertheless."

For stepfathers in combined stepfamilies, money matters

may be further complicated if their biological children live with them full time. Some stepfathers in this situation complain that their children's mothers fail to take an adequate share of the financial responsibility for their children. One stepfather in this situation, who praised his two stepsons' father for being generous, added, "I wish I could say my ex-wife, who earns a good deal of income herself, had made any financial contribution at all." Another stepfather in this situation, who felt his stepsons' father should take more financial responsibility for them, commented, "This is a very touchy subject, since my ex-spouse pays zero support for my son who lives with us full time, but she was previously collecting $350 per month, plus we were obligated for the insurance as well as half of the medical not covered by insurance."

In all types of stepfamilies, another common complaint among stepfathers concerns the ways in which stepchildren's fathers' personalities affect how they deal with money. The two most typical annoying traits are pettiness and rigidity. One stepfather reported, "The financial aspects get to be real fun. He shells out large amounts of money for school. It's a very expensive private school. Somehow he can justify that, because a man of his stature has to do this. But then when the telephone went from ten cents to a quarter, he won't spend the money to call up to our apartment to tell us that he's downstairs—since we don't have a bell—he insists on phoning once as a signal and we'd better not answer it.

"There's some kind of a paper according to which he pays. He does that fairly responsibly. He's also very petty in some ways. If Scott rips open a pair of sneakers or something like that, he'll send him back with the ripped sneakers because he doesn't want to pay for the new ones. He sees the paper as governing everything. It's his pound of flesh."

Another stepfather said, "I feel he takes adequate financial responsibility, except for his rigidity. What he told Hank this year, for example. Hank had used up his allowance. His father said, 'I won't pay you any allowance for another six months.' This is for a sixteen-year-old, and he added, 'But you also can't work to make money.' So that puts Hank in a double bind to say the least."

Another complaint from stepfathers is that they see their stepchildren being generous to their biological fathers with money given to the children by them and their mothers. One stepfather, for example, said he resented his stepchildren spending money that he and their mother give them on gifts for their father, who pays no child support. These feelings became so intense that the stepfather decided to explain to the children how he felt. Having this discussion showed this stepfather how much of a conflict of loyalty there really was for the children, and it helped him to understand them and vice versa. For his part, he began to understand his stepchildren's impulse to be giving to their father even if their father wasn't generous in terms of their support. And the children began to see that their stepfather's feelings could be hurt by actions they didn't realize might hurt him. "What amazes me is that kids are a lot more able than you think in terms of what they can deal with," he told me, reflecting on the whole experience.

"Sometimes I feel resentful about having to do without things I would like for myself," this stepfather added, "but I accept it. It's not the children, afer all, it's their father. This guy is irresponsible and arrogant."

For some stepfathers the major complaint is that they are being asked to do without things they would like for themselves when they are not willing to do so. A stepfather in this situation said, "My wife and her ex-husband have financial responsibility for the kids. Up till a few months ago she and I have been putting our money together to take care of her share. Recently, we had an argument over it because I wanted to hold some of my money back for me. I wasn't crazy about getting new sneakers every three months for the children. I need a suit, I need shoes, I need this and that. I've been putting off things that I want to meet my needs.

"Lately, I've been feeling that I have other needs that have not been met and I've put them off too long. I'm forty-three years old. I have some hobbies like boating that require constant infusions of money. I don't want to feel that I can't do them or that I have to get by with very little all the time. I mean, as far as reserve money goes, I feel that money is mine, too, to fritter if I want.

"I guess we consider money an area that we're not really clear about."

As in nuclear families, continuing arguments about money may be a symptom of other problems in stepfamily relations. In the case of this particular stepfather, as he told me himself in another part of our interview, there are basic disagreements between him and his partner about his role as stepfather, and there are other communication problems between them as well. Thus, his feeling short-changed financially is symbolic of his general feeling about his marriage and his experience as a stepfather. While many stepfathers may occasionally feel frustrated that they are doing without things they would like for themselves in order to give to their stepchildren, men who persistently complain about this may well be signaling a more fundamental dissatisfaction about what they are getting on an emotional level from their partners and from their family life in general.

We've already seen stepfathers who would like to take over the financial responsibility for their stepchildren as a sign of their commitment to them, and how they often feel their step-children's fathers are providing too much child support. Step-fathers may also complain about biological fathers being too generous if they feel it is harming the children. As one stepfa-ther facing this circumstance reported: "Right now, my step-kids' biological father is giving too much to the two boys, who are twenty-three and twenty-two. They're alcoholics, and he's acting as an 'enabler' for their addiction."

For stepfathers who are helping their partners in custody battles, the expenses can be devastating. A young stepfather in this situation complained about the stress of paying a $10,000 legal bill. "I feel like I'm digging my way out of a hole by ac-cepting jobs I would not have accepted had I not gotten my-self involved in this," he told me. "And it puts a big strain on my relationship with my partner." This stepfather—one of the two who identified the stepchildren's father as the biggest problem he encountered in stepfathering—also complained about the distorted information emanating from the man about financial arrangements. "He's lying about insurance coverage and nickel-and-diming us to death," he said. "He's greedy, selfish, and annoying. We're being as patient as possible but it's not easy."

The last area of complaint I encountered from stepfathers about money matters applies to stepfathers in combined stepfamilies where conflicts over who's spending what on which children and who will inherit what from whom can be a problem. "I think one of the reasons that my own kids are stand-offish to me now is because they realize there is an involvement there for me in terms of the parent end of it," explained a stepfather of substantial means with two biological children and one stepchild. "That there are people stepping in who weren't in the financial picture a little while ago. I may be making more of it than it is, but that's there. Not just what's happening now with the money, but what will happen in the future."

One stepfather told me about his partner's very specific complaint about the child-support arrangements between her and her former husband. Although I encountered only one instance of this particular complaint, I think it is worth including because it makes a great deal of sense emotionally and I'm certain many others of today's stepfathers and their partners are facing similar situations. "It's okay with me that Sara's father pays very little child support and hasn't increased the payments," this stepfather told me, "but sometimes it's not with Ann. For the simple reason that he has a new child by his new wife, and she is at home raising the child, she is not having to work, and it raises old animosities, because Ann had to go back to work two weeks after Sara was born, and Sara's father says the reason he can't send more to us is they have only one income, and well, why do you have only one income, you could have two? Well, she wants to stay home and take care of the baby. Ann naturally feels that's unfair."

WORKING IT OUT WITH THE FATHER

In situations where stepfathers and their partners felt biological fathers should increase their child support, different approaches were used in different stepfamilies.

In my case—paralleling the cases of most of the stepfathers I interviewed—when there was a need for additional funds, whether for the children's transportation between households or schooling or to compenstate for the rising cost of living, Cynthia and I discussed the matter, then she spoke to Kevin and Timothy's father.

When it came to discussing the new financial arrangements that would be necessary to pay for a private high school for Timothy, the first agreement that had to be reached was which school Timothy should go to. His father, in the cause of economy as well as education, suggested a religious school that charged a modest tuition. Timothy was not attracted to this idea; and Cynthia and I felt strongly that he would be served best academically, emotionally, and psychologically by a rigorous academic school that attracted children of all religions. Cynthia and Timothy's father talked about this, as did Timothy and his father. Once or twice I had phone conversations with Timothy's father to hear his point of view. The conversations were amicable, and there was a real sense that we were all trying to do what we could afford and what we thought would work for a child we all cared about. Since Timothy lived with us full time, and he would be going to school from our house, ultimately Cynthia's and my view prevailed, and we selected a school three blocks from where we lived. Timothy's father contributed what he could to the tuition. This left a large portion for us to pay, but because we took the initiative in making the more expensive choice, we didn't mind paying the bulk of the tuition expenses.

When it came to choosing colleges, Kevin and Timothy took most of the responsibility for selecting a school for themselves, because they both had very strong preferences. (They both also contributed to their own college expenses through part-time jobs.)

Another stepfather reported that although his partner had most of the responsibility for communicating with her ex-husband and negotiating matters of finance, recently he had begun to participate in their talks, too: "My stepdaughter is getting ready to go to college, and the financing of it is difficult. My wife is acting as a go-between between me and their father to see who would pay what. We have had a few meetings together with the children's father, though. One formal meeting and one informal meeting. This is a very rough time for him, with college for his daughter costing so much and his daughter not talking to him very much. And I think he's feeling left out of the decision-making, but he's not feeling left out of the financing."

When communicating and negotiating with the biological father on an informal level doesn't work because he is not living up to his contract and shows no intention of doing so, most stepfathers and their partners did what the stepfathers I've already quoted in this chapter said they've done: accepted the situation and figured out how to cope with it themselves. Some have hired lawyers to deal with the biological fathers, some have even gone to court. The consensus seems to be that where there is no good will on the biological father's part it's virtually impossible to make him live up to his obligations. Despite righteous indignation, most mothers and stepfathers are not willing to prosecute the children's biological father.

CHILDREN AND SELF-SUFFICIENCY

One of the things that makes stepfathers feel good about taking at least some of the financial responsibility for their stepchildren is when the children themselves are willing to help out by earning money of their own. I've said already how much this has meant to me. Both financially and emotionally, Kevin and Timothy's willingness and ability to work and support themselves as much as they could, given their age and school responsibilities, has made me glad to give them whatever I have been able to whenever it's been necessary.

Whether in a nuclear family or a stepfamily, training children for self-sufficiency begins when they are young. In addition to providing children with experiences that will teach them how to manage money, training them for self-sufficiency also involves helping them to develop high self-esteem, good work and study habits, discipline, and motivation.

The most common means for teaching children some sense of money management is to give them an allowance out of which they must pay for certain things. There are two basic approaches held by parents and stepparents about giving allowances. The first is that allowances should be given to children as payment for specified tasks or chores; the second is that allowances should be given to children just because they are members of the family, regardless of whether or not they have fulfilled their assigned responsibilities. Some parents and stepparents combine the two approaches, docking children to some extent but not entirely if they don't do what they're supposed to. There are also differing views on what allowances should be spent for and how involved parents and stepparents should become in directly teaching children about managing their allowances. Some believe allowances should be spent totally at the children's discretion; others believe in teaching the children to save for things they may want. They may also require children to pay for specified items out of their allowances. Criteria for how allowances should be spent generally change as children grow older, with parents and stepparents expecting them to take more responsibility for handling some of their expenses, whether for entertainment or necessities.

How much a stepfather has to say about these matters depends on whether his stepchildren live with him full time or part time, how much financial responsibility he takes for them, and/or how much decision-making about these matters his partner shares with him. As with discipline, most stepfathers tend to feel their partners are a little too soft with their children in regard to money. As one of the stepfathers I've already quoted indicated, occasionally there is also the feeling that biological fathers can be generous to the children to the point of detriment. The more time stepchildren spend with the stepfather and the more the stepfather and his partner agree about teaching the children to be self-sufficient, the more of an influence a stepfather can have on his stepchildren's concept of money and financial responsibility.

Until Kevin and Timothy became adolescents, Cynthia and I did little to teach them about money management. They, like most of the children of the stepfathers I interviewed, received allowances. Cynthia never received an allowance when she was growing up, but her parents paid for whatever she needed. I received an allowance as well as supplemental money from time to time to pay for extras, all measured to some degree against my performance of my household chores. Generally my father found me lacking but gave me my allowance anyway. Unconsciously, I adopted this attitude with Kevin and Timothy. Neither Cynthia nor I really taught them about saving their money, and we gave them additional money for their necessities and luxuries as the need or desire arose. Part of this, of course, came from the child-support payments their father sent us.

The first idea I really had about setting the boys on the road to financial self-sufficiency came as they approached adolescence. I had been an avid baby-sitter and lawn mower myself, starting at twelve years old, and I earned the money I needed to buy records and books and go to movies and shows—things I could not afford on my allowance alone or even with my parents' additional gifts. When Kevin and Timothy reached the age of twelve, I encouraged them to seek out any baby-sitting, lawn-mowing, or similar jobs they could find in our neighborhood. This worked very well; they were eager to have extra money, and they took whatever baby-sitting and odd jobs they could find.

Next came encouraging them to get actual part-time work after school. Starting at age sixteen, I had worked full time during the summers and part time during the school year, so this seemed the logical next step. Logical though it may have been, it wasn't an easy step for any of us to take. It ended up being a series of steps; and curiously enough it ended up being a different series of steps for each child.

When Kevin was seventeen, we became so fed up with him

ignoring his chores (and being rude and obnoxious) and expecting to be supported in the style to which he had become accustomed that we had a showdown in which we changed our household policy. Late one night, we called him into the living room and told him we would take over his chores and discontinue all his allowance and extra money and that he would have to get a job to earn money for whatever he wanted or needed to buy for himself beyond the food we put on the table. We also told him that he had to show better manners in his way of relating to us. After hearing our ultimatums he said to Cynthia, "You've been a good mother up to now, but now you're making a big mistake." It was after uttering this warning that he ran away from home one night for a couple of hours, then came back, went to sleep, and got himself a job the next afternoon.

Instead of being the mistake that Kevin warned his mother it would be, her request—which I supported—that Kevin get a part-time job after school was the beginning of improved relationships among the three of us and new self-respect and independence for Kevin. It was also good training for us for being firm when Timothy became an adolescent.

With Timothy, there was never a need to tell him to get a job. He always liked having extra money in his pocket, and so from the time he could baby-sit he was always doing some sort of odd job to earn extra money. By the time he was fifteen, he was working after school at the local cheese shop. The problem with Timothy came out of his idea that his earnings were "extra money" when we insisted that, as Kevin had before him, he buy some basic necessities himself. With Cynthia and me having to pay the bulk of Timothy's tuition for private school in New York (and it seemed to both us and his father that moving as we did from California to New York, Timothy was not ready to cope with the local public high school in New York City), our determination to have Timothy take care of a certain amount of his own clothing, entertainment, and even school supply needs himself was more than just wanting to train him for economic independence as an adult. It was a necessity for us.

Whereas the big explosion with Kevin occurred the night we announced our policy, and then the explosion was over, with Timothy there was no explosion, just a slow burn that occasionally ignited into a fire. Every now and then he would become furious at the idea that he should *have* to pay for anything that wasn't in any way a "fun purchase." This feeling is quite understandable, of course; I had it myself at his age. It's even more understandable that Timothy felt this way because at school he was surrounded by many other children whose parents were so affluent that the children were given just about everything they wanted without having to pay for anything themselves—regardless of their behavior toward their parents.

Gradually though, Timothy, like Kevin, developed a mature attitude toward money. He and Kevin are also extremely generous. Having both become self-supporting, they enjoy being able to pay their own way and make their own choices about where and how they live. They also enjoy being able to give to others. It's a pleasure to see that the traits that Cynthia and I and their father and stepmother worked to instill in them during their adolescence have made them comfortable functioning in the adult world.

Most of the stepfathers I interviewed who had adolescent stepchildren or biological children reported that the children, like Kevin and Timothy at that age, were working in part-time jobs or were at least in the talking stage of getting part-time jobs. Like myself, most of these stepfathers encouraged or insisted on this choice both for economic reasons and in order to train the children for independence.

"One of the things that's been very successful in our family is that we've always mandated that the children work from a very early age, to the extent to which they were capable of doing so, to buy things, discretionary items that they would want," a stepfather with six stepchildren, all in their teens and early twenties, told me. "For instance, if they wanted a forty-dollar pair of sneakers, we would, say, contribute eighteen dollars, and they would have to subsidize the purchase with the remaining twenty-two dollars."

Another stepfather, with three stepchildren, commented, "Once the kids are in their mid-teens, I like them working. I think it's important just for the sense of responsibility, for their sense of contributing, their sense of helping out. Because, although we basically do all right professionally, we're not affluent like their father is, or like a lot of people are. We have to be aware of money."

A stepfather, who is also an educator, with two children from a previous marriage and three teenage stepsons, expressed a very definite point of view about children and self-sufficiency: "What we do here at our school with all our kids—mine and the ones I've brought up and taught—is to raise them so that by the time they're eighteen they should be able to support themselves and move away. I think that should happen whether or not they do in fact move away." In terms of what parents and stepparents should pay for and what children themselves should pay for, he added, "I don't feel that I owe my kids anything, whether in the nuclear family or stepfamily. But I certainly include the children in my life. So I tell them what I'm going to do, what they can expect from me, and what I'm not going to do and what they're going to have to expect from themselves."

Another stepfather, with three teenage stepchildren, reported that in his stepfamily, "The kids already have part-time jobs. They're earning spending money. We have a policy that they should pay for the first year's insurance for their car. We're setting goals for the things we feel they should work for rather than just getting those things for them."

While approving of his biological children and stepchildren working after school, one stepfather voiced a concern expressed by others as well: that for some children, balancing schoolwork and a part-time job may pose a problem. "My stepson got a job on his own prompting," he told me. "I don't know how it's going to affect his grades. He hasn't been doing that well in school, so I have some mixed feelings there. But I think by the time they get to their junior year in high school, if not before, they should be earning some money, at least during the summers. Because they're going to have to pay part of their expenses."

WORKING OUT FINANCIAL ARRANGEMENTS

While some stepfathers and their partners are very clear about the financial arrangements regarding stepchildren prior to marriage, many are not. Many stepfathers have only just a vague idea of how much financial responsibility the father is taking and how much the mother is taking, and just as vague an idea of how much the things children need cost. Many also are surprised by how little these ideas correspond to the reality of the situation once they are the children's stepfather. For the outraged stepfather I quoted earlier in this chapter who said, "Is financial responsibility an issue to me? *Yes!* The children's father pays zero. What am I doing? Withdrawing all financial support effective immediately," the surprise was overwhelming. For most stepfathers, the surprise, if there is one, is something they learn to live with, perhaps with some regret and irritation and perhaps with the evenness of the stepfather who told me simply, "I don't recall that financial arrangements had been much of an issue that we talked about before we got married. At some point after we got married it just became part of the routine."

A stepfather's surprise at how money matters really work in his stepfamily depends largely on the personalities of everyone involved, as well as the specifics of everyone's financial situation. The stepfather who responded so evenly to the child-support arrangements his partner had worked out with her husband has, in fact, accepted arrangements that very much gave him and his partner an inequitable financial burden. As with other stepfathers I've already quoted, this was acceptable to him because of his commitment to his partner and her daughter, and because he and his partner earn an adequate income.

With twenty-twenty hindsight, his advice to men who are about to marry and become stepfathers is this: "The whole area of money is a real minefield, because there could be a lot of potential for conflicts there, so at least you have to get it on the table and talk about it. You probably are never going to feel that the child's father is pulling his fair share, or you may feel that the father uses money to try to buy the child's attention or something like that. So obviously there are no pat answers, but at least know it's something you've got to handle and be prepared to open up the subject and look at it closely."

Here is advice about money matters from another sensible stepfather: "If you feel that there are going to be any money problems, I think it should be worked out as much as possible in advance of getting married. I don't think under any circumstances that the new stepfather should depend on maintenance from the natural father to help maintain the lifestyle that they hope to live. Do it on your own, and whatever he sends for the kids, spend it on the kids or put it in a college fund or whatever, but don't depend on it to live on."

CHAPTER TEN

Your Adolescent Stepchild

"ADOLESCENCE IS SUCH an incredible mess. It's so fascinating to watch. There's no way you can be an adolescent without hurting everybody around you and without feeling hurt yourself. And if people grow up without that, there's something wrong and it will come out later. It's the hydraulic theory of biography: If you don't have an adolescence during your adolescence, you're going to have it sometime or other."

"My major fear is that if my girlfriend's son goes through the kind of adolescence I had, I would seriously consider not living with him, because I was a real ball of fire for my parents to handle."

"My partner's older son is now a mature young adult and I feel moderately close to him. The younger son is still in adolescent crisis, and closeness is now virtually nonexistent. It was better previously and will get better again."

These three men are living with adolescent stepchildren; two are longtime stepfathers, the other has just moved in with his partner and her teenage son and has taken on the role of stepfather. Their quotes express what are to me perhaps the

three most essential points for parents and stepparents to remember about adolescence:

1. It is a stage of development through which all of us must
go, and it causes turbulence for the individual going through it
as well as for everybody around her or him.

2. Although we have all been adolescents ourselves—and
have had and caused our own problems when we were—as
stepfathers we may still be tempted to jump ship when our adolescent stepchildren cause problems for us.

3. It is easier to accept the challenges raised for us during
our stepchildren's and children's adolescence if we maintain
the perspective that it will not continue indefinitely.

The reason I think it's important to keep all three of these
points in mind is that, despite my vivid memory of the trouble
I caused my parents when I was an adolescent, when Kevin
and Timothy were adolescents I was still tempted at times to
jump ship, or at least to push the boys overboard. At the same
time as I say this, I also have to make it clear that neither
Kevin nor Timothy caused Cynthia and me any major problems. Overall they were good kids when they were adolescents, just as they had been before, and it was something I was
very thankful for. I liked them as adolescents, especially compared to some of their acquaintances, and on many occasions
we enjoyed each other. This was, as I said, my overall view.
But on a day-to-day, hour-to-hour, and minute-to-minute
basis, sometimes I felt severely tested by the operatics of living
with emotionally tempestuous young people who at times behave like adults, leading you to believe they are adults, and at
other times behave like little children, leaving you feeling a
fool for having believed they were mature and responsible.

Two things helped me to have a better perspective on Timothy's adolescence than I had on Kevin's. The first was the
knowledge that Cynthia and I had survived Kevin's adolescence and so had Kevin. This wasn't enough, however, since
often we would forget that our experience with Kevin had a
direct bearing on what we were experiencing with Timothy.

The second was that when Timothy was fourteen I became an editor at *Parents* magazine, and in that position I began to learn something about what the process of adolescence entails and why adolescents, whether they are one's stepchildren or biological children, act as they do. Suddenly I could see parallels between what Kevin had gone through and what Timothy was going through. I could also see that the differences in their behavior resulted from the differences in their personalities and their particular emotional needs at this critical time, but that they were basically going through the same process—becoming an adult.

Knowing what I now know about adolescence itself, I can see that it's challenging to be either a parent or a stepparent to a teenager, but in many cases it's more challenging to be a stepparent. This is particularly true if we come into our stepchildren's lives when they are already in their teens or when they are pre-teens. In such situations we haven't had the time to begin building bonds with them before the turmoil of adolescence; instead we find ourselves attempting to form these bonds exactly when they may be least receptive to us just because we are adults.

Even when stepfathers enter their stepchildren's lives earlier, their stepchildren's adolescence may very well test the strength of these bonds. When a stepchild's adolescence is especially tumultuous, if the bonds aren't strong enough, stepfathers may find themselves wanting to throw in the towel on their whole marriage. When the bonds are strong enough, of course—not just the stepfather's bond to his stepchild but also his bond to his partner—there is usually more tolerance for the teenage stepchild's behavior. But even so, many stepfathers feel at least occasionally that they are having to serve above and beyond the call of duty by living with their teenage stepchildren, especially if the children live full time with them and only part time with their biological fathers.

Considering how distraught biological parents can become over their teenagers—even teenagers whose troublesomeness is totally within the bounds of ordinary adolescent behavior—

this is only to be expected. Without the biological link and with the inherent demands of coping with the results of divorce and the formation of a stepfamily, stepfathers have another dimension to deal with in meeting the challenge posed to them by their stepchildren's adolescence.

In this chapter we're going to look at what adolescence is like both for the teenager and for the adults in his or her life. As various stepfathers talk about their experiences with their adolescent stepchildren, we're also going to focus on the special problems that are raised by adolescents in stepfamilies. In this way, you'll be able to see that some of your adolescent stepchild's behavior that you may be taking very personally, in fact, has nothing to do with your being a stepfather at all. It is simply a result of your teenage stepchild being a teenager, and he would act "that way" to any full-time resident adult male acting as more or less of a co-parent to his mother. You'll also be able to see, although you may not yet be aware of it, that as a stepfather you may actually have some advantages over your partner in dealing with your teenage stepchild simply because you are one step removed. The point of all this is that the more you know about adolescence, the better prepared you will be to cope with your stepchildren's adolescence and your own feelings about it.

It might be helpful to look at a few of the distinguishing hallmarks of adolescence as identified by Erik Erikson, the psychoanalyst who has studied and analyzed this period of life as part of his work on the successive stages of human development. The basic developmental tasks have to do with what Erikson calls "identity vs. role confusion."* The teenager has to integrate into his or her identity the new feelings of sexuality as well as the skills he or she has developed or has been naturally endowed with in childhood, and also to integrate what Erikson refers to as "the opportunities offered in social roles," which is how teenagers see themselves in terms of future careers. Integrating these elements into a newly forged iden-

*Erikson, Erik H., *Childhood and Society* (W. W. Norton and Co., New York, 1963), pp. 261–263.

tity means that a teenager must develop a higher degree of independence. Being able to do this is a sign of real growth and personality strength, and many teenagers have trouble with it, at least for a time.

According to Erikson, much of adolescent behavior is rooted in the immense biological changes occurring within. The speed of a teenager's body growth—which is as rapid as body growth during early childhood—compounded by his or her newly acquired genital maturity, causes a teenager to question all over again the identity he or she has formed up to that time and even to requestion previous assumptions about life. These inner concerns have very definite consequences on the teenager's outward behavior.

"The growing and developing youths," Erikson says, "faced with this physiological revolution within them, and with tangible adult tasks ahead of them are now primarily concerned with what they appear to be in the eyes of others as compared with what they feel they are, and with the question of how to connect the roles and skills cultivated earlier with the occupational prototypes of the day. In their search for a new sense of continuity and sameness, adolescents have to refight many of the battles of earlier years, even though to do so they must artificially appoint perfectly well-meaning people to play the role of adversaries. . . ."

This is a large part of what makes adolescence so stressful for the parents and stepparents of teenagers as well as for the teenagers themselves. As a parent or stepparent, it's very painful to be turned into an adversary, especially when we know we are well-meaning. One reason for teenagers' propensity to turn adults into adversaries is that despite their desire to be grown up—and their frequent pretense that they are grown up—they are, in fact, still dependent on us and extremely ambivalent about this dependence. On the one hand they resent it, on the other they are aware that they still need us because they are ambivalent about the real prospect of independence. They want control over their own lives, but they are also afraid of it, and at times that makes them resent us all the more.

Treating as "the enemy" those adults—such as parents, stepparents, and teachers—who are in a position to say no to some of their requests is far easier on adolescent egos than admitting their own ambivalence about having some requests granted. Treating us as the enemy is also part of the adolescent tendency to see things in terms of black and white, which also comes from their attempt to forge an identity and escape role confusion.

Erikson analyzes another hallmark of adolescents: their clannishness and apparent obsession with peer groups or idols, values we may not understand at all. "Young people can also be remarkably clannish, and cruel in their exclusion of those who are 'different,' in skin color or cultural background, in tastes and gifts, and often in such petty aspects of dress and gesture as have been temporarily selected as *the* signs of an in-grouper or out-grouper," he says. "It is important to understand (which does not mean condone or participate in) such intolerance as a defense against a sense of identity confusion. . . .

"To keep themselves together," Erikson explains, during this time when they are forming their adult ethics, to fight against role confusion which can be sexual as well as occupational (it is during this period, after all, that they are first really beginning to consider what they will do when they are adults), "they temporarily overidentify, to the point of apparent complete loss of identity, with the heroes of cliques and crowds."

Furthermore, because of teenagers' often distorted concepts of what being "grown up" entails, they are especially sensitive to what they consider their "rights." Their reactions are often exacerbated by the hormonal changes that are part of the biological revolution Erikson speaks about. Given the developmental issues and the emotional sensitivity that accompany the biological changes of adolescence, it becomes understandable that a small matter of a parent giving a teenager unasked for advice about how to do something or telling him or her to finish an uncompleted chore may be viewed by the teenager as a total negation of his or her new identity.

These, then, are the dynamics of what is occurring within our adolescent stepchildren. Let's look now at how stepfathers and their partners are affected by, and cope with, the behavior of the adolescents within their households.

Talking about his sixteen-year-old stepdaughter, one stepfather mentioned many of the characteristics stepfathers typically noted in adolescents that makes it such a trying time for all concerned. "I think she likes to shock me in some ways," he said. "She tells me things about what she is doing, and she expects me to be shocked. She wants to think of herself as a pioneer and precocious; I guess every adolescent needs to."

This stepfather links his stepdaughter's need to be shocking and precocious in her behavior to her underlying concern with the occupational issues that Erikson identified as part of the teenager's agenda. In this young woman's case, her trouble with school seems to put a block between her and her mother—who is extremely intellectual and a high achiever—and also to motivate her to finding even greater closeness with her peers. "I think my stepdaughter is not that confident. She's not that successful; that's a terrible burden for her because she lives in a household with two achieving professionals who don't do badly. She's kind of struggling. She's not as successful a person as we look to be, and I think that bothers her. She has school anxiety. She has some very close friends in whom she tries to encapsulate her entire affective life. She wants people to like her.

"She's actually begun to think about college, which really surprised me. She is more or less realistic; she has worries over where she'll be able to get in."

A teenager's ambivalence about parents and stepparents is very clear in the remark of a stepfather who said, "She'll complain about us not being around when in fact we are around, or maybe for a short while we've just been in a period of not spending a lot of time in the house. But I know if we had been in the house she probably wouldn't have spent the time with us and she might have been spending a lot of time out of the house herself. She has a double standard about that. She's at a point in life where she doesn't like to do very many things with us."

A stepfather in a combined stepfamily spoke about the similarities and differences in the ways the three adolescents in his household expressed their need to become independent and form new identities for themselves: "I think especially my stepson, who is seventeen, and my daughter, who is fourteen, are still going through sort of a rebellious stage, trying to find what they're all about, testing a lot of limits and things. They're very mercurial. My son, who is also seventeen, keeps a lot of it inside of himself, but it comes out a lot as anger."

In terms of adolescents testing parental limits, some stepfathers agreed with the longtime stepfather of six who expressed the sentiments of the majority of stepfathers I interviewed when he said, "I don't think there's any more testing from adolescents because we're a stepfamily than there would be in a nuclear family." Others agreed with the stepfather who expressed his concern that his biological and stepchildren's adolescence might be that much harder on them as well as their parents and stepparents because "on top of being an adolescent, they're also having to deal with the fragmented family stuff."

Another stepfather felt that an additional complicating factor for adolescents and their parents and stepparents is the contemporary culture, with its availability of drugs and alcohol, early sexual relations, and its glamorization of youth. "Parenting in general and stepparenting in particular are difficult undertakings today," he said. "Nowadays there are a lot of forces which tend to pull families apart. I think we live in a time generally in which the authority of parents is greatly diminished compared to twenty or thirty years ago, when I was growing up. The empowerment of parents, the ability to mold and direct and guide your children, is tremendously diminished over what it was several decades ago in comparison with the influence of the culture as a whole—the peer group, commercial forces, and the general climate of the times, which I feel prey on children. Parents and stepparents need a strong ego to withstand the tensions and batterings and the assaults on our self-image and sense of self-competence that occur during our children's and stepchildren's adolescence."

HOW STEPFATHERS REACT TO STEPCHILDREN'S ADOLESCENCE

How an individual stepfather reacts to his adolescent stepchildren is influenced first and foremost by who he is. This was brought out by one stepfather who observed, "The children's adolescence is probably the area of greatest problem for me as a stepfather. I felt myself, in all honesty, to be a more successful stepparent when the children were younger than when they moved into adolescence. That may be idiosyncratic to me; in other words, that may have to do with my own limitations as well as my strengths."

Our reactions to our stepchildren's adolescence are also influenced by another familiar factor: who our stepchildren are and what our relationships with them have been like prior to their becoming teenagers. As this same stepfather said: "The most marked problem has been my relationship to my stepdaughters, not to my stepsons. The oldest girl, also the oldest child, never fully accepted me. She always retained a primary and closer relationship with her father, which was not true for the others. All the others accepted me when they were younger as a surrogate father."

As I mentioned earlier in the book, I had a slightly different experience than this stepfather in how the history of my relationships with my stepchildren influenced my relationships with them during their adolescence. As you know, I had resistance from day one of my relationship with Kevin. Gradually, by the time he entered his teens, things improved. He pushed me to my limit when he reached his mid-teens and began treating our house as a hotel—where he had no obligations except to rest, eat, and go through the necessary bodily functions—but he didn't test me any more severely at that point than he had tested me before. Although there were definitely some very dramatic moments and often I was peeved at him, his adolescence was not a surprise. In fact, simply because we had known each other longer and had developed more trust, our relationship continued to deepen even during our conflicts.

The change in my relationship with Timothy was far more dramatic when he became an adolescent. Because he and I had been so close, the rebellious attitudes he sometimes exhibited during his high school years and his freshman year of college seemed like more of a slap in the face than Kevin's behavior had. What helped me at times to enjoy the wonderful side of Timothy even during this period was, as I mentioned before, my inner knowledge that our family had survived Kevin's adolescence and that Kevin had emerged from it a sensitive, loving, and dynamic young man.

Another stepfather, who was and is very close to his adolescent stepson, reported, "I think the major challenge adolescence presents to any parent or stepparent is staying with the ups and downs, the swings they go through. Thinking of my stepson, for example, the hardest parts for me have always been when he was in one of his closed-down phases not to start feeling either angry at him or scared, like 'My God, we're losing him, what's going to happen?' but instead just to give him his space.

"I don't know if he's typical, but it certainly has worked out well that if we just lay off and give him space, that within a couple of days it feels like he swings around and we have a really neat and enjoyable kid on our hands again. That's one of the things that's hardest. The anger from the adolescent, when it flares up, and when it feels unreasonable, to be able to recognize that that's okay."

What would happen if, upon marrying his partner and becoming stepfather to her teenagers, a stepfather discovered that the children were engaging in legally or morally questionable activities?

The idea of children becoming problem adolescents is every parent's nightmare, but the concept is particularly frightening to an adult entering the stepparenting role. It is even more frightening if the stepparent doesn't know the children well or gets a sense that there may be problems. Without the history and the bond that a biological father has, what kind of an influence can a stepfather have on his teenage stepchildren if they do have the usual or more than the usual teenage problems? What kind of an influence can a stepfather in this situation have on *new* teenage stepchildren even if they have just the usual teenage problems?

The answer depends on several factors: how much time the children spend with the stepfather and his partner; whether he and his partner are in agreement about the children's behavior and about what kind of response is appropriate regarding that behavior; the biological father's influence, and whether he agrees with or opposes the course of action the mother and stepfather wish to adopt; and how open the children themselves are to changing. Sometimes the addition of a stepfather is just what the children need (which doesn't mean they will accept either him or the process of change graciously).

The worst scenario was described by the stepfather with three "juvenile delinquent" stepchildren. As we know, he found himself in a situation where the children were already in their mid to late teens at the time of his marriage to their mother. They did not live full time with them, but when they were there, his partner did not support his taking a tough line with them. On his own, he demanded that if the children wanted to be a part of his life, they had to conform to responsible behavior; if they set that as a goal, he would support them in achieving it. Not only did this stepfather's partner oppose this stance, the children's father opposed him by providing his children with money despite their addiction to alcohol and their anti-social activities. That's why the stepfather called their father "an enabler." As a result of all these forces, the stepfather ultimately told his partner that she had to back him up with her children or he could not go on with the marriage. Then she finally began to listen.

This is indeed the worst situation I heard about from the stepfathers I interviewed. Most found their teenage stepchildren displayed toward them and the world only what may well be called "the typical teenage traits." One stepfather who married his partner when her daughter was a teenager described his stepdaughter at that age this way: "Her general view was that she was her own mistress, and we didn't have very much to say about it. I'll never forget her going to dinner with us one night when she was about fourteen or fifteen and saying, 'You know, you people really don't know what's going on in the world.' That was rather characteristic of her outlook, in that she assumed we were not privy to all the things she knew and that we knew nothing that she didn't know.''

This attitude on the part of teenage stepchildren toward their stepfathers and mothers is a common one, but it is not universal. Some stepfathers whose stepchildren were teenagers actually met with less difficulty, and received more respect, than some stepfathers whose stepchildren were younger. Some stepfathers also met with more resistance from their teenage biological children than their stepchildren.

One new stepfather with a teenage stepson has a generally affable relationship with him because, he said, "I treat him with respect as an individual. I don't push myself on him; I don't try to make him uptight by playing Mr. Authority; I don't talk to him as if he's a little boy. Sometimes if he gets uptight with me I find myself getting uptight with him. But I remember what it's like to be a teenager. I know you don't like too much authority at that age, and so who needs this new man who's just 'taken your mother away' to come in and tell you what to do and act uptight to you? I leave most authority and discipline up to my wife, who is a very good mother, though I'll draw bounds when I'm alone with him and I have to. I make it clear that I'm an adult and he's still a developing person not quite yet an adult. But I also make it clear that I'm a friendly adult."

This stepfather's experience gives every stepfather a major key to developing good relationships with teenage stepchildren. That key is to take the time to look at things from our stepchildren's point of view and not to come on playacting the part this stepfather called "Mr. Authority." Teenagers are impressed with authenticity, whether we are agreeing or disagreeing with them. The more genuine we are, the more that we are ourselves, the more they are likely to hear us and to respect us—though they also may make us their enemies for a while in order to play out the necessary drama of becoming independent.

DEALING WITH ADOLESCENT ANGER

One of the traits evident in the adolescent personality is anger. As one stepfather reported: "With adolescence, Lewis became much angrier, much more into testing us." Another stepfather remarked of his stepson, "He's very quick to cop an attitude of anger. And I react to that, probably because that's how I am myself."

One stepfather observed that while his stepson is prone to anger, he also often tries to suppress his emotions, feeling that it's grown up to do so. As this stepfather puts it, "His general attitude is 'Hey, it's cool.'" This stepfather feels that when his stepson's feelings are strong and he is unable to express them, it's important for him as a stepfather to help his stepson give up the "cool" act and get in touch with what's really happening with him.

I had quite a different challenge with Timothy's adolescence. Rather than trying to act "cool"—which was more in keeping with Kevin's demeanor—Timothy would occasionally explode in anger and upsetness. This was sometimes very difficult for me to take, and sometimes as a stepfather I resented having to take it. But there I was, having to cope because I was there and because I chose to be his stepfather.

Part of my resentment came from the fact that if the cause of his anger was some restriction I had made, then his anger would be directed at me; and it was hard not to react to it emotionally myself. This took a lot out of me. It was also ineffective, I discovered, if I reacted to his anger with anger. Then I would lose much of my power to communicate. This meant that instead of enforcing limits firmly and humanely I resorted to enforcing them through who had the louder voice and the bigger emotional gun. It would become a clash of wills, and I felt I was winning by intimidation instead of simply stating my position as the adult with the authority to make a necessary decision.

Eventually, I learned to allow Timothy to have his reaction, and to keep my center and continue communication. The provocation for his anger may have been my setting an earlier curfew than he liked or not allowing him to fly a glider or not buying him something he felt he needed. Whatever the issue, I learned to handle his anger by accepting it and acknowledging it, and then to continue with the task of setting limits.

SETTING LIMITS

The whole area of setting limits for teenagers is one in which many of us stepfathers need special encouragement. I mentioned earlier in the chapter that our bonds to our stepchildren and our commitment to them may be tested during their adolescence; so may our sense of what rights and power we have as stepfathers. Underlying my own emotional reactions to Timothy's anger was not just resentment and frustration at having to deal with it but the whole question of how much right I had to set limits for him and how much power I had to do so.

I believe that many stepfathers find themselves facing these questions during their stepchildren's adolescence. Even if, by the time they are adolescents, we've been their stepfathers for years, setting limits with teenagers is a whole new experience. Their adolescence is the first time that they are so independently mobile and that they can do so many things that could endanger them. It is also the first time they can resist us so powerfully, both because of their newly gained physical strength and stature and because they are more independently mobile. Suddenly we as stepfathers are called upon to assert ourselves much more in order to set limits, and this in itself may be threatening to us. Biological fathers and mothers have to do this, too, of course; but they don't have to question their right and responsibility to do so.

Just how much of a right and responsibility you have to set

limits for teenage stepchildren depends, of course, on the factors that define your stepfamily and your role within it, not the least of which is your own idea of how much you want to or should do in this area. If, as was true for me, your adolescent stepchildren are living full-time with you and you are co-parenting them with your partner, you may well feel that as a stepfather you have the same right and responsibility to join your partner in setting limits for them as you would for young children. Because teenagers potentially can get into so much more trouble, you may well feel, as I did, and as many other full-time stepfathers do, that you have the added responsibility to set limits that protect your own peace of mind as well as the teenagers' well-being.

In connection with this, I learned another important lesson: that if the reason I was setting a particular limit or saying no had to do with what I myself would be comfortable with rather than right or wrong, it was better to come right out and say that it was my preference rather than to try justifying the choice in another way. This is a good practice with children of any age, and it is a necessity with teenagers, because they do value authenticity so much. Kevin and Timothy, like most teenagers and pre-teenagers, could always pick apart a bad justification. If you tell a child the truth about your reasons from the beginning, the child knows there is nothing to argue with. He may be angry at you for being "too nervous," as Kevin and Timothy sometimes accused me of being, but that's who you are, and the anger dissipates far more quickly than it would if you set yourself up as a self-righteous dictator.

Since Cynthia and I co-parented Kevin and Timothy the nine months a year they lived with us, whenever an issue that necessitated limit-setting came up, whichever one of us was home generally spoke for both of us. If she and I had the foresight to talk about the issue in advance and there was some disagreement between us about it, we negotiated a stance that either of us could articulate to the boys at the appropriate moment. If we hadn't talked about the issue beforehand, then we would wing it, using our own best instincts. If one of the boys felt he wanted to appeal the decision made by the one who was home to the parent or stepparent who was out of the house at the time, that was always his prerogative.

As a stepfather, in rendering a decision to my adolescent stepsons I learned to take a firm stance, to explain why I felt as I did, to hear them out, to digest this, see if it changed my mind, and, if it didn't, to restate my stance. If the topic under discussion involved possible danger to them, after restating my stance I would pray that they would do as I wished. They would know I was taking the stance I had because I was the particular individual that I was and that individual had a lot of good points as well as bad points in terms of making decisions that affected their freedom. Whether I was saying no to something they wished to do or to something they wished me to purchase for them, through my words and attitudes I always strove to communicate that I cared for them. My saying no neither signaled a lack of caring nor a lack of respect for their ability or talent.

WHAT RUBS US THE WRONG WAY

Stepfathers of teenage boys frequently spoke about their stepsons' language. "His language is pretty well colored with 'Fuck this,' 'Jesus Christ,' 'Shit,' and 'Damnit,'" one stepfather said. This stepfather also said that his own language is sprinkled with these words. "So," he explained, "I'm not the one to talk to him about curtailing it. I just explained to him that in certain situations you're really going to make a big mistake if you talk like that. But when you realize you're not setting a very good example, that's the problem: Where do you go from there?"

Setting a good example for the children is a concept that stepfathers came back to time and again, whether in the areas of language, manners, dress, or the most potentially dangerous ones of alcohol and drug consumption and driving, which I'll discuss later in the chapter. Given the significance of the home as well as peer influence on adolescents, it's crucial that what we do in our own lives is consistent with what we tell our adolescents we want them to do. What they see in our behavior as well as the behavior of their biological parents is going to register more than what they hear from us.

Another stepfather, whose speech is not sprinkled with profanity, encountered a language problem with his teenage stepson, and he had this success story to tell: "Zack went through a period where he would react, really losing his cool completely, swearing or making poor-sportsman type of statements and doing unsportsmanlike things after sports events. I sort of let him know at the time that that felt lousy to me. I waited a couple of days to say anything more about it. Then I was driving him to school and he wanted to get a note so he could go in late. His mother said, 'No, I've witten enough of them.' I said, 'I'll tell you what, I'll give you a note if you'll listen to me for three minutes,' and he said, 'Okay.' So I talked to him on the way, and I said, 'I want you to know how lousy it feels to hear you do that. Suppose my parents were there, do you know how embarrassed and ashamed I'd feel if they were to hear you talking like that? I know you get angry, and it's not necessarily fair what's happening in the game, but you've got to come up with a different way of expressing yourself, because it just feels horrible. All I'm asking is for you to listen and think about what I'm saying, and see what you can come up with.' He said, 'Okay.'

"The next weekend he had a game, and there wasn't a single bit of that. I didn't even think about that to comment about. He said to me later, 'Did you notice I didn't lose my cool?' So I felt like there was a real sense that it does matter how I feel; that's what feels nice about that, that he's willing to listen and respond."

Many stepfathers talked about the bad manners of their teenage stepchildren. Kevin and Timothy operated as a team with bad manners, both in the house and at restaurants, acting in a way that Kevin calls "rowdy." Sometimes they drove Cynthia and me to distraction with their blowing straw papers at each other and having food fights in the middle of restaurants. *Animal House* was their favorite movie, and although we also enjoyed it, we were dismayed to find them emulating its heroes. Cynthia and I found that all we could do was to call the boys' attention to their bad manners because at times we preferred to eat out as a family than to forgo their company, problematic as it occasionally was at this stage. We also tried to have a sense of humor about their behavior at the table and keep in mind that it would pass, as it eventually did. Miraculously enough, despite their habitual rowdiness, as teenagers the boys obeyed their mother's edict that they be polite when they were visiting friends' homes; and today as young men they continue to observe their mother's high standards of politeness not just with others but with her and me as well.

In terms of teenagers' choice of clothing—an issue that sends many adults up the wall—stepfathers generally were not irritated, worried, or offended by their stepchildren's individual styles, whatever those styles happened to be. In fact, the issues of a teenager's language, manners, and dress are sometimes easier for a stepfather to handle than for the children's mother. Since her ego is more identified with the children—and therefore she views them as more of an extension of herself—she is more likely than the stepfather to view their going their own way in these areas as more of a personal rejection. Thus, her reaction to these issues as they show up in her children may be a reaction to the rejection she feels rather than to the children's language, manners, or dress.

Obviously, it also depends on the individual stepfather and mother; what are loaded issues for one may be neutral for the other. As one stepfather in a combined stepfamily observed: "One thing that really bothers Debby in terms of my stepson is, for example, that he wears an earring. It really doesn't bother me that much. Or my daughter who is sort of into soft punk—that also bothers Debby a little more than me. But I think we both have our areas where we're a little more strict or a little less strict. Like at the dinner table I'm more strict than Debby."

A stepfather who does not react emotionally to a particular

issue himself may have more success communicating his partner's point of view about it to a teenager than she has, and vice
versa.

TEENAGERS AND SEXUALITY

As one stepfather observed: "I definitely feel an atmosphere
of sexuality in the house with adolescents around."

The point of view of many stepfathers expressed on educat-
ing their stepchildren and biological children about sex was
well stated by the stepfather who told me, "My only concern
about my stepchildren and sex really has to to with their being
aware of safety, responsibility, and their respect for people.
That's what I talk with my Zack about, that's what I've talked
with Julie about. The other message I've given is that when
they're old enough sex is something to enjoy and to have fun
with, and find out what you like and what feels good, and don't
get hung up about it."

Another stepfather, while saying that his primary concerns
were also safety and respect for people, added another value:
"I communicate to my stepchildren and children that I don't
believe in promiscuity." Another added: "Even if they don't
want to hear about it, I talk to my stepsons about the necessity
of contraceptives as well as not rushing into sex. They have
their whole adult lives ahead of them and today there are
many serious health issues connected to sex that make the
1970s free attitude less appropriate. If I had stepdaughters, I
think I'd have my wife address these issues with them, because
I don't know how comfortable I'd be. I think it's more of a
mother's job to talk to her daughters, but I think kids of both
sexes need to know how crucial it is today to be careful where
sex is concerned."

The majority of stepfathers shared the view of one stepfather who said, "I think I try not to be too didactic about sex or
anything else. If something about sex—or alcohol or drugs—
comes up in a conversation I'm having with my stepchildren

or children, I'll talk about it and at least get my view across as to what the problems are."

One stepfather spoke about a special concern connected to adolescent sexuality and stepfathering. "An issue that isn't often spoken about in stepfamilies is that you're dealing with a non-biological child," he said. "Your partner can have an eighteen-year-old or a twenty-two-year-old daughter who's very attractive, and you've got to establish dress codes for both yourself and the child. The child may have lived in a house where she and her mother and another sister were living together without a male for five years, and they walked around in various stages of undress. That's got to change, got to be talked about—not changed in a harsh disciplinary way, that's a terrible thing to do, but it's got to be discussed and new rules have to be made for yourself also. You have to consider also that sometimes you suddenly have two teenage opposite-sex stepsiblings living together and they're not related, and this can create a problem. That has to be talked about. So sexuality is something that must be looked at."

This stepfather definitely sees gender as an influence on how he has reacted to his stepchildren's adolescence. "The relationship with the girls has been strewn with more difficulty especially at this stage," he explained, "in part not only because of Oedipal problems that you'd expect in any father-daughter relationship, and which of course are highly exaggerated in a stepfathering relationship because of the lack of relation by blood, but also because our values are different in many ways.

"As they've become adolescents, what's become more and more clear is the power that their mother has for the girls in being a role model; and, contrariwise, the influence that I've had as a role model for the boys. So the boys are more like me in terms of values, outlook on life and so forth, which has made my relationship with them much smoother than with the girls."

Another stepfather, with three teenage stepdaughters, reported an entirely different perspective: "To some degree being a male in a relationship to girls can be a little easier. Girls are typically more rebellious against their mother than their father, and I've been a surrogate father to them. So that's a plus." As for any sexual self-consciousness with his step-daughters, he said, "They're not real self-conscious, but, like me, they don't parade about nude. They're modest. Which is appropriate."

Another stepfather commented, "I guess I feel there have been periods over the last five years of greater and lesser self-consciousness about having a stepdaughter. At this point there's a recent graduation picture up there, and when we got it I thought, 'God, she's beautiful; what a kid.' But I feel that as sort of very much a paternal pleasure and pride in how pretty she is. I think to the extent that I feel any of that sexually, I focus it on her friends. Some of them are so gorgeous. I keep that displaced."

In the households of some stepfamilies, the sexuality of adolescent stepchildren isn't as easy for stepfathers to handle. Some stepfathers feel their teenage stepdaughters are flirting with them by wearing scanty underwear, and some stepfathers feel drawn into the flirtation themselves, feeling either flattered, attracted, or both. While it's normal for adolescent daughters to compete with their mothers to at least some degree, the fact that in stepfamilies they are competing with their mothers for the attention not of their biological fathers but of their stepfathers undeniably adds to the potential danger of such flirtations. That's why it's particularly critical for dress codes to be established in the house, and to follow the advice of one stepfather who suggested that stepfathers tell their partners to speak to their daughters about dressing more modestly. In stepfamilies where stepfathers have problems coping with their stepchildren's sexuality, individual and, often, family therapy are necessary.

ALCOHOL, DRUGS, CURFEWS, DRIVING, AND OTHER
PROBLEMS

The stepfather who said he tried "not to be too didactic" with his teenage stepchildren also commented, "The areas about which I've been most concerned about getting my point of view across are alcohol and drugs. I know Hank has experimented some with alcohol, and so has my daughter Leslie, so I've tried to deal with it. It's not always an easy thing, because I have a drink every day, too. But they're not in their forties; they're seventeen. Certainly if they want a beer they should have it here; I'm not even sure they should have it here, but I don't want them off at parties or out in an alley or something. And it can become addictive the same way as any kind of drug. I want them to be responsible."

Another stepfather said, "Drugs and alcohol I have a real sense of being concerned about. In my work as a counselor it's frightening how much you see it at an early age. Our kids so far are at the extremes. My stepdaughter reacted very strongly against drugs and was in a lot of ways sort of very straight and almost had troubles from that with the kids in school, because she was so much against it and it was prevalent.

"My fourteen-year-old stepson is very much into athletics and sports. Although that doesn't preclude drugs, he has of yet not tried any. I think we've been pretty clear about our values and our views about it. We've always been clear to him about the importance of talking, of communicating with us about it.

"My oldest stepson was the other extreme. At the age of twelve he was drinking, using street drugs, close to killing himself with these things in some ways. Even after he got away from the edge and was sort of more settled into high school, he was still doing a lot of drinking, and we periodically got concerned about him because of that. What he says now is interesting, because he is at college, and one of his reactions to the kids at college is that they're all getting so heavily into that stuff, and he feels like 'I've already been through that, and I'm not into it anymore.' His experience is that he's glad he's no longer in an out-of-control version of drinking and drugs. But his younger brother saw a lot of that, and in some ways I think we can use that as part of what our concern is about these substances. And also the papers are filled with stories, and we'll bring his attention to those in various ways."

One stepfather, with his partner's support, told his stepdaughter who tried marijuana when she was thirteen that she was not to use marijuana because it was illegal and would damage her lungs and her memory. "As far as I know, she never tried it again," he told me, "but it's easier with a thirteen-year-old than an eighteen-year-old. You have more power. It's not a philosophical question. You just say no, because they're more dependent on you at thirteen, so you have more control."

We had a similar experience with Kevin. When Kevin was thirteen, friends told us they found him with their son in a tree smoking pot. Cynthia and I totally blew our cool. We gave him the same information the stepfather I just quoted gave his stepdaughter: We talked about the illegality of marijuana and its negative effects on the mind, and I said that since Kevin's primary job at thirteen was to be a student, he could not afford it. He had to keep his mind in good shape to exercise and develop it to its fullest potential, just as he might go to a gym to build his muscles. Kevin's big worry at that age was about not fitting in with his friends. "I could smoke pot better than all of them," he cried. "What should I do if they offer me some? I don't want to have to say you told me I couldn't." We told Kevin he should just say he didn't want any; he didn't have to bring us into it at all. Fortunately, he soon became a varsity swimmer with such an intensely vigorous workout and meet schedule that he had his own reasons for not smoking marijuana. For the rest of high school and early college, swimming remained his top priority.

Cynthia and I were grateful for this because we had smoked marijuana ourselves during the time since we had all been together, and we were beginning to realize that we had not set the best example. This incident made us see that in his own mind, whether he said it or not, Kevin was only trying to emulate us in being "hip."

When Timothy was twelve, he came home from a party so full of beer and whatever else he had drunk that he could barely walk up the stairs to kiss us goodnight. Having learned nothing relative to keeping our cool from the pot-smoking incident with Kevin three years before, Cynthia and I immediately became hysterical, afraid that we had raised a child alcoholic. We sat him down and yelled at him about liver and brain-cell damage, told him he was never to drink again until he was legally old enough to do so, and asked how the parents of the child whose party he attended had allowed such a thing. At that point we discovered that the parents had not been home. We got the child's phone number, helped Timothy as he threw up all over the bathroom, put him to bed, went to sleep, and the next morning called the parents of the child who had given the party. Apparently we were not the only parents who called. We never had another drinking incident with Timothy—which was, I'm sure, as much or more a result of luck as it was of wisdom. But since we rarely drank, at least we felt we had behaved responsibly ourselves in this area.

A stepfather with two stepchildren, ages sixteen and eighteen, and three biological children, ages twenty-one, twenty, and sixteen, used a roundtable discussion type of approach for these issues, and found it very successful. "We've never had a problem with drugs, but there was some drinking with the kids," he said, "and there were talks about it—what it might mean, what it certainly means about driving, what can happen with alcoholism. And we try to keep it open so they can talk about it and not feel there's any great rule against drinking occasionally without driving. I find the more leeway you give, the less temptation there is to rebel, and that's pretty much worked. My stepson out of his own initiative is very moral and will not drink. He gets a lot of pressure at parties from his friends who drink, but he sort of says, 'I don't want it.' He didn't get that from me, he didn't get that from his mother. That's his thing."

Another stepfather encountered problems with his daughter and marijuana starting when she was in her mid-teens. As he sees it, smoking marijuana was only a part of a whole lifestyle that became a problem. "My oldest stepdaughter was an extremely rebellious teenager," he told me. "There was a flirtation with drugs and also a flirtation with the less responsible aspects of the adolescent culture in terms of acting out. Never getting into trouble but wanting to stay out very late hours; being extremely defiant; being extremely willful; not listening; being fresh and vulgar very often; and so forth. That has not been true with the other children, certainly to that extent. I mean she was in a category alone.

"We dealt with it by not yielding our authority. Neither my wife nor myself cowed under that sort of thing. We tried to deal with it as best as we could—through necessary restrictions; through attempting to reason; through laying down the law; through consequences that would prevail—but never yielding our own values in the face of her defiance. Even in situations which we could not control, we always let her know what our standards were, and those were articulated. To a great extent you have to live it out, and you have to hope that if you always present what you think are the better values, then in the long run something will have been internalized by the child and something will come back, which has been the case with my stepdaughter. She's now polite. Although she never went to college, which was something that was upsetting to me, she nevertheless has a responsible job, makes a good income, and is a very sensible and attractive young woman."

In dealing with alcohol and drugs as well as any other issue of lifestyle or values, our greatest power seems to me to lie in the example we set ourselves—and the power to feel that we do have the right, as well as the responsibility, to make *ourselves* heard when our stepchildren are living with us and their behavior not only comes under our scrutiny but also affects us.

Of course, the power of our words is that much greater when it is backed by our own actions. While we may rightly feel it is inappropriate for children to smoke marijuana, for example, our arguments based on its illegality are undercut if we smoke marijuana ourselves. Teenagers may also give less credence to the differences in our ages as a significant criterion than they do to the example we set for them.

Dealing with these difficult issues with our adolescent stepchildren, we can only do our best. We cannot possibly control their behavior, but, borrowing the words of the stepfather I just quoted, even in situations we cannot control we have to let our stepchildren know what our standards are, what we feel the better values are. And even then, as he said, it may well be a process of living it out.

This stepfather mentioned his stepdaughter's "wanting to stay out late hours." The issue of curfews is one that always arises during adolescence In dealing with this issue, most stepfathers took the same tack Cynthia and I did: they and their partners arrived at a curfew time that they were comfortable with—which very often was a compromise between what they wanted and what the children wanted—and that became the rule. The younger the adolescent, the firmer the stepfathers and their partners tended to be about enforcing the curfew.

As Kevin and Timothy reached their last two years of high school, when they tended to travel in packs, Cynthia and I were willing to be more flexible with the boys. Most stepfathers reported an attitude change similar to ours as their stepchildren and children reached their mid to late teens. School nights, teenagers had a definite curfew, which could be extended when circumstances demanded it. On weekends, we negotiated a curfew which became later as the boys got older. Sometimes, when they were in their senior year of high school, instead of insisting that they be home at a precise time, we insisted that they call us by a certain hour to tell us who they were with, where they were, and when they would be home. We could then give them permission to remain out and follow their plan, or help them work out a plan for getting back earlier if transportation was a problem. If they wanted to stay over at a friend's house, we would find out who, whether or not the parents were going to be home, and what time we could expect them home the following morning. Following what many stepfathers told me they and their partners did, we were flexible about the curfew but firm about the necessity to call in. Not calling in within half an hour from the time we agreed on resulted in the loss of privileges.

In terms of driving, stepfathers also generally seemed to

agree on the approach we used in our house. We feel the main issue is responsibility. A car is a means of transportation; but it is also a potentially life-threatening instrument. Cynthia and I and every stepfather and mother I spoke to made it crystal clear to the children that they had to take driver's-education or a similar course from a driving school or qualified teacher, and under no circumstances were they to drink and drive.

Once teenagers have a license, parents and stepparents are faced with the issue of car borrowing and car ownership. Stepfathers concurred that the primary criteria for making their car available to their teenage drivers were how responsible the teenager was as a driver and how responsible the teen would be in keeping agreements like filling the car with gas and bringing it home on time.

As for a teenager's getting a car of his own, most stepfathers felt their stepchildren and children had to be able to pay for the expenses or at least the majority of car expenses, including insurance and maintenance.

COPING WITH A TEENAGER'S IMPULSE TO BE RECKLESS

Sometimes children want to do things that we and our partners consider reckless. But as one stepfather commented about his stepdaughter and marijuana: The younger the child, the easier it generally is for us to prevent a course of action or a behavior we disapprove of. When the child is older, we may have to resort to different means than simply forbidding the child to do what he or she wants to do.

"You have to give them room to be the age they are," one stepfather who faced such a situation told me. "When my stepson turned eighteen, he was determined he didn't need authority. We gave him room. Last year he wanted to do things himself, and he tried but it didn't work out. So this year he's much more willing to negotiate with us. He called us at one point and said he wanted to do some flat-track motorcycle racing. My wife came apart. We have a nephew who is in a wheelchair because of motorcycle racing. She said, 'No way you're going to.' Then she and I sat down and talked for several hours. I was trying to tell her that a kid comes to an age when you can't tell them what they're going to do.

"He called back a lot later and said how extremely disappointed he was that she had that attitude. In the meantime she'd loosened up a bit and told him, Well, she didn't feel too good about what he wanted. Their conversation worked out better. I wrote and told him it's okay, but we can't help you, because we've gone through accidents before. We have to keep our distance from the whole thing for that reason. That forced him to put the whole thing together, which it turned out he wasn't able to do financially, so he wound up not doing it. By now I think maybe he's out of the notion. Maybe he thinks he doesn't have time to do it because he's working so hard at school."

There is a difference between a child wanting to do daring, adventurous things—even things we may consider to be reckless but which may not be if proper safety rules are followed—and a child consistently ignoring safety rules that make daring activities truly dangerous or participating in reckless or self-destructive things without asking permission or acting in hostile defiance to us or others. If an adolescent (or a younger child) acts self-destructively, such behavior may well indicate a problem for which the child and the family need counseling or therapy. Also, if a child seems depressed or talks about suicide, it is important to take that behavior seriously and to consult and go with the child to a therapist.

With teenage suicide as prevalent as it is, it's important to be sensitive to signs that a child may be temporarily suicidal. Faced with adolescent development and the associated physiological changes within, many teenagers feel overwhelmed. They themselves may need the reassurance that adolescence is only a stage and that it will pass if they'll just be patient and see it through.

WHEN YOU AND YOUR PARTNER DIFFER

We've looked several times at the worst-case scenario of the stepfather with three juvenile delinquent stepchildren and a partner who has fought him tooth-and-nail about his setting any limits for them. In most stepfamilies there is neither this extreme behavior on the part of stepchildren nor this extreme disagreement between the stepfather and the children's mother. However, there is likely to be at least some disagreement about rules for the children. And since during their adolescence new issues arise that require the creation of new rules, there are new opportunities for disagreement between a stepfather and his partner, too. As always, communication and negotiation are the tools for resolving these disagreements.

Some stepfathers, however, feel that when there is a disagreement about rules for teenage stepchildren, it's really not their place to negotiate for their point of view. One stepfather in a combined stepfamily said that once he shared his opinion with his partner, if she disagreed with it he felt the choice should be hers and the children's biological father's. "With the issue of curfews for my stepdaughter, my moral code is a little bit different from my wife's. I would tend to be stricter than her and the child's father," he explained. "And I feel it's best for my wife to make the decision about it, because her daughter is her daughter. As to whether or not it has an effect on my stepdaughter because she does it her mother's way or my way, of course there is an effect. But I think that either way the child does it there's going to be a negative and a positive. I believe that if my stepdaughter did it my way, it would have been resented by her. So there would be the negative of resenting me along with what I see as the positive of an earlier curfew. I think my wife's philosophy is right about many issues, and she feels my stepdaughter is responsible enough to handle this."

Responsibility is a key word for adolescents themselves and for us as their stepfathers. Adolescence is the time when children become young adults. In making this transition, they learn about being responsible in their relationships with others. They also learn to take increased responsibility for themselves. Our responsibility as stepfathers is to support them in this process. Sometimes, because we are stepfathers and not biological fathers, this means supporting our partners in their view of what their children can handle, as the stepfather I just quoted did when he and his partner disagreed about her daughter's curfew. Sometimes we are unable to live with certain behavior, either because we feel it affects the children's safety or affects us directly. This means we have to do our best to be firm about what we feel, and do our best to convince our partners to change their minds and support us. Sometimes it means going to a therapist, counselor, or support group to resolve continuing disagreements that have us all at loggerheads with each other.

Most often I found that my responsibility as a stepfather was just to be there, to show my love for my stepchildren by a willingness to deal with whatever issues their adolescence presented. Part of this for me meant learning to be able to argue with them one moment, to hug them the next, or laugh at a joke they made. It meant learning not to carry a grudge because sometimes I did have to work hard with Cynthia to set limits for them and, as a result, would temporarily find myself cast as the villain.

The people who taught me not to carry a grudge about such things were Kevin and Timothy—because they never carried a grudge against me. I might be the bad guy in the morning, but in the afternoon I was just Mark again. Through the give-and-take that occurred between Kevin and Timothy and me during their adolescence, and despite the melodrama it sometimes contained, my relationships with both my stepsons continued to grow. Looking back, I feel the difficulties helped to forge the closeness. The fact that I was willing to take the responsibility to be there said a lot about my commitment to them. The fact that they were willing to fight it out with me at times—and not just with their mother and father—said a lot about their trust in me.

Their adolescences through age eighteen set the stage for the next major development in our relationships with each other: their moving out on their own.

WHEN KIDS MOVE AWAY

I mentioned at the beginning of this chapter that one of the things to bear in mind during your stepchildren's adolescence is that it's finite. Parents and stepparents alike often find that as their children and stepchildren reach the later stages of adolescence—first by trying out the semi-independence of going to college, and then by moving out on their own—their relationships with the children begin to improve. In my own case, my relationships with Kevin and Timothy began to bloom when they moved away from home.

Stepfathers are often surprised by how much things change for the better once their stepchildren leave home, whether for months at a time if they go to an out-of-town college, or when they go to live in a place of their own. I know that, for me, I really began to be emotionally close with Kevin when circumstances forced us to be geographically distant. Suddenly, as a result of Cynthia's and my moving back to New York from Los Angeles, and Kevin entering college in San Diego, he and I were three thousand miles apart. This meant that I only got to see him during holidays and summers, and then his time was split between us, his father and stepmother, and his many friends. The obvious growth in him with each passing semester—his greater clarity of who he was, his increased academic and professional skills, increased self-sufficiency, and, what was most gratifying to me, his increased appreciation of me and his increased desire to be close with me—made me more and more eager to see him. Soon his vacations went too quickly for me, and after he spent his first summer working in San Diego, I asked if he'd spend the next working in New York so he could live with us again.

Today, our feelings for each other are so spontaneous and heartfelt and our communication is so good that it's hard for me to believe that this Kevin is the same person I met when he was nine years old, trying so hard to exclude me from his, his brother's, and his mother's life, working so hard not to have me as a stepfather. Today, I know that he respects and appreciates me for having passed my initiation test. I know because he told me. "It's like a fraternity," he told me. "You don't just take someone in—you have to initiate them."

Timothy's moving away from home happened in stages. First he went to an out-of-town high school for a year. Then he came back to live with us and go to high school in New York City. He began college out of town, then left college in the middle of his freshman year. When Timothy said he wanted to leave college, Cynthia and I talked over this decision with him at length. We reminded him of why he chose the school and the positive things he had said about it. But his mind was set. So were ours. If he wanted to leave school, he also had to learn to be independent, we told him. That meant getting a job that could support him. He could come home for a month or six weeks, but after that he would have to come up with living arrangements that he could afford and that were also safe—not an easy challenge in New York. This would probably mean living with roommates, other young men and women who were working. He could not come home and hang out or just depend on us to put a roof over his head as we had when he was in high school. If he was making a decision to go out to work as an independent young adult because school "bored and depressed" him, as he said it did, then he had to follow that decision through.

As it turned out, after being home for a few weeks he took our suggestion to go live in upstate New York, where we had rented a house and where we had friends. Once there, he first got a job as a cook in a restaurant and then started learning carpentry. He also began going through many of the almost ritualized steps leading from late adolescence to young adulthood. He bought his first car, which didn't work when he bought it and never did despite the seller's promises. He expected us to continue supporting him and was annoyed when we didn't come through, even though we had told him we wouldn't when he first left college. He had his first experience getting over a long-term love affair. He asserted himself as an adult and an equal with us one minute and interacted with us as a rebellious child the next, sometimes deliberately breaking agreements he had made with Cynthia and me as a way to test his own limits as well as our limits and reactions. Where we were spared the minutiae of these steps with Kevin because he was so far away, we were geographically close enough to Timothy to be included in his growth process, and often to be cast in the roles of adversaries or jerks.

During this stage, we only saw Timothy when he visited us in New York City or when we went up to the country to visit him. Then, just as he approached age twenty, things began to change. The same traits I had noticed appearing in Kevin in late adolescence began blossoming in Timothy: consideration, gratitude, generosity, and an increased sense of his own identity and purpose. It was glorious.

Around this time Timothy decided to move from the country back to New York City and to get an apartment with friends whom we also knew and liked. Since then my relationship with him and his relationship with his mother have grown easier and easier and more and more enjoyable. As much as I've always loved him, I sometimes used to dread seeing him, because I never knew what new test he would have in store for me. And nobody could drive me as crazy as he could, perhaps because he had the same kind of willfulness and arrogance I had at his age and the same quick tongue. Now I look forward to seeing him, and I think of him as I think of Kevin: very much as a friend, as well as a young man I've raised since childhood. Like Kevin, he is the closest thing possible to a flesh-and-blood son. And just as I miss seeing Kevin more often, suddenly I find myself missing Timothy, too, though he lives just a few miles away from us and we get to see him once a week or so.

Often, the dual process I've just described of an adolescent continuing to grow up and also moving out of the home produces the same kinds of positive results I experienced in my relationships with my stepchildren. As one longtime stepfather told me: "We went through quite a lot with my stepdaughter. Then she got out of high school, went to college, associated with us a lot less. But a person keeps changing all the time. I guess that's the heartening thing about all this—that it never stays the same. She gradually got old enough to realize what our problems were in this whole thing. She could look back on it from a different perspective than being a victim of it. Then she started telling her feelings. So what I'm saying is that you must have the patience, and not jump to conclusions that all is lost and gone. It'll probably work out if you just hang in there. My stepdaughter is married, lives fairly close by, and we get along fine. My stepson is starting his last year of college, and we get along fine, too."

Another stepfather who had a very troubled relationship with his twenty-three-year-old stepdaughter during her teenage years commented, "She's out of the house and independent, so that relationship has changed, and in fact has improved. I don't know if the improvement in our relationship is a result of her moving out of the house; perhaps partially it is as a result of it. I suspect also in terms of her maturation, which is part of it. She lives in the neighborhood and visits when she wants something. But beyond that she's taken a responsible role in terms of running her own household. She comes back to me now in a way that is at least cordial, which was not the case when I was actively involved in raising her."

How We Feel when They Move Out

As their stepchildren approach late adolescence, many stepfathers find themselves longing for their stepchildren to leave home and simultaneously feeling ambivalent about them actually doing it. The ambivalence biological parents feel when their children go off to college, even when they've done little but fight with them for the previous five years, is notorious. Stepfathers often have similar experiences—which often surprises them. Their ambivalence about stepchildren leaving home is increased, of course, when stepfathers have close relationships with their stepchildren.

One stepfather who feels particularly close to his stepchildren told me, "I miss all three kids a lot when they're not home. That's a general thing with me. But I've been going through a hard time with my stepdaughter right now because she's about to leave. Now that she's twenty-two, she's finished with college. This last month I guess I'm very aware of how close we've been and how special she is, and how she's going to move across the country in a couple of weeks, and who knows what's going to happen after that? I just have this feeling of 'I'm not ready yet.' I mean I only got into her life six or seven years ago, and I'm not ready to see her go away.

"Then I sort of tell myself, 'Well, the kids can continue the relationship with their parents after the age of twenty-two,' and that the important thing is that she always knows she's welcome here and that I love her."

It's easy for parents and stepparents to find reasons to criticize children who have reached an age where they are making the necessary decision to go off on their own when we still feel so attached to them. Sometimes we and our partners can serve as a check-and-balance mechanism for each other. So we don't drive them away because we're upset that they're going.

As the stepfather I just quoted observed, "To give you an example that just came up yesterday, we just went through this whole graduation stuff for Julie; and Renée, her mother, was feeling sort of angry with her in general, just feeling that Julie wasn't appreciative enough of what we've done. I was able to say, 'I'm not sure I agree with you, and I think you ought to hold off before you start talking to Julie about it.' That sense of being able to provide checks for each other. I had a sense that my wife was sort of feeling abandoned. She sort of knows that, and she said, 'Okay, I hear you, and I'll wait.' But then it's funny, because this morning Julie was asking me something, and I found myself reacting the same way and feeling like I want a little more appreciation and gratitude instead of her just saying, 'I want more.' So we provide checks for each other."

This stepfather finds assurance for the continuity of his relationships with his stepdaughter and other stepchildren in the strength of the bond they have developed since he came into their life five years ago. "It just feels like they see me as one of their parents," he said. "I feel like we've worked hard at keeping communication open, and that they also very much see us as the type of parents who are into giving; if there's something they need, they'll come for it."

Some stepfathers worry that once their stepchildren go off on their own their relationships with them will disintegrate. "I know stepfathers who have been rejected by the children when the children are grownups in their twenties," one stepfather told me. "It would hurt me if my two stepchildren would cut me off because I was their stepfather. There's a fear that that would happen, that I don't think a natural parent has."

Another stepfather commented, "I look for them to grow up and hope I share with them a sense of values, morals, ethics. I don't know if we're going to have an ongoing relationship. I'm prepared for the fact that there may be some resentment that comes up toward me, because that's what I've heard can happen, that there'll be very little appreciation for what I've done, until maybe they reach a later point in their life."

Another stepfather, who is a therapist, observed, "My first guess about why someone would feel his stepchildren would resent him when they grew up is that there's got to be resentment now, and if there's no resentment now, then why should there be later? A stepfather who says this is either not exactly admitting or dealing with the resentment that's there now, or else he's just insecure."

ENCOURAGING CHILDREN TO MAKE THE TRANSITION

Some of the stepfathers I interviewed felt they had to catalyze their stepchildren's leaving home, both for their stepchildren's good and for their own. One stepfather in a combined stepfamily explained his perspective this way: "We're going to help the kids in growing up—we're going to encourage them to leave. In fact, we told the oldest one, who's twenty-two, that she has to be out by December. She's not crazy about it, but I think she knows it's time for her to go out. Her life right now revolves around work and the health spa and tanning salon. There's more to life than that. She doesn't have time for anything other than those three things. And, hey, there's a big world out there, and you've got to learn to live in it. She's accepted it very well. I think she's ready to go. If she weren't financially ready, we wouldn't force her out. I think she could get an apartment and move in with somebody, and I think everybody will be happier.

"She elected coming out of high school not to go to college. Her attitude was, 'I don't need college. I'm just going to get married and have kids, and I don't need a college education for that.' She had a boyfriend at the time. Now after being out of school and enjoying herself for four years, she's thinking, 'Maybe I ought to go back to school,' and we should pick up the tab. We have said, 'No, you gave that up a long time ago. If you want to go to school, go at night. Your employer is willing to pay the tuition and everything. But you're not going to quit work and go to school full time for four more years. It doesn't work that way.' "

Stepfathers agree that discussion rather than ultimatum usually suffices as a means to support children in making the transition from their home to one of their own, as it did when we talked to Timothy. This is not to say that such discussion is easy. Whether stepfathers and their partners think it is appropriate for children to leave the nest at age eighteen, twenty, twenty-two, twenty-five, or older varies with the particular individuals involved. Whether stepfathers and their partners agree is another matter entirely. In our case Cynthia and I agreed that Timothy had the ability and the stamina to work and become self-sufficient and that we wanted to support that rather than to support him in remaining dependent on us while also being so argumentative with us, clearly needing to pull away. We also felt, in hindsight, that he had gone to college with a very cavalier attitude, not really pausing to think too much about why he was going, where he was going, and what it was offering in the context of what his real likes, dislikes, and needs were. We didn't want his decision to leave college to be cavalier, too; we wanted it to have consequences. If college really did bore him, as he said it did, and he far preferred working and making his own way in the world, then the only way to help him see if that was true was to give him the opportunity to do it.

WHEN CHILDREN COME BACK HOME

Sometimes, of course, for various reasons, stepchildren and biological children come back to the nest. How stepfathers feel about this depends on their relationships with their stepchildren and with their partners. When children are in late adolescence or have just graduated from college, it's not unusual for them to return home for some nurturing and time to assess their options. Parents and stepparents usually tend to be willing to accommodate them. This happened for us in a minor way when Timothy left college and came home and when Kevin graduated and settled in with us for two months before going back to California and facing "the real world."

When children are in their mid-twenties or older and certainly cannot properly be called children anymore, parents and stepparents may be less willing to open their homes to them. They may feel the live-in visitor is coming for a long stay. According to the stepfathers I've interviewed in these situations, the primary motivation for their stepchildren to return to the household as adults is economic or in some other way related to self-sufficiency. Most often, stepfathers with adult stepchildren in these circumstances told me they permitted them to come back to their households because the children's mothers felt it was the best alternative.

One stepfather, for example, confided to me, "This is probably the single biggest irritant that my wife and I have ever had in this marriage—my stepson, who is thirty, living with us again. In fact, I was seriously thinking about three years ago that it cannot go on this way. I love my wife very much, but I was willing to say this is it.

"But even when it looks the bleakest, I hang in there. Because I always go back to what we have. We are very good for each other; we enjoy each other. I always think of these things. But if I was just to look at the balance sheet for the week, I probably would have left. But we have too much invested in each other. Where this boy's going, I don't know. Right now I really feel we don't have any privacy. I just feel this is not my own home. We were on the verge of putting him out, and then he got sick. I don't care how intolerable he is, I cannot put him out on the street in his medical condition. But we have to do something. My wife and I have to have a talk; we're going to have to decide one way or the other.

"I don't want to have to sell my house to get away, because then I'm running away from something, and I don't run away from things. I will stand there and either fight or work them out. I feel that I have to work this out, because if I don't work it out now, will I have to work it out wherever we move to?"

For the next five months, this stepfather worked to get his partner to support his decision that when his stepson was well enough they had to insist he get a place of his own and become financially self-sufficient. His partner did eventually come to agree with him. She even came to see that her doting attitude toward her son was encouraging him to remain sick. The stepfather also talked with his stepson about his feelings about him and his expectations of him, and he discussed what he was willing and not willing to give him. Five months after our interview, the thirty-year-old stepson had recovered sufficiently from his medical condition that he was able to live on his own. He moved into an apartment with friends and began working toward self-sufficiency again.

Some families, both step and nuclear, spend years resolving relationships with children and attempting to meet children's needs and solve problems that may come up and not go away. With the stepfathers I've interviewed, even among those whose problems have been most severe, there is a real sense of progress, at least within the marriage, where there is love and communication between husband and wife, a mutual commitment to each other and to doing whatever they can to meet the needs of all concerned.

I have one more happy story to tell in this regard—not happy in the storybook sense, but happy in terms of dealing with the kinds of difficulties many people experience today. This story is about a stepfather whose stepdaughter in her mid-thirties has severe mental problems and has periodically shown up on his and his partner's doorstep. "I have to do everything I can for my stepdaughter," he explained, "both because I feel it's right spiritually and because it's best for my marriage. Being a mother is part of my wife; I can't ignore her needs as a mother; I want to support them. My wife also wants to support our marriage. Now we feel we don't want Elissa home living with us anymore—we know that doesn't work for her and doesn't work for us, we've tried it—so we're doing everything we can to support her outside of our home. And it's working for her and for us. We've just come back from visiting her and helping her to get a new apartment, and she's doing very well. Her problems are going to continue, of course, but she is doing well. And we all do better when we're not in each other's hair. Working together to work out these problems has made my wife and me even closer."

CHAPTER ELEVEN

The Rewards of Stepfathering

For me, the chief rewards of stepfathering are my relationships with Kevin and Timothy, two people I love very much. But there are other rewards as well, rewards that have come, and keep coming, from the process of stepfathering. These have to do with what being a stepfather has taught me about myself: my strengths, my weaknesses, my sense of commitment, my ability to give and to receive.

Because I became a stepfather at age twenty-four and my stepchildren were ages ten and six, I had to grow up as fast as I could in order to catch up to the demands of being a stepfather to them. I had to be less childish, because *they* were children. My becoming their stepfather enhanced my own personal growth. Today, as a result of being Kevin and Timothy's stepfather, I approach my thirty-ninth birthday a far more well-rounded person.

Another part of the reward of stepfathering is seeing a bit of myself in Kevin and Timothy—not my jawline, eyes, or nose, of course, but my sense of humor, my ideas and values, and some of my personal style. Part of the reward is seeing them mimic me with affectionate humor, as only they know how, imitating my mannerisms and my voice, whether it is what I say when I answer the phone or how I walk into the wall because I'm not watching where I'm going. I've learned a lot, not just from being their stepfather but from living with two young people who in many ways taught me by their good examples. I mentioned earlier that I learned from both of them not to carry a grudge. I learned from Kevin to develop a greater acceptance of people and from Timothy to develop a more positive attitude. I learned from both of them to enjoy physical activities instead of just mental ones. I also learned from both of them to be more at ease in expressing physical affection.

After fifteen years of stepfathering, I feel not just that the rewards far outweigh the work I've put into it, but that the rewards are that much more precious. As one stepfather said in assessing his hard-won relationship with his stepdaughter: "I feel I've earned the closeness." We've all worked to create the bonds that now exist among us. For me, it adds a special dimension to our relationships to know how much these bonds have grown in strength and love over the years, and that all of us have had to invest ourselves to create them.

WIDE RANGE OF REWARDS

When I asked stepfathers about the rewards they have experienced from stepfathering, the responses ran the gamut from one stepfather who told me the rewards are "the same as the rewards of biological fathering" to another who said merely "none." The stepfather who told me the rewards are "the same rewards of biological fathering" has been a stepfather for seventeen years, ever since his stepson was four years old, the boy's biological father having passed away in the child's infancy. This stepfather also has a loving and mutually supportive relationship with his wife. The stepfather who said the rewards are "none" has been a stepfather for four years, has his stepson only part time, still meets with resistance from him, and receives no support from his wife for any of his ideas as a stepfather. Their respective conclusions are hardly surprising. The responses below are from other stepfathers whom I asked to comment on the rewards of their role. They range from loving to thought-provoking to poignant. Many combine all three of these qualities.

"The rewards of stepfathering go beyond description," one stepfather of ten years with a combined stepfamily told me. "A relationship with two extraordinary kids who have taught me about being very alive."

The stepfather of three and a half years who described his three stepchildren as "juvenile delinquents" commented, "So far the rewards I've realized are none! It's been nothing but headaches and heartaches and bloodshed because of the nature of my stepkids. I surmise that had I had nicer stepkids the rewards could have been beautiful and enriching."

"The rewards are the closeness that you feel with your children, the actual realization that, Hey, you are forming a new family, that you've gone through a lot of problems, actually solved a lot of problems, and you're being successful at it," a stepfather of four years with a combined stepfamily commented. "At the time you're doing this problem-solving it doesn't seem like you're getting anywhere, but one day you wake up and you look back and you say, 'Gee, we did it, it worked out, and we did it pretty well.' In fact, things are working fairly well. Those are the things that make me feel good about being a stepfather.

"There are emotional feeling type things: when a kid runs up to you and gives you a big hug when you've come back from a trip, happy to see you; when kids respond to you when you give them advice and they thank you for it; the feeling of unity of all the people in the family when you enjoy something together. All of those are the things that are the rewards that make me enjoy stepfathering."

A stepfather of seven years with a combined stepfamily said,

"A very touching thing happened on my birthday this year. My stepson gave me a present and wrote on a card to me, 'To a wonderful person and a great stepfather.' I found that very touching. I think we have a solid relationship."

A stepfather of sixteen years told me, "The rewards are the relationships resulting from the *difficult* times. The kids and I both know what we went through, and we survived it and are all the better for it. We love each other because we want to—not because we are supposed to; with biological children there is no choice."

A stepfather of ten years, with two stepchildren and two biological children, reported: "My initial impulse is to say there are no rewards in stepfathering and that all stepparent roles are either thankless or nearly so. But I guess I would have to say that contributing to their being functional, happy adults is important to me. When my wife and I look back at our former marriages, if we had stayed in those marriages, these children would have been much worse off, very much worse off. I also get the reward of giving my wife the gift of supporting her and helping her in raising her children."

"The biggest rewards for me are just the great new experiences of the expanded family," a stepfather of eight years with a combined stepfamily remarked. "It was just incredible watching and being part of all the new interactions. The growth that we all had to undergo to be in this new situation was really exciting, and there were some tough times, but most of it was very positive. Just living in an expanded family is an experience that I think nuclear families are cheated out of, I really do. I really know a lot of stepchildren who have biological fathers and are loved by a lot of sets of people, and they have a lot more advantages than nuclear children that way."

A stepfather of three years said simply, "The biggest rewards are being around kid energy."

"I absolutely feel some satisfaction from being a stepfather, and grateful also for the personal growth in me," a stepfather of eight years commented. "It's very hard-earned and a bit late in life. It's what anybody should learn from being a parent;

there's nothing unusual about it: humility. In the sense that there are things you have to be bloody careful about, because if you're not, you'll hurt somebody. In all kinds of complicated life situations I've been mildly aware of that. I mean, two marriages and other relationships and so on. You screw up, but it's much easier to blame the screw-ups on somebody else or to not assume complete responsibility. But in this kind of situation, when you're relating to a child, if you do something that's costly to somebody else, then it's costly to somebody else, and you can't run away from it and quit. There are errors of omission and commission that I'm aware of that I don't think I was aware of before. Now I know that if I do not alter my behavior at least a trifle to what's going on, it may be costly to my stepdaughter. That's a lesson."

"The biggest rewards of stepfathering are the stepkids," a stepfather of sixteen years said. "Talk is cheap, but I can say I would really hate to not have the relationships I have, especially with my wife's daughter. That's a thing I would have missed out entirely on. And I hope I'll have a long time to enjoy the relationship with her. And with my stepson, I don't feel all that much differently with him than . . . Well, when you move in with a little kid that small, it probably isn't all that much different than with a normal family, actually."

"Stepfathering feels like it's been an enormous completion of me as a person somehow," a stepfather of five years told me. "Learning to really take responsibility for them and to put them first in a lot of ways; letting their needs determine what their mother and I do. I get a sense of needing to protect them, and at times shelter them, sort of care for them—all of that; it just feels like it's added an enormous amount to my life.

"A week ago I was going through this thing about my stepdaughter and her graduating. I was aware one morning of feeling like I don't know what she's going through, and is it different being a mother or father than being a step? There's always that awareness of that dimension as possibly being a determining or differentiating factor. So I was aware that I didn't know what my stepdaughter was going through, and it was my sense of being separate from her right now because I was 'only' a stepfather, and what did I really mean to her. Then my wife wrote me this letter—about being a stepfather.

"She said, 'I've been thinking about stepfathers today, preparing to leave for the graduation. While no definition feels quite adequate, here are some things I know about my daughter's stepfather. Her stepfather helped build her room, helped her with history, tells her often how beautiful she is, watched the soaps with her, supports her financially and emotionally, got up early in the morning to rescue her from a disastrous vacation, and loves her dearly. Her stepfather feels sad that he missed her early years, but accepts that. He built a relationship with deep love and patience. Her stepfather is a sensitive, gentle, and strong partner to her mother in their parenting— always there, never demanding of his own needs in the face of her needs to parent in her own way, respectful of her judgment and holding her often. My daughter says about this man that he is her parent, an internal but clear definition for her. As for me, I feel gifted to have experienced watching you become this special stepfather, a process that has seemed so often to be one I could never have managed. Thank you. P.S. We did good.' "

STEPFATHERS' WIT AND WISDOM

After each interview, I asked stepfathers if they had any additional comments about the stepfathering experience that they'd like to share with the stepfathers and prospective stepfathers who read this book. The following observations and advice represent what are to me the most cogent, important, and/or original responses to my request. If you are having a momentary or a longer-than-momentary crisis in your stepfamily, in reading over these remarks you will find some commiseration, some productive suggestions, some humor, some encouragement, and possibly some inspiration.

"What makes it work is the willingness of the parent and stepparent to go at the rate the kids are able to integrate them.

That's one element I feel is the key: not pushing it faster than the kids are ready for.

"The second thing that feels key to me is the biological parent's role in bringing the stepparent in. During the time that I felt totally hopeless about my role as stepfather, and like I'd never feel solid being there with the children, my partner's supporting me and reinforcing me in the role, and also her willingness to encourage me to jump in at times and to back me up with the kids so that they know they can't play games with either of the two of us, that's made all the difference."

"The first thing I would say is one has to work to insure that one's primary relationship—that is, one's relationship with one's wife—is as strong as it can be. Because the relationship with the children cannot be better than the primary relationship. That's a precondition for one's effectiveness as a stepparent.

"I would also say, and I realize that this is a matter of choice, that, especially if the children live full time with you, one has to dedicate oneself to one's stepchildren and, where the scenario permits, involve and invest oneself as greatly as possible.

"Third, I think one has to be prepared for rejection, for assaults on one's ego, for being able to confront one's own inabilities and weaknesses and not to be thrown by them.

"Which leads me to my fourth point, which is that if you feel you're doing the right things and your relationship with your wife is a strong and mutually respectful one, you have to have the faith, in the final analysis, that what you're giving out to your stepchildren will on some level, even if it's not articulated by them, be picked up by them and internalized by them, and that they will prosper and grow as a result of what you've put into that experience."

"Accept the things you cannot change, affect the things you can change, but above all learn rapidly the difference between the two. Learn early and quickly which problems are yours, which problems are your spouse's, and which are the children's. In this way you can *avoid* some mighty big pitfalls and

STEPFATHERING

bruises. Stay away from the 'pity pot.' Find resolutions—don't garbage-dump on yourself, your spouse, or the children.

"The fantasy that stepfamilies are like normal families is critical to avoid. Stepfamilies are a process apart. So long as I remember that, I find that all is well (or as well as I might reasonably expect)."

"Like any human relationships, steprelationships are two-way; they are reciprocal. They cannot be any better than both parties—the stepfather and the stepkids—make them."

"My main advice is that biological parents be as searchingly honest as possible when viewing their own kids. Biological parents may tend to see their kids as they wish them to be. The biological parent is entitled to her hopes and to her pride in the positive things her children do, but the stepparent is also entitled to his feelings and observations. She can't discount them just because she doesn't like hearing them."

"Joining a stepfamily group or going to a counselor can be critical. We now belong to a stepfamily group, and that's been helpful and has actually provided me with a feeling of having been more successful in stepfamily situations than I thought I was. And believe me, that feels good after the hard struggle."

"If a person wants a challenge and to be tested, this is it. You have to parent, even though you're not the parent. And then, unlike an intact nuclear family, there's also that other person, that other parent, the biological father. He doesn't just disappear from the face of the earth. So the kids come into it sort of torn, fragmented, and I think you do, too. Maybe there's a positive in this, too; maybe as the kids develop, they can make more independent relationships with the mother, the stepfather, and the biological father, too."

"They should have a pension for stepparents, like they do for veterans, and special hospitals."

"Stepfathering is not an exact process. It's a process that you have to work on an awful lot. You can be a miserable failure at it or you can be a success at it. I don't think it has all that much to do with the chemistry of the stepchild and yourself. I think it has a lot to do with how you deal with your stepchild's biological parents, and I mean both of them, and how you treat your own children if you have them. I guess you have to let a lot of things go by that might upset you; you have to leave yourself a lot of space and admit that you make mistakes—be very open about that, say that you're not unhappy with that.

"You probably deeply can wish that they'd move, but that's not possible, because you provide a home. It's not an exact science and it never will be. It's like anything else: If you want to make it right, you have to work at it. And we all get tired sometimes and cranky ourselves, and we don't want to deal with it.

"In the long run, I think we're turning out a batch of real good children. That's what I believe our goal is. We try to make them live in a world that probably we feel slightly guilty that we've created for them. They're no longer in the same house that they were in when they were in a nuclear family.

"You know, it would be great if we were perfect. It would be really great. Because then we could just set down all the rules for this and everything else. But we wouldn't be on earth; we would have risen a long time ago. That's not the way it works."

"Communication is the whole key."

INDEX

Index

alcoholism, in biological father,
183
allowances, for children, 220
anger:
adolescent, 239–40
in re-entry period, 181
authority, 119–48
different forms of, 135–43
as male role, 119
problems with, 126–30
resolving disputes over, 129–30
stepchildren's resistance to,
123–24, 133–35, 139
stepfather's reluctance to assume, 129
see also discipline
authority figure, stepfather as, 34,
46, 144

baby, new, in stepfamily, 89–90,
116–17
biological children of stepfather,
70–71
adjustments by, 29, 124
stepfather's bonds to, 101–7
stepfather's closeness to stepchildren vs., 102–3
stepfather's favoritism towards,
107–11
stepfather's financial responsibility for, 207–19
stepfather's physically affectionate relationships with,
103
biological father, 12, 49–50,
177–206
adjustments by, 92–93
alcoholic, 183
blocked out of children's lives,
188
children's dependence on, 169
children's relationships with,
63–64, 103, 192–95
child-support payments of,
207–19
dead, 23, 205

as "enablers," 237
"escaping" of, from stepfather,
177–78
ex-spouse's relationship with,
187–88
genetic links of, with children,
57
home of stepfather vs., 182
influence of, on stepfamily,
49–50, 177
jealousy of, 50
new partner of, 197–98
non-interacting, 196
personality of, 214
pettiness of, 214
positive re-entry interaction between stepfather and, 185–87
preformed opinions of, 179
as presence in children's lives,
31, 49–50
severity in stepfather's dealings
with, 191
stepfather's adjustments to, 50,
92–94
stepfather's communication
with, 189–91, 195–97
stepfather vs., 22, 38, 43, 56–58,
168, 192–95, 198–200, 205–6
Bohannan, Paul, 22–23
bonds:
in adolescence, 229
father's, to biological children
and stepchildren, 101–7
mother-child, 47–48, 69
new baby and, 90, 117
partner's support in development of, 91
with post-adolescent stepchildren, 61
shared activities and, 155–59
"Brady Bunch, The," 67

child-rearing:
partners' agreement on, 47
see also discipline

children, *see* biological children;
 stepchildren; stepsiblings
child support, 207–19, 225–26
 in combined stepfamily, 213–14,
  217
 negotiating new arrangements
  for, 218–19
 range of arrangements for,
  209–13
 stepfather's attitudes about, 208,
  209
 stepfather's gripes about,
  213–17
closed-door policy, 175
clothing, of adolescent stepchildren, 244
combined stepfamily, 42–43,
 99–118
 adjustments in, 88–90
 adolescent sexuality in, 246
 child-support in, 213–14, 217
 communication in, 111, 113
 equal treatment of stepsiblings
  in, 39–40, 108, 110
 fairness and favoritism in,
  107–11
 formation of, 37–40, 99
 jealousy in, 109
 loyalty conflicts in, 39–40
 major issues in, 101–18
 new baby in, 89–90, 116–17
 problems of, 39–40
 re-entry period in, 115, 180–87
 stepsiblings' relationships in, 76,
  114–16
 in television programs, 99
communication, 275
 adjustments and, 87–88
 between biological father and
  stepfather, 189–91, 195–97
 cutting off, 35
 discipline and, 141
 between partner and stepfather,
  30, 111, 113
counseling, 31, 126
 for stepfamily, 49

courtship:
 getting-acquainted stage and,
  27, 28, 32–33, 38–39
 secret, 33–34
curfews, of adolescent stepchildren, 252, 255–56
custody:
 battles for, 64, 173, 216–17
 split, 173

dating, getting-acquainted stage
 and, 27, 28, 32–33, 38–39
discipline, 119–48
 adolescents and, 139
 age of children and, 142–43
 conflicts with partner over,
  120–21, 122–23
 elements of, 141
 family lifestyle and, 124
 gender roles and, 120–21
 as insecurity issue, 126
 problems of, 126–30, 143–44
 punishment and, 141–42
 re-evaluation of, 143–46
 responsibility of, shared by stepfather and partner, 120–21,
  122, 138
 stepchildren's resistance to,
  123–24, 133–35
 and stepfather's attitudes and
  background, 130–33
 stepfather's stake in, 125–26
 strategies in, 135–43
 see also authority
divorce, 22–23, 50
 and children's resistance to authority, 123–24
 mother-child bonds after, 69
divorce rate, 12, 25–26
driving privileges, of adolescent
 stepchildren, 252–53

Einstein, Elizabeth, 136
Erikson, Erik, 230–32, 233

family, *see* combined stepfamily;
 stepfamily

as role model, 56
role of, in stepfamily, 54–74
stepchildren's time alone with,
  149–60
stepfamily problems defused by,
  30–31, 48–49
steps in becoming, 22
support for, 49, 128
tested by stepchildren, 36–37,
  87
variables shaping role of, 60–72
wit and wisdom of, 272–73
stepmother, 111–14
stepsiblings:
  jealousy among, 109, 114
  new baby and, 89–90, 116–17
  relationships among, 76, 114–16
  see also stepchildren

suicide, in adolescence, 254
"superman fantasy," 48

territorial conflicts, 79–80
testing, by stepchildren, 36–37, 87
time, adjustments and, 31, 50–52
time alone with stepchildren,
  149–60
  awkwardness in, 159–60
  benefits of, 151–55
  as priority, 155–59
"tough love," 145
"triangle" relationships, 69–70,
  160
"turn-off/turn-on period," 86

wife, *see* partner
women's liberation movement, 13